Caryl Churchill
Plays: 1

Owners, Traps, Vinegar Tom, Light Shining in Buckinghamshire, Cloud Nine

The plays in this volume represent the best of Churchill's writing up to and including her emergence onto the international theatre scene with *Cloud Nine*.

Owners: 'Churchill possesses creative gifts that are almost singular among her contemporaries: a poetic imagination, an idiosyncratic vision of reality, and a sense of variousness in her characters . . . her themes are subtly evoked through the interplay of character and action.' *Observer*

Traps: 'A fascinating script . . . offers plenty of sinewy lines and joyous juxtapositions and Churchill's most confident and creative deployment of stagecraft to date.' *Plays and Players*

Vinegar Tom: 'is set in the world of seventeenth-century witchcraft, but it speaks, through its striking images and its plethora of ironic contradictions, of and to this century's still deep-rooted anti-feminism and women's oppression.' *Tribune*

Light Shining in Buckinghamshire: 'It unflinchingly shows the intolerance that was the obverse side of the demand for common justice. Deftly, it sketches in the kind of social conditions . . . that led to hunger for revolution . . . The play has an austere eloquence that precisely matches its subject.' *Guardian*

Cloud Nine: 'A marvellous play – sometimes scurrilous, always observed with wicked accuracy, and ultimately, surprisingly, rather moving. It plunges straight to the heart of the endless convolutions of sexual mores . . . and does so with an acrobatic wit.' *Guardian*

Caryl Churchill has written for the stage, television and radio. Her stage plays include *Owners* (Royal Court Theatre Upstairs, 1972); *Objections to Sex and Violence* (Royal Court, 1975); *Light Shining in Buckinghamshire* (for Joint Stock, Theatre Upstairs, 1976); *Vinegar Tom* (for Monstrous Regiment, Half Moon and ICA, London, and on tour, 1976); *Traps* (Theatre Upstairs, 1977); *Cloud Nine* (Joint Stock at the Royal Court and on tour, 1979, De Lys Theatre, New York, 1981); *Three More Sleepless Nights* (Soho Poly and Theatre Upstairs, 1980); *Top Girls* (Royal Court, London and Public Theatre, New York, 1982); *Fen* (Joint Stock, Almeida Theatre and Royal Court, London, and on tour, and Public Theatre, New York, 1983); *Softcops* (RSC at the Pit, 1984); *A Mouthful of Birds*, with David Lan (for Joint Stock at the Royal Court and on tour, 1986); *Serious Money* (Royal Court and Wyndhams Theatre, London); *Icecream* (Royal Court, London, 1989); *Mad Forest* (Central School of Speech and Drama, London, 1990); *Lives of the Great Poisoners* (Arnolfini, Bristol, 1991); *The Skriker* (Royal National Theatre, 1994); and a translation of Seneca's *Thyestes* (Royal Court Theatre Upstairs, 1994).

by the same author

CHURCHILL PLAYS: TWO
(Softcops, Top Girls, Fen, Serious Money)
SERIOUS MONEY
SOFTCOPS and FEN
TOP GIRLS
ICECREAM
MAD FOREST
THE SKRIKER
LIVES OF THE GREAT POISONERS
(written with Orlando Gough and Ian Spink)

also available

CHURCHILL THE PLAYWRIGHT
by Geraldine Cousins

CARYL CHURCHILL

Plays: 1

Owners
Traps
Vinegar Tom
Light Shining in Buckinghamshire
Cloud Nine

methuen | drama
LONDON · NEW YORK · OXFORD · NEW DELHI · SYDNEY

METHUEN DRAMA
Bloomsbury Publishing Plc
50 Bedford Square, London, WC1B 3DP, UK
1385 Broadway, New York, NY 10018, USA

BLOOMSBURY, METHUEN DRAMA and the Methuen Drama logo are trademarks of
Bloomsbury Publishing Plc

This collection first published in Great Britain in 1985 by Methuen London Ltd
Reissued in this series in 1996 by Methuen Drama
Reprinted by Bloomsbury Methuen Drama 2013, 2014, 2015, 2016, 2017, 2018 (twice), 2019 (twice)

Owners first published in Great Britain in 1973 by Eyre Methuen Ltd
© 1973, 1985 by Caryl Churchill
Traps first published in Great Britain in 1978 by Pluto Press Ltd
© 1978, 1985 by Caryl Churchill
Vinegar Tom first published in Great Britain in 1978
by TQ Publication; and in 1982 by Methuen London Ltd in *Plays by Women: Volume One*
© 1978, 1982, 1985 by Caryl Churchill
Song 'If You Float' © 1976, 1978, 1982, 1985 by Helen Glavin
Light Shining in Buckinghamshire first published
in Great Britain in 1978 by Pluto Press Ltd
© 1978, 1985 by Caryl Churchill
Cloud Nine first published in Great Britain in 1979
by Pluto Press Ltd and Joint Stock Theatre Group; revised ed. 1984
© 1979, 1980, 1983, 1984, 1985 by Caryl Churchill
Lyrics 'Come Gather Sons of England' © 1902
by Anthony Wilkin; 'A Boy's Best Friend' © 1897 by Joseph D. Skelly;
'Cloud Nine' © 1979 by Caryl Churchill and Andy Roberts

Introduction © 1985 by Caryl Churchill
Collection © 1985 by Caryl Churchill

A catalogue record for this book is available from the British Library.

A catalog record for this book is available from the Library of Congress.

ISBN: PB: 978-0-4135-6670-6
ePDF: 978-1-4725-3673-0
ePUB: 978-1-4725-3674-7

Series: Contemporary Dramatists
Printed and bound in Great Britain

To find out more about our authors and books visit www.bloomsbury.com and sign
up for our newsletters.

CONTENTS

A Chronology of Performed Plays

PLAY	WRITTEN	PERFORMED [s=stage, r=radio tv=television]
Downstairs	1958	1958 s
You've No Need to be Frightened	1959?	1961 r
Having a Wonderful Time	1959	1960 s
Easy Death	1960	1961 s
The Ants	1961	1962 r
Lovesick	1965	1966 r
Identical Twins	?	1968 r
Abortive	1968?	1971 r
Not . . .not . . .not . . .not . . .not enough oxygen	?	1971 r
Schreber's Nervous Illness	?	1972 r
Henry's Past	1971	1972 r
The Judge's Wife	1971?	1972 r
Owners	1972	1972 s
Moving Clocks Go Slow	1973	1975 s
Turkish Delight	1973	1974 tv
Perfect Happiness	1973	1973 r
Objections to Sex and Violence	1974	1975 s
Traps	1976	1977 s
Vinegar Tom	1976	1976 s
Light Shining in Buckinghamshire	1976	1976 s
Floorshow (contributor to)	1977	1977 s
The After Dinner Joke	1977	1978 tv
The Legion Hall Bombing	1978	1979 tv
Softcops	1978	1983 s
Cloud Nine	1978	1979 s
Three More Sleepless Nights	1979	1980 s
Crimes	1981	1981 tv
Top Girls	1980–2	1982 s
Fen	1982	1983 s
Midday Sun (with Geraldine Pilgrim and Pete Brooks)	1984	1984 s

A Mouthful of Birds (with David Lan and Ian Spink)	1986	1986*s*
Serious Money	1987	1987*s*
Fugue (with Ian Spink)	1987	1987*tv*
Icecream	1988	1989*s*
Hot Fudge	1989	1989*s*
Mad Forest	1990	1990*s*
Lives of the Great Poisoners (with Orlando Gough and Ian Spink)	1991	1991*s*
The Skriker	1993	1994*s*
Thyestes (trans. Seneca)		1994*s*

INTRODUCTION

Owners wasn't my first play, more like the twentieth now I count them up, and certainly the fifth full-length stage play. But the earlier stage plays were student productions or unperformed, and most of my work had been on radio for the previous ten years. Since *Owners* I've worked almost entirely in the theatre. So my working life feels divided quite sharply into before and after 1972, and *Owners* was the first play of the second part.

I'd written constantly since I was a child, mainly plays since I was about 20. A one-act play, *Downstairs*, went from Oxford to the NUS drama festival in 1958-9, and two full-length plays had student productions, *Having a Wonderful Time* at the Questors Theatre in 1960 and *Easy Death* at the Oxford Playhouse in 1961.

I'd listened to radio a lot as a child, and wrote *You've No Need to be Frightened* for voices in 1959, which again had a student production. When I wrote *The Ants* in 1961 I thought of it as a TV play, but my agent Margaret Ramsay sensibly sent it to radio, where it was directed by Michael Bakewell, and over the next ten years I wrote seven radio plays (see list) all directed by John Tydeman. I can think of about ten other plays I wrote during this time, some for the theatre (*The Finnsburgh Fragment*, 1960 and *The Marriage*, 1968) and some for TV. *The Judge's Wife* was done on BBC-TV in 1972, directed by James Fermin.

In 1972 Michael Codron commissioned me to write a play. I wrote *Owners* and it was done in the Theatre Upstairs at the Royal Court that autumn, directed by Nicholas Wright.

The next year I wrote a science fiction play and in 1974 *Objections to Sex and Violence*, which was done on the main stage of the Royal Court in early 1975, directed by John Tydeman while I was resident writer there. The earlier play, now called *Moving Clocks Go Slow* was done in the Theatre Upstairs by John Ashford. Meanwhile two of the radio plays were done as lunchtime plays, *Schreber's Nervous Illness* at the King's Head in 1972 by Kenneth Haigh, and *Perfect Happiness* at the Soho Poly in 1975 directed by Suzanna Capon.

I wrote nothing in 1975 and three plays in 1976, all in this volume. First I wrote *Traps*; by Easter I was reading books about witches for Monstrous Regiment, and wrote a draft of *Vinegar Tom* before starting work with Max Stafford-Clark and Joint Stock in May on a workshop about the seventeenth century revolution; and wrote *Light Shining in Buckinghamshire* that summer. It opened at the Edinburgh Festival, toured and came twice to the Theatre Upstairs; in the autumn I worked with Monstrous Regiment, finishing *Vinegar Tom*, and it opened in November, directed by Pam Brighton, touring widely and playing in London at the Half Moon and the ICA. Then came the production of *Traps* in January 1977, directed by John Ashford, in the Theatre Upstairs. Working with companies for the first time, while before I had always worked very much alone, made the year almost as much of a watershed as 1972.

Looking back it's not surprising that I didn't write much in 1977. I contributed with Michelene Wandor and Bryony Lavery to Monstrous Regiment's cabaret, *Floorshow*, early that summer, and in the autumn was thinking about ideas some of which finally came out in *Cloud Nine* and *Top Girls*, but I didn't write a stage play that year. In the autumn I wrote *The After Dinner Joke* for Margaret Matheson's series of 'Play for Today' on BBC-TV, and while it was being made, directed by Colin Bucksey, the transcript of a trial in a Diplock court in Northern Ireland came into my hands, and we decided to make a 'Play for Today' of that. This was *The Legion Hall Bombing*, directed by Roland Joffe. The BBC removed our voice-over explaining the background of the Diplock courts, as being political comment, and put their own voice-over on; we removed our names in protest.

In 1978, excited by reading Michel Foucault's *Surveiller et Punir*, which fitted in with things I'd been thinking about, I wrote *Softcops*, the first stage play since *Light Shining*, which I then put away and forgot. It was done much later, 1983, by the RSC, directed by Howard Davies. In the autumn I started work with Max Stafford-Clark again for Joint Stock, this time with a workshop on sexual politics. I wrote *Cloud Nine* that autumn and it opened in February at Dartington College, toured, and played in London at the Royal Court. A year later the production was revived at the Royal Court with a different cast, co-directed by Les Waters, and in 1981 it was produced by Michel Stuart, directed by Tommy Tune, at Lucille Lortel's Theatre de Lys in New York, where it ran for two years. So *Cloud Nine* was another kind of watershed.

OWNERS

Onward Christian Soldiers,
Marching as to war.
Christian hymn.

Sitting quietly, doing nothing.
Spring comes and the grass grows by itself.
Zen poem.

Owners

I was in an old woman's flat when a young man offering her money to move came round – he was my first image of Worsely and one of the starting points of the play. Another was wanting one character with the active, achieving attitude of 'Onward Christian Soldiers', the other the 'sitting quietly, doing nothing' of the Zen poem. The active one had to be a woman, the passive one a man, for their attitudes to show up clearly as what they believed rather than as conventional male and female behaviour. So Marion and Alec developed from that train of thought. I'd read Figes' *Patriarchal Attitudes* not long before, which may have affected the character of Clegg, and had recently reread Orton's *Sloane*, which may have done something to the style.

C.C. 1984

Owners was first presented in the Royal Court Theatre Upstairs, London, on 6 December 1972 with the following cast:

CLEGG	David Swift
WORSELY	Richard O'Callaghan
MARION	Stephanie Bidmead
LISA	Anne Raitt
ALEC	Kenneth Cranham
ALEC'S MOTHER	Eileen Devlin
MRS ARLINGTON	Lucinda Curtis
TWO CUSTOMERS	

Directed by Nicholas Wright
Designed by Di Seymour

Marion was played by Jill Bennett in the previews. She was injured and the part was taken over by Stephanie Bidmead.

CLEGG is dowdy and getting fat. He's unattractive but not so grotesquely that it's impossible to imagine Marion having married him when he was younger. Forty.

WORSELY is tall and thin, with greasy black hair, not long; dark blue suit; shiny blackpointed shoes. Early twenties.

MARION is thin and edgy and moves about a lot, often eating. Strong face rather than pretty. Her clothes are expensive but often badly matched, coming undone, slightly askew. Thirties.

LISA has a weak pretty face losing its prettiness with strain. When dressed up her hair, eyes and clothes are elaborate: other times it is all let go. At the beginning of the play she is six months pregnant. Late twenties.

ALEC is tall, rather plain and ordinary, but attractive. Thirties.

ALEC'S MOTHER is senile.

MRS ARLINGTON is very young, well dressed, well bred, with the good nature of someone who has never met difficulties or been disliked. No need to send her up – she can be as nice as possible and still be intolerable to Lisa. About twenty.

CUSTOMERS can be any age and can be played by the same actress, but as two different customers, not one.

Act One	Scene One:	Clegg's butcher's shop
	Scene Two:	Room in Alec and Lisa's flat
	Scene Three:	A strip club
	Scene Four:	Marion's office
	Scene Five:	Room
	Scene Six:	Room
Act Two	Scene One:	Kitchen, in Clegg and Marion's house
	Scene Two:	Marion's office
	Scene Three:	Hospital cubicle
	Scene Four:	Room
	Scene Five:	Clegg's bedroom
	Scene Six:	Marion's office
	Scene Seven:	Marion's office
	Scene Eight:	Clegg's new butcher's shop

The play takes place in a developing bit of North London.

Originally the play opened with Scene Two, followed by what is now Scene One. We swapped them round in rehearsal as it seemed a more effective opening to the play. Then we realised that causes a problem of chronology, since Scene Three follows directly on Scene One. It doesn't seem to matter. But the play could be performed in the original order.

ACT ONE

SCENE ONE

Inside CLEGG's *butcher's shop.* CLEGG *and* CUSTOMER.

CLEGG: Lovely day dear. Been sitting in the park in the sun? I know you ladies. Twelve ounces of mince. And what else? Some nice rump steak dear? You don't keep a man with mince. No? Twenty p, thank you very much. Bye-bye dear, mind how you go.

> [*She goes.*]

Old cow.

> [*He starts chopping chops.* WORSELY *comes in. His wrists are bandaged.*]

WORSELY: Give us a chop.

CLEGG: Have six if you like for the price. It's the last day. Marion tell you?

WORSELY: Said you was closing down. Pongs a bit.

CLEGG: Old stock. I can let you have some kidneys.

WORSELY: I don't go for offal. It's too much like insides.

CLEGG: Nice rabbit?

WORSELY: Rabbit's one of those things I think of you know as a rabbit. Horse the same but the French manage it all right. A nice lamb chop though is definitely a dish.

CLEGG: Have ten.

WORSELY: Aren't they a bit grey?

CLEGG: Lamb always smells a bit strong. You don't want to mind the smell. Run them under the cold tap when you get home.

WORSELY: I like lambs in a field mind you in the spring time. I had quite a pet lamb one holiday when I was a kiddy.

CLEGG: Marion still in the office is she?

WORSELY: Hard for a child till it gets the knack. If the lamb's a pet don't hurt it. If the lamb's a chop, it's not got a name.

CLEGG: Marion very busy I suppose?

WORSELY: Waiting for a big phone call. She's got two buyers after them three houses in a row in the square. Playing them off sort of thing.

7

CLEGG: One thousand five hundred and seventy-five people die daily in England and Wales.

WORSELY: Fair number.

CLEGG: It's only a matter of making her one of them.

WORSELY: It's not so easy. Speaking as one who knows.

CLEGG: She's physically a very strong woman. And mentally in some respects.

WORSELY: But you weren't thinking of unarmed combat?

CLEGG: She did karate once in an evening class. When she had more time on her hands. No I must find the right tool for the job.

WORSELY: Is the idea to kill her at all costs or do you count on getting away with it?

CLEGG: I hadn't planned on being caught, no.

WORSELY: Then a knife might be too much of a clue.

CLEGG: What I'd prefer is a convenient accident. If she could topple off a cliff.

WORSELY: A day trip.

CLEGG: You could come with us as a witness.

WORSELY: A witness is what you don't want.

CLEGG: To say you saw me not push her. An accident.

WORSELY: Are you serious?

CLEGG: How do I know? I know I dwell on murder day and night. I can't see any life for myself till she's gone. And she's in much better health than I am.

WORSELY: Why not leave her?

CLEGG: I tried that once. But where would I go? And she didn't mind at all. Hardly. Not enough. She can stand on her own two feet which is something I abominate in a woman. Added to which she has what you might call a magnetic personality. We got that out of a machine once on a pier in happier times that said your character. It was so like it made you wonder just what is above. My card said exactly the same as hers, which was a mistake on the part of whoever filled the machine, so I don't know my true character. But she's a magnet all right. I gather round. So do you. You kept dropping in all the time till she said you could work for her and now you work for her all day and half the night and you still drop in. You're drawn in. What for?

Just to be there when she's there. You see?

WORSELY: Aren't you afraid I'll tell her?

CLEGG: I have to talk to somebody now and then. I'm very fond of the dog mind you.

WORSELY: Are you getting another job?

CLEGG: I've been a butcher twenty-five years. And my father before me. He killed his own meat. Not in London, there isn't the opportunity, we had the good luck to live in a suburb that had a small field adjoining the shop. Then we moved here. It seemed like progress at the time. But now it's all done by machine a lot of the dignity's gone out of it. But you still don't see a lady butcher. Apart from the physical weakness a lady has a squeamishness which is very proper in the fair sex but shameful in a man. We were taught to look up to my father. My mother literally worshipped him. I've seen her on her knees. And he would raise her up, very gracious. She knew how to give a man the right support. He had his chair. The tea was hot on the table when he came in. We never made a sound.

WORSELY: It was Sainsbury's opening next to you did it was it?

CLEGG: I don't know why people want meat in polythene. It's like going round with your head in a plastic bag.

WORSELY: You could get another shop better placed. Wouldn't Marion buy you a shop?

CLEGG: I don't let her buy me a drink. I was going to be big myself, you don't seem to realise. That was my intention as a young man. I had none of your difficulties Worsely. I was thrusting. I envisaged a chain. Clegg and Son. I was still the son at the time. I would have liked a son myself once I was the Clegg. But now I've no business I don't need a son. Having no son I don't need a business.

WORSELY: You need a hobby. Have you no interests?

CLEGG: I could have any number.

WORSELY: Pick one or two and throw yourself in wholeheartedly. You need to keep busy.

CLEGG: I've always been my best under pressure. I thrive on competition. I put two men out of business when I was only twenty-seven years old.

WORSELY: That's where we differ. The slightest pressure from outside and I fall in. Because inside me there is very nearly a vacuum. The balance is just so. I was top in the lower forms of the grammar school. I liked marks then. I sometimes look around now to be marked. Or I mark myself. [*He looks at his bandaged wrists.*] B minus. Could have tried harder.

CLEGG: Isn't it painful cutting yourself like that? I know when I have the odd slip with a knife I don't half give a yell.

WORSELY: An accident makes you feel got at. If you mean it, the pain's more on your side. Because nobody dies without discomfort. I take it as an occupational hazard. You don't get anything of value without working for it, as the headmaster liked to say at assembly. Per ardua ad astra.

CLEGG: But do you intend to be dead?

WORSELY: I try to. My doctor says I'm so safety prone I must have a lifewish. I have a sense of humour about psychiatrists.

CLEGG: I've every respect myself for the mental profession. When Marion was in hospital they tried to tell her she'd be happier and more sane as a good wife. Comb your hair and taken an interest in your husband's work. Find a hobby. She had her painting, which was all right. Creative hobbies are very nice for a woman. I appreciate anything pretty and artistic. But she wouldn't listen. She came out of there with staring eyes and three weeks later she bought her first house. It was only fifteen hundred pounds. She had five hundred left by her dad. And I did the rest for her on a mortgage because the mortgage company was understandably reluctant to deal with a lady. She's paid me back since of course. I would have lost the money gladly and forgiven her and not said another word about it if only she would have stayed with painting and been content. Everything I had was hers. I always said. She only had to ask.

WORSELY: I was sorry she didn't stay in hospital longer. I used to dance with her at the socials.

CLEGG: Mental hospitals aren't altogether moral. That's the one fault I find. They don't care if what a patient does is good or bad, just if it's good for her or bad for her. Dancing can be very dangerous if it's not watched.

WORSELY: I wouldn't say she danced with everyone. She's not everyone's type.

10

CLEGG: That I put up with this sort of talk. Or seem to. In fact I bide my time. If I thought for a moment she had dishonoured me, then without hesitation or a thought of the police – [*He plunges knife into meat.*] And also into the heart of the thief. I am more an Othello than a Hamlet. Out out damned candle! She is legally mine. And one day she will die knowing it. And another satisfaction of my shame is the proof that it's she who is infertile.

WORSELY: But Marion's on the pill. I daresay.

CLEGG: I would never give my name to another man's child. He would be robbing me not only of my helpmate but my chain of highclass butcheries. Clegg and Son. Pork butcher. Clegg and Son. Family butcher. But still she's Mrs Clegg. I am even proud of her. I look at her sometimes and think I am the one this powerful rich property developer swore before God to honour and obey. Whether she does or not. You won't deny she is a wonder. It's very like having a talking dog, and it's on the front page at breakfast, the radio at dinner, the television at night – that's mine, look, that's my clever dog. But a time comes when you say, Heel. Home. Lie down.

WORSELY: You know what you were saying about a plastic bag. Suppose I put a plastic bag over my head and tied it tightly round the neck. What could possibly go wrong?

CLEGG: Some of them nowadays has safety holes.

WORSELY: Not all. I would have a look.

CLEGG: There couldn't be any possible situation in which Marion might put her head in a plastic bag?

WORSELY: Clegg you have no experience of taking life.

CLEGG: I get my ideas mainly from books. I can't ever put Agatha Christie down. And newspapers are great fun too. But people do die in real life. Daily. In large numbers.

WORSELY: I've tried to kill myself six times. And I'm a willing victim.

CLEGG: I know it's one thing to think about it. When I see her in real life I'm always surprised at the bloom of health.

WORSELY: I saw a poster saying Suicide – ring the Samaritans. So this very pleasant young fellow came round and I told him I want to kill myself and could he help. He said in a very feeling

11

voice he would certainly try. But does he hell. The bastard's always trying to stop me.

CLEGG: It's half past five. Time to close. There should be some ceremony to help. As a funeral does.

[MARION *comes in.*]

MARION: One hundred thousand.

WORSELY: That's it.

MARION: I held out.

WORSELY: I knew you would.

MARION: I admitted there was competition.

WORSELY: Made him jump.

MARION: I gave him a deadline.

WORSELY: Put him on the spot.

MARION: He came through on the telephone like a lamb. He could after all see his way clear.

WORSELY: Should have asked a hundred and twenty.

MARION: No dear I should not. It was worth perhaps eighty. Don't show off.

CLEGG: Congratulations my love.

MARION: We shall celebrate. It stinks in here, Clegg. Does it always? No wonder you've no customers. Throw it all away. Shut the shop. Whatever's that you're clutching, Worsely? Meat? You won't want it, you'll eat out with us. Chuck it in the bin. What about the rest of it, Clegg? Will you pay the dustmen to take it away? I think I'm turning into a vegetarian.

[*Pause.*]

I know very well it's a sad moment, I can't be a failure just to help. We will all go out together and celebrate. Commemorate. Make an occasion.

SCENE TWO

ALEC *and* LISA's *room. A lot of furniture in a small space. Bed stripped, chair overturned, drawers pulled out, clothes on floor, china smashed.*

ALEC *is sitting in the armchair, unconcerned.* LISA *is rummaging*

among the clothes on the floor. She's about six months pregnant.
She's dressed up, as they've been out for the evening.

LISA: What's gone? They've taken the transistor. Have they?
  Where did you leave it? They have taken it. They didn't have to
  smash the bambi. Oh, oh no, yes, the ring. My engagement ring.
  I took it off to do the washing and left it – unless it fell down.
  [*She rummages among clothes on the floor, tossing them aside*
  with distaste.] Help me look. I can't ever have another one.
  It's my one and only engagement ring and it's gone. And what
  else? Try and look around. Here's the tin had the housekeeping
  in it. And where's the clock? I'll be lost in the morning. Oh Alec
  get the police, get it all back. Run out to the phone.

ALEC: Let's not get the police, Lisa.

LISA: If we're very quick they might just catch them.

ALEC: I wouldn't want them caught.

LISA: What is it now?

ALEC: If he wants the things that much, perhaps let him have
  them.

LISA: I want the things very much. And they're mine.

ALEC: If you have the police you've all the bother. You may not
  get anything back. I don't want them catching somebody for
  me.

LISA: If we'd come in when he was still here, you wouldn't have
  grabbed him.

ALEC: No.

LISA: If we'd found him murdering the boys you'd have stood
  there.

  [*Pause.*]

  I'm going to get the police.

  [*Pause.*]

  I can't get the police if you won't. Please Alec.

ALEC: You can if you want.

LISA: Anyone in their right mind would get the police.

ALEC: All right but don't ask me to do it for you.

LISA: I don't like the way you're stopping me.

ALEC: I'm not stopping you.

LISA: I can't do it if when they come in you're just going to sit
  there.

13

ALEC: If you want police go and get some. If you don't let's forget it.

LISA: Any other man would get the police himself. He wouldn't put it all on me. You never worry about nothing.

ALEC: So why do you?

LISA: Someone's got to worry to get things done.

ALEC: What really has to be done can just be done. You worry before and you worry afterwards. Most things needn't be done at all.

LISA: Yes, I've noticed. Like work. I often wonder what you're doing all day while I'm washing hair. The boys are kept busy at school. Your mum was busy when she could be.

ALEC: Sitting here quietly. Doing nothing. The day goes by itself.

LISA: I wish you'd see a different doctor who'd find something really wrong with you. Then I could hope you'd get better. I forget normal people are like me. Why can't we try and get our things back?

ALEC: Yes, you must leave me if you want to.

LISA: I always hate it when you say that because what you mean is you want to leave me.

ALEC: No, if I wanted to I would.

LISA: Yes, you would, wouldn't you. You wouldn't worry about us at all. You wouldn't wonder how I'd bring up the kids. I can't go on working with a little baby you know. You'd go away and forget all about us.

ALEC: But I'm not forgetting. I don't want to leave. Here I am.

LISA: Plenty of men do leave their wives but at least they feel guilty about it.

ALEC: Why not sit down? You must be tired out, you look awful.

LISA [*sitting down*]: Angie says, you're not still working, Lisa, not after six months.

[*Pause.*]

ALEC: It's better you know without that clock ticking. Nothing's moving at all.

LISA: The baby is.

[ALEC *puts his hand out to feel it. Downstairs the front door shuts. Footsteps come upstairs.*]

LISA: I shall scream.

ALEC: If you want to.

    [*Footsteps. Knock at the door.*]

  It's not locked.

    [WORSELY *comes in.*]

WORSELY: I hope I'm not intruding. Mrs Crow said she was sure you wouldn't mind if I had a look round.

LISA: A look round what?

WORSELY: My name is Worsely. Mrs Crow may have mentioned me. I am a prospective buyer of the house.

LISA: She never said nothing to me.

WORSELY: I think she told you she was intending to sell.

LISA: She said she was thinking about it. That was only a couple of days ago.

WORSELY: She went to see an estate agent yesterday and the house is on their new list out today.

LISA: I didn't think she was certain in her mind.

WORSELY: I think she is now.

LISA: It's a bit late at night isn't it for buying a house?

WORSELY: When I viewed the rest of the property this morning there was no reply to my knock. Mrs Crow kindly lent me a spare key because she goes to bed –

LISA: You've got a liberty. What do you want to come frightening people for?

WORSELY: I'm nervous myself. Why am I frightening?

LISA: Have a look round by all means, have a good look round, and you'll see every single thing we own tipped out on the floor. What you don't see is what they took which is what was worth something.

WORSELY: A burglary? I didn't like to wonder. I thought perhaps some matrimonial . . . are the police making enquiries?

LISA: We haven't told them yet. We've just come in.

WORSELY: Just now? You must be in a state of shock. Can I make some tea? Or wrap you in a blanket? We must get the police at once. What a nuisance there's no telephone in the house.

LISA: No, I'm sorry.

WORSELY: You must be about to rush out to the callbox on the corner. Don't let me detain you. I'll just make myself at home.

LISA: That's all right.

WORSELY: My business can wait.

LISA: We thought we'd leave the police till the morning.

WORSELY: The sooner you go –

LISA: Thank you ever so much. I'm sorry. We're leaving it.

WORSELY: Don't let me interfere of course.

LISA: Do look round at anything you like. The cooker and sink's out on the landing. I expect you saw. I'll clear this lot up. I hardly like to touch my own things. They feel . . .

WORSELY: Sullied. You could put them all in the drycleaning machine.

LISA: It seems a bit extravagant

WORSELY: It's what I'd do myself.

LISA: This lot can go to the launderette.

WORSELY: You hear of cases where intruders relieve themselves on the furnishings.

LISA: I don't think I could go on living in a room where that had happened.

WORSELY: I hope you didn't lose anything of great value.

LISA: My engagement ring. That's the worst. And a quite new transistor radio –

WORSELY: And then there's the sentimental value.

LISA: Well there is. I was just saying to Alec.

[*They look at him but he doesn't respond. He is lying on the bed by now and stays there for the rest of the scene.*]

I don't know what you want to see or I'd show you. It's not a very good room I'm afraid. There's a lot of damp up in that corner. It gets in through the roof. It don't look bad now but it comes up worse in the winter.

WORSELY: I'll have a surveyor of course to see what repairs are necessary.

LISA: It will be nice if you can fix the damp because it's only going to get worse if it's left and it worries me for the winter with the baby.

WORSELY: The back room?

LISA: Yes, would you mind being very quiet because the kids are asleep in there, and Alec's mother. I'm sorry.

WORSELY: I won't go in. I wouldn't dream of it.

LISA: Please do.

WORSELY: I didn't come to wake up your children. That wouldn't be a very good start to our relationship. It's like the room below.

LISA: I've never been in Mrs Crow's rooms. We painted it yellow last year. I don't know if you care for yellow.

WORSELY: Two boys, I think Mrs Crow said. And your mother-in-law?

LISA: Of course when we came it was just my husband and myself. We used to hope we might get a house.

WORSELY: And soon there will be six of you.

LISA: Of course nobody with a decent place would want us in it. I wouldn't myself if I was letting rooms. I'd have single English steady office workers, one in each room. People like you.

WORSELY: Very true.

LISA: So we manage all right.

WORSELY: I expect when Mrs Crow sells the house you'll want to leave.

LISA: I hadn't thought of it.

WORSELY: I thought as you've been friends all these years you might not feel so comfortable when she's gone.

LISA: We're not what you'd call friends.

WORSELY: Especially as you're so overcrowded here.

LISA: Not that we're on bad terms at all.

WORSELY: I'm sure you'd be happier somewhere else.

LISA: Are you turning us out? Is that what you're saying? You can't do that. Alec? We're not furnished you know like the basement.

WORSELY: Turning you out? What an old-fashioned idea. I was hoping I could do you a favour.

LISA: Because this is an unfurnished tenancy.

WORSELY: Moving house is always an expense. You'll want new things for the baby. And then there's your losses tonight. What would you say to two hundred pounds?

LISA: We haven't got two hundred pounds. What do you mean?

WORSELY: No, I'm going to give you two hundred pounds.

LISA: What for?

WORSELY: I was going to say one hundred but seeing I've come at such a catastrophic moment, which I really do sympathise with, I can see my way to making it double.

17

LISA: How do you mean?

WORSELY: To assist with the removal expenses. To enable you to afford a bigger place. A ground floor perhaps and use of the garden for the kiddies.

LISA: You want to give us two hundred pounds? For nothing?

WORSELY: It's a bit like winning the pools. In a small way.

LISA: Two hundred pound notes?

WORSELY: I like to see people happy.

LISA: You're very kind. Are you sure you can spare it? You're not just sorry for us are you? You've caught us at a bad time.

WORSELY: The delightful thing is we both get something out of it. I get the rooms, you get the money, we're both happy.

LISA: But they're not our rooms to sell, they're Mrs Crow's. Shouldn't she have the money? I'm getting all in a muddle, I'm sorry, but I'm not used to property at all.

WORSELY: Mrs Crow is getting a good price for the house and this is a little bit extra for you because I like to do things properly.

LISA: Is this what usually happens?

WORSELY: Very often.

LISA: It's all new to me. Well what an excitement.

ALEC: I'm not moving.

WORSELY: Did your husband say something?

LISA: Have you been paying attention, Alec? Mr Worsely's giving us two hundred pounds. We mustn't feel bad about taking it because we'll have the trouble of moving and he'll have the rooms.

ALEC: We'll have the trouble and he'll have the rooms.

LISA: We can use the money to pay for a bigger place.

ALEC: How much did you say?

LISA: Two hundred pounds.

WORSELY: Two hundred pounds is a lot of money.

LISA: Of course the rents round here have shot up. We'll be lucky to find something even this size for less than ten. We only pay two pounds here because it goes back a long time.

WORSELY: But your new flat would be of a higher standard.

LISA: That's eight into two hundred . . . It's less than six months.

18

Is that right? Then we'd have to find all that extra. Don't think I'm being ungrateful.

WORSELY: You're taking a very unrealistic attitude. I'm only trying to be of assistance.

LISA: I wish it could work out. It seems such a shame.

WORSELY: These conditions are most unsuitable for bringing up a young family. [*To* ALEC.] All these stairs for your wife. [*To* LISA.] Three kiddies and their grandmother in one small room.

LISA: What I'd really like is somewhere of my own. I never thought we'd still be here. I saw my life quite different.

WORSELY: You may never have another chance of making a new start. If you try to stay here I think you'll regret it.

LISA: But we don't have to go whatever you say.

WORSELY: Under the new act your rent here will of course be adjusted to a fair rent.

LISA: How much is that?

WORSELY: The property will be so much improved that the rent to be fair – well, we'd have to wait and see, wouldn't we. The builders may find it necessary to take out the stairs for a time. The roof of course will have to come off.

LISA: The roof come off?

WORSELY: You mustn't let that worry you because I'm quite sure that before that happens you'll be snugly installed in some new accommodation. Only don't leave your decision too late because I can't keep my offer open indefinitely.

LISA: It's still open now?

WORSELY: Oh yes, still open for the time being. Suppose I give you a few days and call back one evening next week and we can finalise our arrangements to the greatest benefit of all parties. I wish you luck in getting back your property. You'll need luck as well as the police. I can find my own way down.

[WORSELY *goes.*]

LISA: We'll never have two hundred pounds all at once to hold in our hands. But it wouldn't last long. I don't know.

ALEC: The best thing is just ignore him.

LISA: We can't ignore him if he walks in. And what did he mean about taking the stairs away and the roof?

ALEC: He wants us to go.

LISA: If he really wants us to go he might offer us even more money. Then we'd have to take it. In our own interests.

ALEC: We don't have to do anything.

LISA: I don't want to stay where I'm not wanted. It's not like home any more. And all our things . . . Are we getting the police or not?

[Pause.]

Still I've always got the boys, that's what matters. I've got you.

SCENE THREE

Music. MARION, WORSELY, *and* CLEGG *are at a table in a strip club. They have all been drinking,* CLEGG *most.* CLEGG *is watching the stripper, the others not.*

MARION: I will not sell leasehold. I'll have the freehold first.

WORSELY: You'll have to wait.

MARION: Then I'll wait. And the buyers will wait. The price can only rise.

WORSELY: Arlington understood you would sell.

MARION: I understood I could buy the freehold.

WORSELY: He's expecting —

MARION: But you'll tell him he made a mistake. You're wonderful, Worsley, at anything unpleasant. It's what you're for. Interest him in another property. Forty-two.

WORSELY: We haven't got vacant possession of forty-two.

MARION: But you're working on it, so we soon will. Enjoying yourself Clegg?

CLEGG: Aren't you watching?

MARION: Half.

CLEGG: You're not really entering into it. Doesn't the gun do something for you, Worsley?

WORSELY: It would in my own hands.

CLEGG: She would in my own hands.

MARION: If you want a girl, Clegg, I'll buy you one.

CLEGG: She's never bought me a drink until tonight. Pride. I

20

have my pride. Tonight's a special occasion. A fling. The end of
Clegg and Son. The end of me.

MARION: Have you been to forty-two?

WORSELY: Three times.

MARION: The basement's no trouble.

WORSELY: The basement's furnished.

MARION: Upstairs. A couple I think with children. And an old
lady.

WORSELY: That's the ones.

CLEGG: Oh now look, did you see that, Marion? Keep a sharp eye
out, Worsely and you won't miss it.

MARION [to WORSELY]: How do they seem?

CLEGG: How's that for flesh?

WORSELY [to MARION]: Dicey.

MARION [to WORSELY]: How far have you gone?

CLEGG: Ooh.

WORSELY [to MARION]: Five hundred.

CLEGG: Ooh. Ah.

MARION [to WORSELY]: No luck?

WORSELY [to MARION]: I could manage the wife.

MARION [to WORSELY]: The man?

CLEGG: Ah. Ah.

> [*Climax. The gun fires.* CLEGG *gasps.* WORSELY *jumps and
> spills the wine.*]

WORSELY: I hate bangs. I'm so sorry. I do apologise.

MARION: I was throwing the dress away in any case. I hate old
clothes. I love to throw them away. And get new ones.

WORSELY: That doesn't look old.

MARION: Old enough.

WORSELY: You don't look old.

MARION: I should hope not. You're no good at flattery, Worsely,
but luckily I'm too vain to mind.

CLEGG: Wasn't that . . . quite . . . interesting really? Worth every
penny.

MARION: I believe I know the tenants at forty-two.

WORSELY: Minton.

MARION: Lisa Minton. She does hair. And . . . Alec?

CLEGG: What?

MARION: Fancy them being my tenants.

WORSELY: Friends are they?

CLEGG: What?

MARION: Do you remember Lisa and Alec, Clegg?

CLEGG: What do you mean, do I remember?

MARION: Do you remember?

CLEGG: You sound as if I might have forgotten.

MARION: It's some time.

CLEGG: It is indeed.

WORSELY: Old friends?

CLEGG: Friends of Marion's.

MARION: You liked Lisa.

CLEGG: I liked Lisa.

WORSELY: You found him a bit odd, I expect.

CLEGG: Marion got on with him all right.

[*Music starts again.*]

MARION: It's a long time ago.

CLEGG: Why have they come up?

WORSELY: Marion's bought the house they live in.

CLEGG: What for?

MARION: To sell. Look, it's starting again and none of us watching. What a waste.

CLEGG: Worsely deals with it does he?

WORSELY: I call from time to time. They're trying it on.

CLEGG: I'm sure Worsely will deal with it very well Marion. You won't need to go round yourself.

MARION: I trust Worsely to do everything I would do.

CLEGG: Let him do it then.

MARION: Do look, Clegg. I do think these girls are so clever. I would never dare. Would I? I don't think so.

CLEGG: You? Dare? You'd better not, Marion. It's all right for them, it's what they do. We pay for it. You haven't got the figure in any case, so remember your place. Loose talk costs lives.

MARION: What if I did it for you?

CLEGG: For me? Would you? Like that. Look, Worsely, you're missing the best – look at that, Marion. Remember that. Ah, that was close.

WORSELY: You know them then?

MARION: Some time ago. We lost touch.

WORSELY: You remember them quite well.

MARION: Lisa phoned me this morning. She said was it right I knew about property these days because she was in some trouble and needed advice.

CLEGG: Oh Marion look at the size of them . . . oh I'd like to get hold. Oh I'd like to gobble . . .

MARION: I said she could call at the office on Wednesday morning. So you might keep clear for a start.

WORSELY: Be careful.

CLEGG: Oh stop it. Ooh.

MARION: I always am.

WORSELY: I know.

CLEGG: Ooh. Aah. Oh my goodness gracious. Ooh.

MARION: He's busy.

WORSELY: Careful.

MARION: Do as you're told.

[*They kiss.* CLEGG *is intent on the strip.*]

SCENE FOUR

MARION's *office. Large desk and large street map.* MARION *and* LISA. MARION *is on her feet, eating a bar of chocolate.* LISA *is sitting in a chair on the client's side of the desk, huge and tired.*

LISA: Mrs Crow keeps saying, Nobody wants a property with tenants. As if it was rats. Why don't they put poison down? She says, If you're an owner, dear, you expect to own. Why don't you save up and get your own place like I did. She got that house before the war for two hundred pounds and now it's twenty thousand. I wasn't born when I could have got it for two hundred. So I don't care if that Worsely won't like the noise. I'll tell the kids they can shout all they want and get up at six and jump off the bed onto the floor. One thing if we don't have stairs I won't hear him coming up them. My blood runs cold. He comes at night just to make it worse. He takes a look all round the room to see how he's going to improve it. He'll get rid of the old wallpaper, he'll get rid of the damp, he'll get rid of us.

MARION: Five hundred pounds is a good offer.

LISA: If it was just me I'd go.

MARION: Not enough?

LISA: He don't seem to notice Worsely at all. You know what he's like.

MARION: Not really.

LISA: You don't, do you. Not now. You'd see a change. He's very queer. Oh Marion he is. The past is over isn't it Marion? I wouldn't have come to you for help if I hadn't thought all that was such a long time ago. But we all had some good times once. I don't know who else I could ask that knows about houses. And really I'd rather have him unfaithful than like what he is now. It's half·what you expect from a man. My mum always said not to take on and they'd soon be back. And it's quite true, nothing ever lasted. Because men know in their hearts where they belong. But she never said nothing about someone being like Alec is now. He hasn't been at work for six months. He don't remember to eat if I don't make him. He's very nice to me all the time. But I sometimes wonder if he knows who I am. I think he'd be nice to anyone. I went to see the doctor about him and he gave me some pills to take myself but that don't make Alec any better it just makes me put up with it. And now they've stopped cheering me up anyway. And I'm worried, Marion, they might have hurt the baby. I don't think Alec would care if it was a good pretty baby or a monster. I don't think he could tell the difference.

MARION: What does he do? What does he talk about?

LISA: Nothing at all. He don't get bored. He was always rushing about wasn't he? Marion, I'm really frightened by him. I can't start looking for a place with him like that. If I have to do one more thing I'll scream. When I think of the nights and nappies I hope this baby's never born.

MARION: Alec was never stubborn. He always rather gave in to what you wanted.

LISA: If I insisted he might give in. But I don't know what I want any more. And in a funny way he does. He just wants nothing. He seems to feel everything's all right.

MARION: He stays in all day? And in the evening?

LISA: It's not like it was. There's nobody else. It's almost like a very happy time. If things was different. He's lovely with the boys when he bothers.

MARION: Does Alec want the baby?

[*Knock at the door.* MARION *opens it. It is* WORSELY. LISA *doesn't look round.*]

No, not now. Five minutes. Go away.

[*She shuts the door.*]

Now, Lisa, what are you going to do?

LISA: I don't know. I came to ask you. Since you know about property. You don't know of somewhere we could go?

MARION: Not at the rent you're paying now of course.

LISA: Mr Worsely says it's going up. He won't say what to. So you might as well go, he says. But go where?

MARION: Would Alec go if I found you another flat?

LISA: Perhaps if you could come and talk to him. You could tell him it's what you recommend as an expert.

MARION: If you really think that would help.

LISA: I tell myself Mr Worsely's just saying things to frighten me but he does frighten me. I wouldn't ask you if I wasn't desperate. I didn't want to see you again. But I can't have a baby with the roof off.

[*Knock at the door.*]

MARION [*answering the door*]: I said – oh it's you. What's the matter?

[CLEGG *comes in.*]

CLEGG: I just thought I'd drop in. I got a bit bored indoors. Sambo's excellent company for a dog. He does just what he's told as if he was human. I pretended to be cross, just to see, and he lay down with eyes so sad just like a real member of the family, and then I said, Good fellow, come –

MARION: Lisa.

CLEGG: And he leapt – well well. Expecting again. Congratulations.

LISA: We was always such friends.

25

CLEGG: It's a long time. Things were very different. You've heard our tragedy I suppose? I've had to close the shop.

LISA: Oh no, you've never had to do that. What an awful thing. Your very own shop all gone.

CLEGG: That's what I say. All gone. My very own.

LISA: You're as badly off as me.

CLEGG: It's a man's job to put a stiff upper lip on the face of it. To lend a supporting arm. Your chin can tremble.

LISA: It's such a relief to feel I'm with real old friends.

CLEGG: Sympathy may not do any good but it does help.

LISA: Oh it does. I'm so glad. Oh forgive me. [*Cries.*]

CLEGG: There there. A real woman. A good cry. Best thing.

MARION: Can we get on?

LISA: I'm so tired of it all.

CLEGG: There there there.

LISA: Oh oh.

CLEGG: Poor little flower.

LISA: Oh.

[*Knock.* MARION *opens the door. It is* WORSELY. MARION *is about to stop him, then gives up.*]

MARION: Oh what the hell.

[WORSELY *comes in.*]

CLEGG [*to* WORSELY]: A moving moment.

MARION: Come over here where we can hear ourselves think. Has Arlington seen forty-two yet?

WORSELY: He'd like it with vacant possession. Is that her?

MARION: You're very white.

WORSELY: It's the gas.

MARION: What, last night?

WORSELY: That Samaritan friend of mine dropped in just as I was going off nicely.

MARION: Had you invited him?

WORSELY: You know me better than that Marion. I do try.

LISA: Mr Worsely?

WORSELY: At your service as always. I hope you've come to a happy decision.

LISA: You know him?

CLEGG: He's Marion's employee my dear. He goes about to all

26

her properties dealing with the tenants. Have a hanky. Blow.

LISA: You mean it's you buying the house? It's all you, Marion, is it? I always hated you, you horrible bitch, you cunt cunt cunt –

CLEGG: I hate to hear a lady use language.

MARION: Have a cry. Have a good cry. Then we'll see.

SCENE FIVE

Room. ALEC *is on the bed and his* MUM *is in the armchair asleep. From time to time she slips down and has to be propped up.* MARION *is standing, eating a banana taken from a bowl on the table. She gives him an orange, which he takes but doesn't eat.*

MARION: I'm always hungry. But thin. I don't put on. Nothing to show for it. Moving about all the time is what does it. I eat in bed. I work at the table and sleep at my desk. Burning it up.

ALEC: Help yourself.

MARION: I do. Is something wrong with your legs?

ALEC: No.

MARION: Or your head?

ALEC: No.

MARION: Why don't you get up?

ALEC: If you like.

[*He gets up.*]

MARION: Alec you know it's me that's bought the house.

ALEC: Lisa told me.

MARION: Worsely acts for me.

ALEC: She said.

MARION: I want vacant possession of my house.

ALEC: I gather.

MARION: Lisa suggested I came and talked to you. I can offer alternative accommodation. I wouldn't have come otherwise.

ALEC: No.

MARION: I would have come anyway.

ALEC: Yes.

MARION: I knew you were here when I bought the house. That was why. Also the property itself. Desirable investment. How

27

could I have bought it without knowing unless I'd forgotten the address and I couldn't do that. I've a great memory for details. All sorts of little details.

ALEC: Marion, what do you want?

MARION: I'll give you a thousand pounds to go away.

ALEC: I don't want a thousand pounds.

MARION: What do you want?

ALEC: Nothing at all. I try to want things for Lisa. For the boys. For mum even though she's past wanting anything she can have. I don't know what I could lose that would make any difference to me.

MARION: Lisa?

ALEC: No.

MARION: You don't love her.

ALEC: I didn't say that.

MARION: If you love someone you want to keep them. I want to. So not Lisa. Your mum? Lisa says you won't part with her. You won't let her go to hospital. Do you cling to your mum?

ALEC: She'll die soon.

MARION: Are you sorry?

ALEC: Everyone dies. Unless they were never born.

MARION: Are you glad then?

ALEC: No.

MARION: Have you got no feelings at all?

ALEC: Not of indignation.

MARION: But you wouldn't want to lose your children.

ALEC: No.

MARION: There then.

ALEC: But children do die sometimes. It could happen. Why not to mine as much as someone else's?

MARION: But if it did happen to yours, that should be a horror for you. We're not talking about other people.

ALEC: I could probably bear it.

MARION: I'll give you a thousand pounds for Lisa. For your mum. For the boys. Whatever you like to think it's for. And find you somewhere to live. This flat is ridiculous.

ALEC: You seem to want this house very much.

MARION: What I want is you to wake up. We were going to better

28

ourselves. What did we go to evening classes for? We both felt we'd missed something. You were never sure what subject was the answer. Everything seemed to lead to something else you wanted to get hold of. There were books in the bed. You couldn't let a single fact go.

ALEC: Learning things wasn't any use.

MARION: If you wanted it to be some use you should have concentrated on one thing and got a qualification. I got on in the end in my own way. I always said I wasn't the butcher's wife. You could have done something even greater.

ALEC: But why should I?

MARION: You've no stamina. [*Pause.*] I've got a garden flat you could have.

ALEC: Basement.

MARION: Basement flat.

ALEC: Do you want us to go really?

MARION: Two thousand pounds to get out of my house.

ALEC: Why do you think I want two thousand pounds?

MARION: You should want it. For Lisa's sake. For your sons. What are you up to, Alec? Of course it wasn't in your interest to go for two hundred or five hundred or whatever little sum it was. Even a thousand doesn't touch the profit I'll make. I respect you for hanging on. But two thousand? Two five.

MUM: Edie. Edie.

ALEC: Hello there.

MARION: Are you Edie?

ALEC: She likes someone to answer.

[*He goes over to* MUM *and props her up.*]

MARION: My God, I hope I don't live as long.

ALEC: She's not in pain.

MARION: Marvellous.

ALEC: It's a great deal.

MARION: But she doesn't know what's going on. Does she remember her own life? Does she even know who she is? I'd kill myself if I felt my mind beginning to drop away like that. Suppose I said, Alec, Alec, and someone else said Hello there. And I didn't know it wasn't you. Because it would be you I called for even if I was eighty.

29

ALEC: I've always thought of that as over. In fact I never think of it at all.

MARION: My face will go like hers one day. I keep what I can. I don't want to die.

ALEC: It was all here before you were born and you don't resent that.

MARION: But once you have things you don't want to give them up. It's quite different.

ALEC: No, it's just the same.

MARION: But I want to hold on. Everything I was taught – be clean, be quick, be top, be best, you may not succeed, Marion, but what matters is to try your hardest. To push on. Onward Christian soldiers, marching as to war. That was my favourite song when I was seven. Fight the good fight. Where's your fight? I know the bible stories aren't true but that makes their meaning matter most. God gave him dominion over every beast of the field and fowl of the air. Gave the land to him and to his seed forever. Doesn't evolution say the same? Keep on, get better, be best. Onward. Fight. How did man get to the moon? Not by sitting staring at an orange. Columbus, Leonardo de Vinci, Scott of the Antarctic. You would be content on a flat earth. But the animals are ours. The vegetables and minerals. For us to consume. We don't shrink from blood. Or guilt. Guilt is essential to progress. You'll tell me next you don't feel guilt. I don't know how you know you're alive. Guilt is knowing what you do. I see the children with no shoes and socks in the houses I buy. Should I buy them socks? It would be ridiculous. But I feel it. That gritty lump is the pearl. Swine. And what would happen to work without guilt? I was never a lazy girl, Marion tries hard. I work like a dog. Most women are fleas but I'm the dog.

ALEC: I don't at all mind leaving if you want it very much.

MARION: Two five?

ALEC: No money.

MARION: Lisa will want it.

ALEC: All right, if you like. If she likes. Talk about it to her.

MUM: Edie.

ALEC: Hello. [*He goes across to sit her up.*]

30

MARION: Wouldn't you rather stay here?

ALEC: I don't mind.

MARION: You could stay.

ALEC: Of course I could.

MARION: I mean there would be no more pressure.

ALEC: Yes Lisa doesn't like Worsely much.

MARION: No more Worsely.

ALEC: Good.

MARION: Are you with me?

ALEC: I don't think so, no.

MARION: You could stay here as long as you like. If we could go back.

ALEC: Back where?

MARION: To each other.

ALEC: I wasn't at all the same person then.

MARION: You were mine then and you always will be.

ALEC: I've changed. Skin and all in seven years.

MARION: The mind's the same. Don't wriggle, Alec.

ALEC: I don't know what mind you mean.

MARION: You can say what you like but it's still recognisably you. Of course you're not exactly the same. Everyone changes. But this you is in place of that you. It's still you. It's not someone else altogether.

ALEC: I think it might just as well be. You talk about the past and the future but it doesn't apply. Here I am now.

MARION: What you're saying is you've had a breakdown.

ALEC: Or up. Or through.

MARION: I've been in a mental hospital myself. Just after.

ALEC: I heard.

MARION: I don't care if you're mad or sane, Alec. I'm yours whether you want me or not. Have all the money and stay here too if that's what you want. Empires have been lost for love. Worlds well lost. We men of destiny get what we're after even if we're destroyed by it. And everyone else with us. We split the atom. Onward. Love me.

ALEC: I'm not what you want.

MARION: You are what I want. I want you badly now.

ALEC: Now?

MARION: And always. I'm keeping you Alec.
ALEC: I could now. Easily. If you want. But I don't keep.
MUM: Edie. Edie.

SCENE SIX

Same. Old MUM *has slipped well down in her chair and almost fallen out.* LISA *is lying on the bed. She has come in from work.* ALEC *is standing near.* MARION *is eating.*

LISA: Might have known.
ALEC: It wasn't planned.
MARION: Speak for yourself.
LISA: I wouldn't have come in early if this hadn't started. I might never have known.
MARION: Yes it was bad luck.
LISA: It was not. I like to know. So I can forgive him. Or not. Whichever I want to do.
MARION: You were just in time if you want to know. If you're technically minded.
LISA: I don't need to know the details. Here's another.
MARION: You're meant to relax I've heard. You won't do that with me here.
ALEC: Shall I get the ambulance yet?
LISA: Don't you dare. I'm not lying round in hospital a minute longer than I need to. Alec, you'll have to do the boys' tea.
ALEC: Don't worry.
LISA: Tell them where I've gone.
ALEC: Don't worry.
MARION: You can stay here, Lisa, by the way. I lose quite a few thousand pounds. I must ask Mr Arlington if he's prepared to buy the house with sitting tenants. And if not find him another house. And this house another purchaser. So don't mention all your thanks.
LISA: I'm not staying here. With you two.
MARION: If you go you don't get any money.
LISA: I'll see you in hell. Hold my hand Alec.

32

ALEC: You're lovely.

MARION [*propping up old* MUM]: Up she comes.

LISA: It's three weeks early.

ALEC: Don't worry.

LISA: I'm not bringing a baby home to this. I am not. I'd sooner kill it.

MARION: You were quite happy to stay here before. You refused our offers of financial assistance with the move.

LISA: I was never happy.

MARION: You mean you want to go? All right, go. I'll be only too glad.

LISA: I don't know.

MARION: Stay then. Are you staying?

LISA: You can have it. If you think it's so easy.

MARION: I don't want it to live in.

LISA: You can have the baby.

MARION: What does she mean? Having a baby you have to do yourself.

LISA: Afterwards. You have it. I'm not.

MARION: Have the baby?

LISA: I'm not bringing a baby back to this room.

MARION: I'll take it, yes.

LISA: You take it then. I never want to see it.

MARION: I'll take it then. I'll keep it.

LISA: Yes keep it.

ALEC: I'm getting the ambulance, Lisa.

LISA: Both of you go.

MARION: I could stay with you if I have to. Though I wouldn't know what to do.

LISA: Alec, don't leave me alone with her.

ALEC: All right?

　　[ALEC *and* MARION *go out. Old* MUM *slips right down, starts, wakes.*]

MUM: Edie? Edie. Make you cuppa tea.

　　[*She gets up and walks across the room. She goes out onto the landing. She comes back in with the kettle and puts it on the table. She walks slowly around looking for the tea. She finds the teapot and takes it to the table. She finds the matches and puts them on the table. Dizzy for a moment, she holds onto the table. She pours water from the kettle to the teapot, spilling most of it over the matches. She sits trying to strike the matches.* LISA *is lying on the bed. Once her face creases and she breathes deeply as she has a contraction – no exaggerated moaning or writhing about. Then she lies limp as before.*]

ACT TWO

SCENE ONE

CLEGG *and* WORSELY *in* CLEGG's *kitchen. Large pram.* CLEGG *is heating a baby's bottle in a saucepan of water.* WORSELY *is making tea. His neck is bandaged.*

CLEGG: Weedkiller.

WORSELY: Sugar.

CLEGG: Two for me.

WORSELY: I wouldn't try to hang myself again.

CLEGG: Weedkiller in Marion's soup. In a garlic soup. Would it taste?

WORSELY: Try some and see.

CLEGG: I read of someone got just a splash in an orange drink and poured it away when she tasted but even so that sip was fatal. It took a week mind you.

WORSELY: You'd have a job explaining.

CLEGG: I don't care. I don't care. I've had enough bottling up. Something must explode.

WORSELY: My befriender the Samaritan believes life is God-given. At first he was too sensitive to say so but now in the interests of our befriendship he talks about his real feelings. Life is leasehold. It belongs to God the almighty landlord. You mustn't take your life because it's God's property not yours. I tell him if there's anything I own it's what I stand up in.

CLEGG: That old suit?

WORSELY: My flesh and blood. The contraption I am in. The contraption I am.

CLEGG: It's not illegal now I'm glad to say. I couldn't have let Marion employ a criminal.

WORSELY: Why was it illegal? The life as property of the state?

CLEGG: In the free world?

WORSELY: In wartime it is.

CLEGG: In wartime, naturally. No, I believe it was against the law because it was wrong morally.

WORSELY: And now it no longer is?

35

CLEGG: Apparently not.

WORSELY: Though in any case the law's not for morals so much as property. The legal system was made by owners. A man can do what he likes with his own.

CLEGG: Try telling Marion.

WORSELY: A house the same. Your own. You knock the floor out if you like. That's what it's for. A car the same. You drive how you like. Within a reasonable speed limit. My flesh and blood the same.

CLEGG: A wife the same.

WORSELY: A wife is a person.

CLEGG: First and foremost a wife. One flesh. Marion leaves me.

WORSELY: She's basically fond.

CLEGG: Every morning she leaves me to go to work.

WORSELY: Work's a virtue.

CLEGG: And every evening she leaves me, leaves me, leaves me.

WORSELY: Goes out?

CLEGG: Or stays in. But not with me. Not being my wife. Not paying attention.

WORSELY: She's a lot on her mind.

CLEGG: Like what?

WORSELY: The baby?

CLEGG: And?

WORSELY: Business?

CLEGG: And?

WORSELY: I'm not specially close to Marion to know her thoughts.

CLEGG: Not close?

WORSELY: No.

CLEGG: These days.

WORSELY: Pardon?

CLEGG: Not so close as you were?

WORSELY: She's a bit absent-minded as you say.

CLEGG: I will chop her mind into little pieces and blanch them in boiling water.

WORSELY: Baby's looking well.

CLEGG: You are looking, Worsely, at a man who has killed a man.

WORSELY: Pardon me?

36

CLEGG: More than you have done. Manhood, Worsely. Some of us may think we have it when really it is someone else.

WORSELY: How do you mean?

CLEGG: I changed a living human being into a carcass.

WORSELY: Who was it?

CLEGG: I don't know who it was, that's not the point, who it was. It was me did it, that's the point. 'Who was it'!

WORSELY: When was it then?

CLEGG: Twenty years ago.

WORSELY: I was only a toddler.

CLEGG: I was a man.

WORSELY: Before my time. I'm not an accessory?

CLEGG: Man to man.

WORSELY: Some time back. No repercussions?

CLEGG: How do you mean?

WORSELY: Of course most murders do go undetected. The police don't publicise the fact.

CLEGG: It wasn't a murder.

WORSELY: You mean we're talking about an accident? I ran over a little boy with my motor scooter when I was seventeen, I don't make a song and dance.

CLEGG: It was in the army. National Service we men had to do.

WORSELY: Oh the army. Why didn't you say so? Anyone can kill somebody if they're in the army. Was it one of the enemy?

CLEGG: It was a guerilla.

WORSELY: You were claiming just now it was a man.

CLEGG: Guerilla, little chappies in the bushes.

WORSELY: Oh, I thought you meant – never mind.

CLEGG: It was him or me.

WORSELY: It doesn't count if you were in uniform. Everybody knows it's not the same thing as killing another person.

CLEGG: It does count.

WORSELY: I've a cousin in America reckons he killed any number. But what does he expect in the situation they've got in? I don't think that makes him special.

CLEGG: But did he see them?

WORSELY: He didn't say. It was just a postcard.

CLEGG: I can see it might not be the same if you don't see them. Bombing from a plane.

WORSELY: Bombing's not what I call killing.

CLEGG: Not at all.

WORSELY: You can't feel over a certain distance.

CLEGG: Well in my case at about twenty feet I felt quite a shock.

WORSELY: I dare say you might.

CLEGG: Just so long as you know who it's the wife of you're dealing with.

WORSELY: Bottle's hot.

CLEGG: Blast.

WORSELY: Cool it.

CLEGG: Damn nuisance. Night time too. [*He puts the bottle in a bowl of cold water.*]

WORSELY: Does he wake you?

CLEGG: You try spending the night here some time.

WORSELY: I wouldn't mind.

CLEGG: Watch your tone of voice.

WORSELY: I mean I quite take to that baby. I always thought they all looked alike. But I'd know him.

CLEGG: How?

WORSELY: Sort of dimple.

CLEGG: Plenty of them about.

WORSELY: It's the general look. I saw a baby yesterday in the street. I looked in the pram and it wasn't him. Same colour pram. Same size baby. But different look.

CLEGG: You give him the bottle. You be dad.

WORSELY: If he gets kidnapped any time and you have to go and identify him you can take me. Marion wouldn't know.

CLEGG: She sleeps like the dead. I kick her. Punch her in the kidneys. No avail.

WORSELY: He's not awake for his bottle.

CLEGG: It's bottle time.

WORSELY: You don't wake him?

CLEGG: He's got to learn regular habits. He won't make a family butcher without a sense of responsibility. Waking in the night's no substitute.

WORSELY: Butcher is he?

CLEGG: Marion thinks she's bought me off. I've a gun upstairs.
[WORSELY *was about to pick up the baby but now forgets about it.*]

WORSELY: Real one?

CLEGG: Old customer did me a favour. Get all sorts buying meat. No questions asked.

WORSELY: Loaded?

CLEGG: Wait and see.

WORSELY: I couldn't borrow it could I one night? I would have finished with it by tomorrow.

CLEGG: How were you planning to give it back?

WORSELY: I want it.

CLEGG: Of course if I was to think I had any reason to suspect anything of you, Worsely, then I might help you on your way.

WORSELY: Me?

CLEGG: Tell me plainly do you fuck my wife? Or does she jerk you off? Or do you touch her up? Or snog? Fumble? Grope? Caress? Brush against? Or come very close to any of these.

WORSELY: You've got the wrong man.

CLEGG: How close?

WORSELY: Alec.

CLEGG: Proof.

WORSELY: Beyond a reasonable doubt.

CLEGG: Seen?

WORSELY: I wouldn't look.

CLEGG: Said?

WORSELY: Changed, just she's changed.

CLEGG: Changed to you?

WORSELY: All round.

CLEGG: You mean she used to and now she won't.

WORSELY: Anything I can do Clegg as an old friend of the family and employee of your wife I will gladly do to rid us of Alec.

CLEGG: To rid me of Alec.

WORSELY: That's what I said. Don't push me Clegg. It makes my head wobble.

CLEGG: Weedkiller.

WORSELY: Let's have a look.

CLEGG: It says poison in red here.

39

WORSELY: I know it is. [*He takes the packet and keeps it.*]

CLEGG: There's the gun. But I was keeping that for her.

WORSELY: I'm jumpy of bangs. Though I could if it was myself because you wouldn't hear, would you, the explosion causing your own extinction?

CLEGG: What I had in mind, Worsely. What I have had in mind for some time. Was a fire.

WORSELY: Like an electric fire dropped in the bath? But I doubt if he uses the Arlington's bathroom.

CLEGG: Set the house on fire. Set the house on fire.

WORSELY: Easily said.

CLEGG: Easily done. Petrol and so on.

WORSELY: There are other people.

CLEGG: They would get out. They would probably all get out.

WORSELY: Alec would get out.

CLEGG: Never mind, he might not. It's the idea. The threat to him. The damage to Marion. Her property you see.

WORSELY: Arlington completed last week.

CLEGG: It's somewhat symbolic. Think of the terror.

WORSELY: What do I get out of it?

CLEGG: You could try pouring petrol on yourself.

WORSELY: I think I should be paid.

CLEGG: Fifty pounds? Hundred.

WORSELY: Look, Marion will pay, don't you see? You get the money off Marion. You only have to ask.

CLEGG: What have you got against her, Worsely? I'm prepared to sink any differences in a common cause. Afterwards I'd like you to leave the area. You could set up in property yourself. London is full of property.

WORSELY: Thousand?

CLEGG: Leaving me with my wife and son to bring up as I please.

[WORSELY *pours two more mugs of tea.*]

WORSELY: I think I'll just pop out and kill some weeds. Very weedy garden.

CLEGG: A baby's a full time job. I'm not a gardener.

WORSELY: So I'll do a bit for you. All right?

[*He sets off out of the back door with weedkiller, mug of tea, packet of sugar.*]

CLEGG: Don't take all the sugar. What about me. I take two.
    [WORSELY *has gone.* CLEGG *feels the temperature of the*
    bottle: too cold. He mutters and puts it back in the saucepan
    to warm up. Loud explosion. CLEGG *opens the back door.*]
    Christ, Worsely, you've blown off your hand.

SCENE TWO

Marion's office. MARION *and* LISA. MARION *is walking about*
eating. LISA, *no longer pregnant, hair a mess, face a wreck, baggy*
old dress, is sitting in a chair, crying.

LISA: I can't stop crying.

MARION: What about?

LISA: I don't know.

MARION: Then it doesn't matter. So long as you're not sad about
    anything. I should just cry.

LISA: It's the pills they give me.

MARION: There's plenty of tissues.

LISA: You never cry.

MARION: Not over nothing, no.

LISA: I'm getting worse and worse. I want to get better, Marion.

MARION: Home soon.

LISA: Marion I want . . .

MARION: Tissue.

LISA: No no, I want . . .

MARION: Get on with it.

LISA: To see him.

MARION: Who?

LISA: My baby.

MARION: He's not here.

LISA: I want to see him.

MARION: No you don't.

LISA: I want to.

MARION: It's not supposed to be good. You're not even meant to
    see me. Just the third party. That's Worsely but he's late.

LISA: Why not?

MARION: In a third party adoption, Lisa, each party sees the third
party and all emotion is thus kept out.

LISA: I want him.

MARION: You want to get better, Lisa, and look after your boys.
Alec's taken his mother to hospital. Right? So you've got to
look after your big boys. That's your duty, Lisa, to your family.

LISA: I can't stop crying.

MARION: Cry then for God's sake. Nobody's stopping you.

LISA: I may not earn so much as you. But I'm not worth nothing.

MARION: Nobody said you were not worth nothing.

LISA: I'm sorry Marion, it's the pills. There's nothing wrong with
me.

[WORSELY *comes in. His right arm is heavily bandaged.*]

MARION: Late.

WORSELY: Mr Nicolaides barred my way with a poker.

MARION: Haven't they gone?

WORSELY: The wife died of cancer.

MARION: I don't see how that helps. Where are the papers?

WORSELY: Here we are. What's the trouble, Lisa?

MARION: He doesn't expect an answer. You sign here.

LISA: What is it?

MARION: Just a formality.

WORSELY: To make you feel secure in your tenure.

LISA: What?

WORSELY: The flat. You're staying in the flat, Lisa. I won't ever
call on you again.

LISA: Is that what it says?

WORSELY: Legal jargon.

LISA: It swims about.

MARION: Terrible small print, I quite agree.

LISA: What does it say?

WORSELY: It just confirms all the arrangements.

LISA: What does it say about the baby?

MARION: Nothing new.

LISA: What? I can't read it.

MARION: No need.

WORSELY: Sign here.

LISA: After can I see the baby?

WORSELY: Don't drip all over the paper.

LISA: I want to see he's all right.

MARION: Of course he is.

LISA: Because later when I'm better I'll have him back.

WORSELY: He's very well taken care of. I wouldn't lie.

[LISA *signs the paper*.]

LISA: Can I see him now?

MARION: He's at home in his own pram with his own daddy. Now that's all done. Good. Finished.

LISA: I can't stop crying.

WORSELY: I wish you would Lisa, you make me feel quite ill. Cheer up. You're the sort of reason I do myself injuries.

LISA: I can't stop. I can't stop. I can't stop.

[MARION *slaps her. She stops crying*.]

MARION: That's the thing to do. If it was me I'd do the same.

WORSELY: I'll take you home, Lisa, in a taxi.

LISA: You've got so kind again Mr Worsely. Like the first time you came. You won't suddenly take off the roof?

[LISA *goes out*. WORSELY *turns back at the door*.]

WORSELY [*to* MARION]: All right? And I'm going home after.

MARION: You don't have to work for me you know.

WORSELY: I'll tell you when I've stopped.

MARION: She's not fit, you see. And I need it more. I'll make far better use.

WORSELY: I'll still do almost anything for you. Marion?

MARION: Not yet.

WORSELY: You'll turn to me one day and find me dead.

MARION: I'll take the risk.

WORSELY: The times that are unbearable come closer together and last longer. What when they all join up?

MARION: Do what you want. Get what you can.

SCENE THREE

Hospital cubicle. ALEC's MUM *in bed, fixed up to a drip.* ALEC *is sitting by the bed. After a moment* MARION *comes in. She has brought a bunch of grapes, which she soon starts eating.*

MARION: Any change?

ALEC: Not that I've noticed.

MARION: You can't say they don't try.

[*Pause.*]

There's a girl along there been unconscious six months. It's marvellous how they can keep you alive once they get you on those machines. The machine just runs on and you're part of it. An expensive way of life. And what is it they're keeping alive? It still looks like a person of course, which is why they go to all the trouble. If it looked like a vegetable marrow, which is how it behaves and probably how it feels, they wouldn't bother.

[*Pause.*]

Still she might suddenly sit up and then you'd be sorry if you'd let her die.

[*Pause.*]

On the other hand, what a life.

[*Pause.*]

Still a vegetable is a vegetable. You don't smash it up just for being a vegetable.

[*Pause.*]

On the other hand there's plenty of other people.

[*Pause.*]

Still if it was you I expect I'd be glad you were still there. In some sense. I could still recognise it as you.

ALEC: It wouldn't matter.

MARION: What?

ALEC: If it was there or not.

MARION: Not to you. To me it would make all the difference.

ALEC: I don't mind for myself the way you go on but you won't get what you want.

MARION: I was talking about matters of general interest. I do try not to grab at you.

44

ALEC: Next Monday I'll be back at work.

MARION: What as?

ALEC: A glazier, like I was.

MARION: I thought you stopped because you didn't like it. You're not stretched. You have still got ambition whether you want to or not.

ALEC: It's hard to say really why I stopped.

MARION: You couldn't see a future. I'm sure you have a great career ahead as something you hardly dream of. There's no limit. It's finding where to start. Before I started on property I just had no idea of myself. You don't know what you're capable of till you suddenly find yourself doing it. Does property appeal to you at all?

ALEC: I'd rather not have an idea of myself.

MARION: At least you'll be doing something again. That's a start. Do you feel better now?

ALEC: Nothing special.

MARION: I couldn't go up high on those big buildings. I've no head. I think you're wasting yourself.

ALEC: I knew a man fell fifty feet once and he wasn't hurt. Then on the way home he stepped under a bus.

MARION: But usually if you fall fifty feet you do get hurt. There's always traffic but falling's extra.

ALEC: Some people take care of themselves and they're all right. Some people take care and they're not. Some don't take care and they're all right. Some people don't and they're not.

MARION: But still there is what's probable.

ALEC: Not certain.

MARION: Insurance companies make money on it.

ALEC: It does work, yes.

[Pause.]

MARION: Do you stay here all day?

ALEC: I'll stay a bit longer anyway.

MARION: Does she know if somebody's here?

ALEC: I don't think she knows anything does she? I shouldn't think.

[Pause.]

MARION: Some men were playing music in the tube. I heard it

45

floating up round the corner as I came down the stairs, and I thought whatever's that, that's nice. I like music, specially if it's a surprise. I expect they get moved on though because it's public property. The boy that took my money smiled right in my eyes, and later when I saw my reflection in the train window I was smiling and smiling. I hardly knew it was me. Of course it is a very dark reflection. But after all what is all that? I don't know him. He doesn't know me. It could have been anyone. All that smiling would still have happened.

ALEC: But it was you.

MARION: But he didn't know it was me. Not who I know I am. Not what I know is important about me. Not my ideas. And what I've done. And what I've got. Not me.

ALEC: But nor do I.

MARION: You try not to. You try not to know me. I know all I can about you.

ALEC: Let it go.

MARION: After she's dead, leave Lisa. I'll leave Clegg. You can choose where we go to. I can pay for anywhere in the world. Couldn't you do with some sun? Or snow. Snow might suit you better. We could go somewhere in the arctic circle where you wouldn't see anyone for weeks. Wherever you look it's white. You have to wear dark glasses for the glare. On and on, on sledges, and never anything different to see. You always did want to travel. You've a restless nature. You always felt tied by Lisa. I wouldn't tie you. I don't expect you to believe that. But you can't imagine how wonderfully I could let you be once I was sure of you. Just say yes, and we'll be gone. I'll arrange every detail myself.

ALEC: No.

MARION: But you don't love Lisa more than me. Compare us and I'm better in every way. She's not so clever. Not so attractive. To you she's not, not just objectively. She's not even got a particularly nice nature. Though even not particularly nice might be nicer than me, but she's not much of a personality. She doesn't even begin to understand you. I do begin. She's not your equal and I am. I love you more than she does. I'd give up more. I've more to give up. And you know yourself you love me more than her.

ALEC: I don't think I could say I loved anyone more than anyone else.

MARION: You love me more than a complete stranger.

ALEC: I couldn't say for certain. I can say I love you and Lisa. But it wouldn't matter if I never saw you again.

MARION: It's no use being loved like that. You love your children more than someone else's.

ALEC: Not necessarily. You see.

MARION: But you've got to. Everyone loves their own . . . loves.

ALEC: Slowly everything . . . fell through. Lisa, children, work – there was no point. There was no point in the things I wanted instead. There wasn't any point in killing myself. That went on for some time. I didn't know how to make things better. I didn't care if they were better or not. I didn't know what better meant. But now the same things seem quite simple. Lisa, children, work, why not?

MARION: If you got bored with them before you'll just get bored with them again.

ALEC: I longed very much one morning for the sea in winter. Grey sea, I thought, gritty sand. So I leapt up from the bed, grabbed a train, went. I got there and it was nothing special. Grey sea, like I thought, gritty sand.

MARION: A let down.

ALEC: No, not at all. Just right. I saw what it was. Grey sea –

MARION: Yes, you said. Gritty sand.

ALEC: It's just that I'd had a lot of difficulty. Wanting things. Or seeing no point in them. And since then I haven't.

MARION: Are we talking about a mystical experience? I've met people who've had those before. I knew a girl who thought she was Joan of Arc and kept setting fire to herself. When I hold up a grape – look at the grape – is it some blinding sort of – symbolic sort of – revelation that you get?

ALEC: No.

MARION: What is it then?

ALEC: A grape.

MARION: And what about me? What am I? What about me?

ALEC: There you are. I can't say. How can I? There you are.
   [*Pause.*]

MARION: Are you staying here with your mother all night?

ALEC: No, I'll go home in a minute.

MARION: I wouldn't mind what you said you felt or didn't feel. If you do what I want and come away with me.

ALEC: How would that help?

MARION: What can I do to you? What do you care about? I'll find something. One day I'll have the pleasure of knowing you're screaming. Even if you do it silently.
   [ALEC *disconnects the drip.*]
   What are you doing? Don't touch that. Alec. What are you doing?

ALEC: There. That saves a lot of bother.

SCENE FOUR

ALEC *and* LISA *in their room.* LISA *with hair and eyes again — she's back at work, but tired, wearing slippers.*

LISA: I hate that black paint as you come up the stairs. Anyone who deliberately puts that on their walls can't be right. If they're all that keen on painting they could come and do some up here. Not her colour chart, I wouldn't have that. I'd choose my own colours.

ALEC: I'll paint it. What colour do you want?

LISA: He's the landlord isn't he? Let him keep it in good repair.

ALEC: It is in good repair. The damp's gone.

LISA: Then it's all ready for him to paint, isn't it.

ALEC: I thought you liked him.

LISA: Oh I do, I think he's lovely. So well spoken and well paid. His trousers are too tight.

ALEC: I'll get the paint Saturday morning then.

LISA: She's lovely too. Isn't she lovely?

ALEC: All right.

LISA: I'd be lovely in clothes like that.

ALEC: You are anyway.

48

LISA: That came a bit slow.

ALEC: Buy a new dress. It's a long time since you bought anything.

LISA: Just buying a dress wouldn't do it.

[*Pause.*]

I never thought I'd miss your mum, but she was company in a funny way.

[*Pause.*]

There's always been people like that. We just didn't live on top of them. Why do they have to leave their doors open? I don't want to see that kitchen all white and steel and everything in it the same height. No handles. Knives on a magnet just held to the wall. I don't want to know. And that enormous room just for a baby. Why should I have to see that every time I'm coming up with the shopping? I will not feed their bleeding cat while they're in Italy.

ALEC: I don't mind the cat. The boys like it.

[*Pause.*]

LISA: Alec I'm not going to get upset so you're not to stop me talking about it. Don't you miss the baby?

ALEC: I can't say I do, no. He's very well. It's not as if he's missing us.

LISA: I don't care if he's well or nearly dead. What good is it to me him being well in Marion's house? I want him here.

ALEC: You signed the papers.

LISA: How could I tell what I was doing? I wasn't in my right mind. I couldn't even see.

ALEC: It's done now.

LISA: Do something else, then, and get him back. What can we do? I think I might snatch him from the pram. Or even someone else's baby. I'd tell the police and the papers I'd give that woman's baby back if they got me my baby back. Why shouldn't I do something for once? Other people do all the things. Never me. I'm done things to.

ALEC: Shall we have another baby?

LISA: Another baby's got nothing to do with it. I'm getting this baby back home.

MRS ARLINGTON [*calls off*]: Lisa? [*Knock at door.*] Lisa.

49

LISA: Coming.

    [She doesn't stir. After a moment ALEC *gets up and opens the door.* MRS ARLINGTON *comes in.]*

MRS ARLINGTON: Oh thank you. I'm awfully sorry to disturb you. I was just saying I've fixed up the intercom so if she does wake up you should hear all right but I don't think she will because the last three nights she's actually slept through. Anyway I've left a bottle in the fridge so you'll only have to warm it up, and don't worry if she doesn't drink it all because I've made it a bit big so there's sure to be enough. And the nappies are in the airing cupboard. But as I say I don't think she'll wake before we're back and I hope not at all. We won't be later than one. Is that all right? You do look tired, Lisa. Go to bed early. I've got the volume switched up full so if she does cry she'll wake you up.

LISA: I always do go to bed early.

MRS ARLINGTON: Perhaps that's the trouble. You ought to go out more. I know I get terribly fed up if we don't go out a couple of times a week, and you're always babysitting for us and we gladly would for you but you never ask.

LISA: We never did go out very much. And once when we did for a couple of hours somebody broke in, which just shows. No, I don't believe in leaving children. You don't have them to leave them.

MRS ARLINGTON: If there's someone you can trust in the house –

LISA: I've never been in the habit of doing it.

MRS ARLINGTON: But one simply has to get out sometimes or one would go mad. I know I can trust you perfectly to look after Katie if she wakes up.

LISA: You wouldn't know if I didn't.

MRS ARLINGTON: Have you ever not gone to her? Have you left her crying? Have you?

LISA: She's never woke up yet.

MRS ARLINGTON: But what are you saying? Are you saying you'd leave her to cry?

ALEC: Of course she's not saying that. Go on and enjoy yourself.

MRS ARLINGTON: No but I'm not going till she promises she'll go

to Katie the minute she hears her cry. To leave her half an hour
or something like that could damage her mind for life.

ALEC: Go on, it's all right.

MRS ARLINGTON: No, not till she promises.

MR ARLINGTON [*voice off*]: Penny!

MRS ARLINGTON: You're making us late for the theatre.

[*Pause.*]

All right, we won't go out.

LISA: I don't care what you do.

MR ARLINGTON [*off*]: Penny!

ALEC: If the baby does wake up I'll go and see her.

MRS ARLINGTON: Are you sure?

ALEC: I wouldn't let Katie cry. Now go along.

MRS ARLINGTON: If it's really all right.

MR ARLINGTON [*off*]: Penny!

[MRS ARLINGTON *hesitates, then goes.*]

ALEC: Cup of tea? I'll put the kettle on.

[*He goes out to the landing.*]

LISA: I'm not something that goes with the house.

[ALEC *comes back.*]

Right. I'm leaving.

ALEC: How do you mean?

LISA: I'm not staying here.

ALEC: You're leaving me and the boys? Or just me?

LISA: Leaving this place. Of course I'm not leaving the boys, don't
be stupid. They go wherever I go. And what's more I'm getting
the baby. I didn't mean leaving you but if you won't come then
I will leave you because I'm leaving here and that's certain.

ALEC: I don't mind leaving here.

LISA: You can't live right in the same house with someone and
they've got everything and go out all the time.

ALEC: We can go out.

LISA: I don't want to go out. I don't want to live here with them
going out. I don't want to look like her and paint the walls
black. But I don't want to live in her house where the walls
should be black if it's her house and look at this old wallpaper
sitting here all night in my old dress.

ALEC: We'll have to find a place.

LISA: All right then we'll have to find a place. People do. They're not all sleeping in the streets are they, you'd trip over them. So they must all be somewhere. At least you're earning again. What I do mind is we could have had all that money to go and now we're doing the same thing for nothing. Marion's going to have a good laugh. But I don't want a corner in their house. They can have their whole house for theirselves. Two black guest rooms.

[*Pause while* ALEC *goes out and comes back with tray of tea.*] I don't see that signing a bit of paper makes him hers. He is mine. His blood and everything. His looks. His – everything he was born with, what he's like. Is yours and mine.

SCENE FIVE

CLEGG *and* LISA *in* CLEGG's *bed, him on top, bouncing up and down under the bedclothes.*

CLEGG: An eye for an eye. A mouth for a mouth. A cunt for a cunt. Vengeance is mine. I will repay. In full.

[*He collapses on her and lies still. After a moment* LISA's *head comes out from under the blanket.*]

LISA: I only came to see the baby.

CLEGG: See him again after.

LISA: You will do all you can for me, won't you?

CLEGG: I just did. What do you want now?

LISA: The baby. You'll sort out the law, sort of thing.

CLEGG [*lifts off her and rolls heavily over onto his back*]: I'm quite puffed. Unaccustomed exertion. They say it's like a five mile run. Or walk is it? Best way of keeping the tum down. Marion's fault I've lost my figure.

LISA: What shall I say to Alec?

CLEGG: Rub it in. Tell him just how marvellously good I was.

LISA: I don't know if I want to tell him at all.

CLEGG: What's the good of it if he never knows? I'll tell him myself. Let him just try and make a fuss. He doesn't know who he's dealing with. What have I had from him that he hasn't had from me? And he's still had most. I've plenty more owing. Plenty more where that come from.

LISA: I feel so funny. I think it must be guilty. Yes I'm sure it is. I felt the same when the headmaster found me behind the apparatus with Nutter Jones. He put his hand right inside my knickers. The headmaster, I mean, in his office. I felt in such a muddle and it all seemed to be my fault though I didn't see what I should have done to make it happen different. And I don't see now. One thing led to so many others. It wasn't really what was in my mind. Nutter Jones come off his motor bike a few years after and smashed his head. He should have worn a helmet. It's always been Alec done it before. I've only ever had to forgive him.

CLEGG: Your turn now. You've every right.

LISA: He's being ever so nice at the moment. Really normal. A perfect husband and father. I'd hate to upset him. I might not tell him about this. Just say I came to see you and you gave me the baby.

CLEGG: No I didn't.

LISA: You will though.

CLEGG: Give you the baby?

LISA: That's what it was for.

CLEGG: What that was for? No it was not. It was my revenge. A teeny little bit of my revenge.

LISA: We agreed before we started.

CLEGG: We did not.

LISA: Half way through then.

CLEGG: Nobody's responsible for what they say in the heat of passion. If I had said at the time, I love you, you wouldn't ever have thought I meant it. So if I said anything it's the same. I don't remember us saying anything. Just heavy breathing and mutters.

LISA: I want my baby.

CLEGG: He's my baby. Marion's bought him a shop.

LISA: Bought him a shop?

CLEGG: A brand new family butcher. Gold lettering. Clegg and Son.

LISA: But he's *my* son.

CLEGG: Lisa, listen to me. I didn't mean to hurt your feelings when I said what I did was for revenge. I also thought what a very sweet girl you are. I always did look at your bottom in the old days. Nice bit of rump. Marion's more like something for a stew. She's all gristle. But you melt in the mouth.

LISA: You taste like a mouthful of sawdust off your floor. Look at you sweating like a bit of hot fat, which is what you are. With your belly sagging like a black pudding and your poor little pork sausage. Give me my baby.

CLEGG: It's not your nature to be offensive. I understand you being upset. Marion's enough to upset anyone. But if I was to give you the baby I wouldn't dare see her again. I don't care how angry you are, it's nothing like. With Marion it's like a mad person, you don't want to be in the same room, you don't want their attention to fall on you. It's not something I'd expose myself to.

LISA: I'll take him. You can say I took him and you couldn't stop me. She'll believe that. And it's true.

CLEGG: She'd have the police. Or she might commit a crime. She's very near some edge just now and I wouldn't want to push her off. In a mental sense. I don't trust her in a hospital, she takes advantage of the facilities. So just wait, I know a better way. A real winner. I'll admit I do get fed up with him though he is as nice a bit of little baby as you'll see. Turns the scales now at fifteen pounds, and I'm the one fattened him up and no one else. But when I start working again I'll have more important things to think about. A man can't be expected to stay home and look after a baby. He can do it of course because it's not difficult. Even a woman can do it easily. But it is a waste of real abilities.

LISA: I'll take him now.

CLEGG: He's Marion's and my little son, legally adopted. In some states of the United States the penalty for kidnapping is death. I think we can come to an arrangement. Someone's got to look after the little sod while I'm at work, and you won't get Marion stopping home. So maybe, if you're very suitable – I'm not promising anything mind you – you could take care of him for us, on condition you see that he is still my son and will not be stopped by you from following his trade. Because I will not let that shiny new sign over my shop tell a lie.

LISA: So long as I have him.

CLEGG: We'll have to put it carefully to Marion. Where are you going?

LISA: I want to see him.

CLEGG: I didn't say you could get up. You won't be suitable unless you lie flat, did you know that, very feminine and do just as you're told. On your back and underneath is where I like to see a lady. And a man on top. Right on top of the world. Because I know what you ladies like. You like what I give you. I didn't say you mustn't move at all. But just in response.

SCENE SIX

MARION's *office*. ALEC *alone*. CLEGG *comes in with the baby in a carrycot. When he sees* ALEC *he stops, then changes and comes in firmly. At first a silence.*

CLEGG: Some people think they're born lucky. Just walk through. Take what they like. Fall on their feet. I wouldn't count on finding a new flat without a great deal of effort and difficulty.

ALEC: I don't, no.

CLEGG: You say don't, but you do. You think you can do what you like. You think everybody loves you just because one person is out of her mind. You're in for a very nasty shock.

ALEC: Housing is a problem, yes.

CLEGG: Lisa told you about our little plan? How we might let her mind our son part of the time? You've come to take part in the discussion. You feel an interest as the former father. Did she tell you where we talked it over?

ALEC: Yes.

CLEGG: In bed.

ALEC: Yes I can see how it might have happened. She is very upset about the baby.

CLEGG: She's told you, has she? She said she wouldn't. Woman's like that. Deceit is second nature. Due to Eve. But I'm too crafty for them by half. I know their ins and outs. You keep her rather short of it I'd say. Unless it was me that specially appealed to her. Yelping for more. I expect she told you. Or did she not bring out that side of it? I keep myself a little in reserve. You never know what else may turn up. I wouldn't want to waste myself on something as second rate as your wife. She was quite useful. A handy receptacle. But quite disposable after. Isn't that your attitude to Marion?

ALEC: No.

CLEGG: You make a big mistake about Marion. She's not like other women in just one important respect. She is mine. I have invested heavily in Marion and don't intend to lose any part of my profit. She is my flesh. And touching her you touch me. And I will not let myself be touched.

[*Pause*]

You pretend not to notice what I do to Lisa. I can do worse. And touching her I touch you. That's just one of the ways I'll be reaching you. You'll feel me. You'll come limb from limb for me one day. I'll think of you when I'm at work. Chop. Chop. Chop.

[WORSELY *comes in. His wrists, neck and arm are still bandaged. His left leg is in plaster.*]

ALEC: Hurt yourself?

WORSELY: I had a fall. I was climbing down at the time and I slipped.

CLEGG: Down what?

WORSELY: A fire escape.

CLEGG: Were you in a fire?

WORSELY: No. No.

CLEGG: Another time perhaps?

WORSELY: You never know.

CLEGG: I prefer a house that doesn't have any fire escape.

WORSELY: We'll have to talk about it some time. I think we're here to talk about the baby. I don't know why it's all dragged up again. The feelings involved make me quite sick.

CLEGG: How it came up was yesterday afternoon when I was having intercourse with his wife.

WORSELY: Lisa? You?

ALEC: Yes.

WORSELY [*to* ALEC]: Tell me why you always act so calm.

CLEGG: He's pretending, to try and make me feel I don't matter, but I know I do.

WORSELY: Pretending? Are you?

ALEC: No.

WORSELY: He's not, you know. What he is, is nuts. I wonder what it is Marion sees.

CLEGG: It soon won't matter what he's like. I can tell you what Lisa sees in me.

WORSELY: I'm completely stunned she even looked at you.

CLEGG: Why?

WORSELY: No offence.

CLEGG: Why are you so stunned? She's not Miss World. She's not even Miss South West Islington.

WORSELY: If I'd ever dreamt it was possible and without any rucking from him I'd have had a try myself.

CLEGG: Be my guest.

WORSELY: It's her bottom.

CLEGG: It is definitely her bottom.

WORSELY: It's hard not to go in for this style of talk once it's available. In fact I like Lisa. I feel quite shocked. Is there really no row? Don't get me wrong. I don't like rows very much. I can't stand anything very much. I'm not looking forward to this discussion. It's going to get very high pitched. My head's already aching from it. I don't see why you had to bring the baby. It screws it all up that much tighter. Something's got to snap. Have you had a good look at Marion lately?

CLEGG: She's always very smart and does me credit.

WORSELY: She's not in a good state. [*To* ALEC:] Interested?

ALEC: I'm sorry to hear it.

WORSELY: You'd better be. She was all right. She was fine. She was a success. Before you turned up again. I thought I might punch you in the face but I don't think you'd notice. And anyway I'd probably fall over. Have you ever tried to kill yourself?

ALEC: No, I don't need to.

WORSELY: Are you dead already? I can't think how else you avoid

57

it. The thought of Marion alone is bad enough and it should be worse for you.

CLEGG: I think it's my role not yours, Worsely, to worry about the state of my wife's health.

WORSELY: Worry, then.

CLEGG: Of course he doesn't need to kill himself. Most of us leave it to something or someone else.

WORSELY: I hear what you say.

CLEGG: You haven't forgotten our little arrangement? The central heating?

WORSELY: The central heating? Yes, that's good.

CLEGG: The financial side is taken care of. I've a cheque here made payable to T. Worsely. Signed Marion Clegg.

WORSELY: Didn't she ask why?

CLEGG: I think she'd better see a doctor.

WORSELY [*taking the cheque*]: This is very welcome of course. But I'm not quite happy. I have some doubts.

CLEGG: I thought it was going ahead for tonight.

WORSELY: Can we talk about it some other time?

CLEGG: You said you had everything prepared.

WORSELY: I have, yes.

CLEGG: Then what's the problem? I'm counting on it, Worsely.

WORSELY: It's a great idea. There's nothing at all wrong with the idea. Except putting it into practice.

CLEGG: How dare you let me down? Give me the cheque. How dare you?

WORSELY [*giving cheque back*]: I'm very brave.

CLEGG: You're a coward. A woman. A baby.

WORSELY: I didn't say I wouldn't. I'm just having a hesitation.

CLEGG: Then you'd better get moving again, sharpish.

WORSELY: I've too much on. I'm caving in. I owe a great deal to Marion and I don't altogether want to – do anything she'll disapprove of, however much she's – disappointed me.

CLEGG: I shouldn't come into my shop to be served, unless you have good news. With knives to hand the temptation might be irresistible for someone of my hot blooded disposition. I'm not in a mind for set backs. I had to have my dog put down.

WORSELY: Whatever for?

CLEGG: He bit me. I was teaching him a trick. I couldn't feel the same to him again. He made himself into just another animal.
   [LISA *comes in.*]
LISA: Where is he? [*She goes to the carrycot.*] Can I pick him up?
CLEGG: He's asleep.
LISA: No, he's wakies, my little lamb. What blue blue eyes. Smile for mummy.
CLEGG: Better not. You don't want to get her against you from the start.
LISA: I'll put him down the minute she comes in.
CLEGG: I said leave him. What I like about you is you do what you're told.
WORSELY: You can pick him up later on, Lisa.
LISA: Oh what have you done now? Broken your leg. Were you skiing?
WORSELY: Not exactly, no.
LISA: I hope it doesn't hurt very much. Look at him smile.
WORSELY: When I talk to you it helps me forget the pain.
LISA: My grandmother was a Christian Scientist. Perhaps I've some power of healing. I've never seemed to have any before. I never seem to have any effect on anything. That's why you've got to help me get the baby because I know I can't manage Marion myself.
WORSELY: You can count on me. That's a lie. I wish my head — you haven't any aspirin?
LISA: How many?
WORSELY: Fifty would be nice.
LISA: Three. You will help me won't you? I know she listens to what you say. And Clegg tells me you're really fond of the baby.
WORSELY: The trouble is I'm getting fond of too many people. I'm not against you. That much is clear.
   [*He turns away, is seized by* CLEGG.]
CLEGG: We have a contract. I'll sue you for breach. We're sworn to revenge. It's the next step. Oh, Worsely. First him, then her. Then perfect peace.
LISA [*to* ALEC]: We'll get the baby and get out of here, Alec, we'll get far away and have a new life.
ALEC: We may do.

WORSELY: Oh, if my head would stop drumming.

[MARION *comes in.*]

MARION: I know my own mind. The legal position is perfectly clear. What can there possibly be to discuss? I won't have tears, Lisa. Clegg and I are united as the child's parents in our opposition to any interference. Worsely will say the same. You can't pretend Alec wants the baby. It is just your hysteria, Lisa, against the reasonableness of the rest of us.

LISA: I'm not crying this time. Too bad for you. I can see what I'm doing this time.

MARION: Won't you take her home? I have work to do.

LISA: Alec and I both want him. It's just a game to you, Marion. You don't want him really. You just want to win.

MARION: He's legally my child. His name is Clegg.

LISA: But I'm sure it can't really be the law. Can't we go to a court and tell them I didn't know what I was signing?

MARION: It would take a lot of time. A lot of money. Meanwhile he's used to us and our home. Have you a home that would impress a judge?

LISA: You're only doing it to be cruel to me. Why should you? How can you?

MARION: I shall do as I like. Worsely, please make them all go away.

CLEGG: But Marion, my dear, wait a moment. I'm sure we can come to some arrangement.

MARION: Why should we? We've nothing to gain.

CLEGG: I can't look after him properly in the shop. Suppose we employ Lisa as a daily help to look after him while we're at work.

LISA: In my own home. I'd want him in my own home.

CLEGG: Provided you register with the council as an official babyminder.

MARION: Are you mad, Clegg? Giving him away? Once she's got her hands on him he won't be ours any more. You'll lose your little butcher.

CLEGG: I don't want that. We'd have to have a written agreement about his future.

MARION: There are plenty of people to look after babies. He will have a trained nanny.

CLEGG: But Lisa –

MARION: I said he will have a nanny. Are you going against me, Clegg? It was entirely for you I got the baby. I bought him a shop, for you. If you don't like the arrangements you can go. Clear right off. It would be a delight never to see you again.

LISA: I went to bed with him yesterday afternoon.

MARION: Is she mad?

CLEGG: Well what happened, in a manner of speaking –

MARION: I don't know which of you I'm most sorry for. Perhaps you'd like to take Lisa and the baby and set up house together, Clegg? I'm sure Alec and I wouldn't mind.

CLEGG: No of course I don't want that. It was just –

MARION: Then don't waste my time. Lisa doesn't come into our plans at all.

LISA: Don't let her frighten you Clegg.

MARION: Worsely, please, clear them all out.

WORSELY: One thing, Marion, perhaps . . .

MARION: Go on.

WORSELY: I don't like to contradict you . . .

MARION: What?

WORSELY: It might be better for the baby. If it was to go back to Lisa. Entirely.

MARION: Better for the baby? Why?

WORSELY: I don't think you like him very much.

MARION: I adore him.

CLEGG: I'm rather fond of the little chap myself. I wouldn't want to completely give him up.

WORSELY: I like him. More than Clegg does. Far more than you do, Marion. But I'm not saying that makes him mine. Let him go back where he belongs. You're letting yourself go mad, Marion. I've seen you in pieces. I don't know whether I want to smash you up or keep you safe. But you won't get Alec like this. You'll just damage the baby. Keep going, be a success, make a fortune. Use me for anything you like. You can still be magnificent.

[*He bursts into tears.*]

MARION: I think everyone's had their say. None of you has any effect on me.

[LISA *picks up the carrycot and tries to rush out of the door.* CLEGG *grabs her, and they struggle briefly. He gets the carrycot and shuts the door.*]

I think I'm going to send for the police.

CLEGG: The advantage of having Lisa to mind the baby is that if anything should happen to you, his mother, he would have you could say another mother in Lisa, which a nanny however trained could never be.

MARION: Why should anything happen to me Clegg? More than to anyone else?

CLEGG: I must have second sight, Marion. I see you dead within a few weeks.

LISA: Oh what else can I do? Alec.

ALEC: I should like him back.

MARION: Say it again.

ALEC: I should like him back.

MARION: Again.

ALEC: No.

MARION: You'd like him back. Have you actually got a feeling? Put it under glass and it might grow. Wouldn't a different baby be just the same? Do you really mean you prefer your own baby? Next thing we know you'll say you prefer Lisa to me. Or me to Lisa. There's no telling what you might say once you start saying you want something.

ALEC: I should like him back. I can do without.

MARION: I can't do without. He's my bit of you. Not a bit of me. That doesn't matter. Not a bit of Clegg, thank God. But a bit of you.

ALEC: We're leaving the flat.

MARION: Leaving?

ALEC: Leaving London.

MARION: Leaving London?

ALEC: So let us go and take the baby with us.

MARION: Up till now, right up till now, I might have let you have the baby. What is it to me? But if you go it's all I'll have left.

LISA: If you let me mind the baby, Marion, in my own home, we would stay in London for that.

MARION: No. No no no. Very clever but I won't be caught. Leave me if you like but you won't get the baby. I will keep what's mine. The more you want it the more it's worth keeping. But you can't just go like that. I haven't paid you to go. Every one of you thinks I will give in. Because I'm a woman, is it? I'm meant to be kind. I'm meant to understand a woman's feelings wanting her baby back. I don't. I won't. I can be as terrible as anyone. Soldiers have stuck swords through innocents. I can massacre too. Into the furnace. Why shouldn't I be Genghis Khan? Empires only come by killing. I won't shrink. Not one of you loves me. But he shall grow up to say he does.

SCENE SEVEN

Office, later. WORSELY *and* MARION. *The carrycot is on the floor near the door.*

WORSELY: I was up on this very high ledge. You could get across to it from the fire escape. Even with one hand. So there I was. If I had jumped it could only have been fatal. Barring accidents. And what could have intercepted me? If I'd hit a pigeon on the way down I'd have smashed it down with me. A high building. So I sat there with a great easing of misery because it was all so possible. A crowd gathered, and so on. Sirens. I took no notice. It was every moment in my power – on or off, be or not. And then there turned up beside me of all people that Samaritan friend. I think I've mentioned him. Very on-going. I'd made a new will in his favour because I thought he always meant well and put in a good deal of effort. B plus. He'd come up on the ledge to squat beside me and talk me down. We had a chat. Just this and that. I was just about to drop off, suddenly, in the middle of what I was saying, to take him by surprise, when I saw he had turned quite pale. He can't have had much of a head for heights. And the next thing, he'd gone. I was quite right to think the distance would be fatal.

MARION: What about your leg?

WORSELY: I was climbing down the fire escape and I slipped. I must have fallen about six feet and landed with my leg sort of twisted. It was quite painful.

MARION: Worsely, could you do something for me? Something to hurt Alec.

WORSELY: Like what?

MARION: Think of something.

WORSELY: Fatal?

MARION: I wouldn't mind.

[*Pause.*]

WORSELY: Like set the house on fire?

[*Pause.*]

MARION: What a good idea. What a very nice thought.

[WORSELY *gets up and goes to the door.*]

WORSELY: I may meet my own death in the blaze.

[MARION *doesn't react at all.* WORSELY *waits a moment, then, unnoticed, picks up the carrycot and goes out with it.*]

SCENE EIGHT

CLEGG's *new butcher's shop.* CLEGG *and* CUSTOMER.

CLEGG: Nice chicken, won't keep you a moment. [*He takes a chicken and cutting off its head cleans it while he talks.*] Lovely day, dear, been in the park? Wish I could get away myself and have the lazy day you housewives have. Giblets dear? Shame to waste them. Eighty-five p altogether darling. Ninety, one hundred. Thank you very much, good morning.

[CUSTOMER *goes out.* MARION *comes in.*]

Slept in the office did you? You look like it. By yourself? Take a bit more pride in your appearance, Marion, it's slipping again.

MARION: You haven't seen Worsely? He hasn't come into the office. I've left him a note. I've come up here.

CLEGG: What did you do for a bottle then?

MARION: Bottle?

CLEGG: I thought you'd come home with him later. Did you have to go out and buy him one? Still it never hurts to have a spare.

MARION: What are you talking about?

CLEGG: Baby Clegg of course, do wake up.

MARION: I haven't got him.

CLEGG: Of course you've got him.

MARION: Where?

CLEGG: Marion, what do you mean? I left him with you at the office.

MARION: I thought he was at home with you.

CLEGG: You insisted I leave him there. Mine, you kept saying, mine, don't you remember? Where is he?

MARION: In the office?

CLEGG: Is he in the office?

MARION: I seem to remember you did leave him, yes.

CLEGG: Didn't you feed him? All night? Didn't he cry?

MARION: He never cried. I never heard him cry.

CLEGG: Marion, you've let him starve to death.

MARION: I haven't. He wouldn't. He'd cry if he was hungry.

CLEGG: He must have cried.

MARION: I'll go back.

CLEGG: I'll go. You can't be trusted.

[WORSELY *comes in. His face is partly bandaged from a burn. Other bandages and plaster as before.*]

WORSELY: Alec's dead.

CLEGG: How?

MARION: In the fire?

CLEGG: You didn't do the fire after all? And killed him?

MARION: It was my idea.

CLEGG: It was mine, but I never thought it would come to this. Let's shut the shop.

MARION: Is he dead?

WORSELY: I got a few burns myself.

CLEGG: No one can say it was me. You assured me you were not going to do it, Worsely. I never even gave you the cheque.

MARION: It was me. I asked Worsely to do something to Alec. He chose fire.

CLEGG: Did you? Did she? You amaze me. And meanwhile she's lost the baby.

65

WORSELY: I took him to Lisa.

MARION: What? When did you?

WORSELY: When I left yesterday evening. You weren't looking. I bet you never thought did you, till today? He's not your baby, Marion, by any stretch of the imagination. I delivered him to Lisa anyway. She was very glad. So was Alec. The Arlingtons were out as it happened. So on the way down I did my bit with the petrol in their sitting room. Very tasteful trendy furnishings altogether.

CLEGG: You gave my baby butcher away?

WORSELY: What worried me a little I must say was the thought of the baby in the fire. Since I'd gone to the trouble of bringing him round. So after I'd gone down to the street and seen it get started I went back in and shouted Fire, fire. The stairs were already aflame so none too soon. But in no time they were all rushing down, Lisa shrieking as you can imagine, her hair singeing, Alec with the baby, the boys stumbling hanging on her hands, and all of them shot out onto the pavement.

MARION: But Alec?

WORSELY: At this point I thought myself of going back in. Fire has a terrible attraction. As it leaps and licks up, like a creature taking over, when really of course it was the house turning into fire because of the high temperature it was reaching rather than a fire consuming the house. Strictly speaking. I went back in through the front door. It was very hot. I went on. It was smoky so I couldn't properly see. I went on, you must give me marks for perseverance, and no, I certainly can't kill myself by fire, it is far too hot.

MARION: But what about Alec?

WORSELY: I was just coming out, and meanwhile I heard the fire engines, when Alec came in through the door, walking quite calmly considering the heat. 'The other baby, you see' is what he said and set off – I would say up the stairs but I couldn't exactly see them in the flames. But he rose as if climbing the stairs. Turning into fire quite silently. We waited but of course he didn't come out and nor did the Arlingtons' baby. It was too hot.

CLEGG: The grand climax of my revenge was to be shooting you,

Marion, here in the shop. Every woman wants to be loved like that. It's more than he would ever have done. Look, here in the drawer is the murder weapon. But now he's gone, and you wanted him gone, wanted the same thing I wanted, we are one again. I forgive you everything. If the police come, say nothing. Leave it all to me. I certainly never intended such a shocking fatal accident as that, and I'm sure you didn't. I will protect you.

MARION: I'm not sorry at all about Alec. Or about that other baby. Not at all. I never knew I could do a thing like that. I might be capable of anything. I'm just beginning to find out what's possible.

[WORSELY *picks up the gun and takes up a stance, placing it by his temple. He fires.*]

WORSELY: Missed.

TRAPS

Traps

When we were casting *Traps*, we found ourselves repeating the same two things to actors as some kind of introduction to the play. First, that it is like an impossible object, or a painting by Escher, where the objects can exist like that on paper, but would be impossible in life. In the play, the time, the place, the characters' motives and relationships cannot all be reconciled — they can happen on stage, but there is no other reality for them. Second, that the characters can be thought of as living many of their possibilities at once. There is no flashback, no fantasy, everything that happens is as real and solid as everything else within the play.

Performance notes

The card trick. The person who chooses a card puts it back on top of the pack. It stays there when the cards are shuffled. If ten cards are dealt off the top of the pack and those cards then put on top of the pack again, the chosen card will be the tenth card.

Mobius strip. Cut a strip of paper and turn one end over before joining the two ends to form a loop. The loop has only one surface. If you cut along the middle of the strip right round the loop, it makes one larger loop.

The jigsaw. I've only occasionally specified where a character should do the jigsaw. Bits can be added at any convenient time by anyone so that it's nearly finished by the end of the play.

Traps was first produced at the Royal Court Theatre Upstairs, London, in January 1977. The cast was as follows:

SYL, 30	Catherine Kessler
JACK, 20s	Nigel Terry
ALBERT, 35	Anthony Milner
REG, 30	Tim Piggott-Smith
DEL, 20s	Hugh Fraser
CHRISTIE, 20s	Catherine Neilson

JACK *is* CHRISTIE's younger brother, and REG *is her husband.*

Directed by John Ashford
Designed by Terry Jacobs

ACT ONE

A room with door, window, table, chairs.

Bluish gloom of early evening, the curtain not drawn and the light not on.

Plenty of clutter: large jigsaw half done on the floor, large pot plant, newspapers in various languages, oil lamp, cards, airgun, cake, pile of clothes washed but not ironed, ironing board and iron, towels, broken bowl, guitar, suitcase, picture, carrycot, clock showing real time.

JACK is sitting in a chair, eyes closed. SYL is walking up and down with a baby on her shoulder, getting it to sleep.

A dog barks downstairs as someone comes into the house and comes upstairs.

SYL is afraid the noise will wake the baby. JACK doesn't react.

ALBERT comes in, snapping on the light, banging the door.

ALBERT: Pissing down . . .

> [*ALBERT realises SYL is putting the baby to sleep, goes quiet, puts off the light.*]
> [*SYL puts the sleeping baby in the carrycot and takes it out.*]
> [*ALBERT puts on the light. He takes off his wet coat and shoes.*]

They're after me, Jack.

> [*JACK doesn't react to this or the next things ALBERT says.*]

Fletcher says, what do I do in the evenings.

He pretends he wants me to watch blue movies.

You see?

What he's doing is try to find out if I belong to any political party.

I'll tell him I got married. You want to go?

You could.

Pissing down out there.

Jack, people are looking at me in a funny way.

> [*JACK's eyes are still shut.*]

JACK: Dog barks at you, too.

73

ALBERT: It does, exactly, it smells trouble. I used to pat that dog one time. Animals can sense . . . You busy?

JACK: No, I'll go in my room.

ALBERT: No, I'll shut up. I'm getting flu, that's all.

[JACK *opens his eyes.*]

JACK: No, I've gone. Keep talking.

ALBERT: Like earthquakes. Animals sense.

[JACK *gets up.*]

[SYL *comes in.*]

SYL: Going out?

JACK: Just upstairs. All right?

[JACK *goes out.*]

[SYL *and* ALBERT *embrace.*]

SYL: She kept waking up all afternoon. I wanted to kill her.

ALBERT: I'm getting flu.

SYL: Cold.

ALBERT: Flu. Syl, people are looking at me in a funny way. Not just that. There's somebody following me. I could have said before. But I wanted to let it pile up till there's no doubt.

SYL: Babe's got a snuffle.

ALBERT: Kiddies do.

SYL: Gave her some gripe water.

ALBERT: That right? For a cold?

SYL: What? You give her something. I know you've brought up a fine family. You stop indoors with her then. She likes gripe water.

ALBERT: Booze, init? Takes after her daddy.

SYL: Had a swig of gripe water myself. Quarter to three.

ALBERT: He keeps just the distance he thinks I won't notice. He reckons he's nondescript. Light brown raincoat, medium height, between thirty and forty years of age, dark hair thinning on top, small face, doesn't wear gloves.

SYL: Do you keep looking round?

ALBERT: Not all the time, what do you take me for? One day the raincoat, next day the hair, I build it up.

SYL: It is always the same man?

ALBERT: Mole on his cheek.

SYL: Every time?

74

ALBERT: Twice is enough.

SYL: Why don't you stop and let him go by?

ALBERT: I don't want them to know I know, do I? Lose the advantage.

SYL: I put her down to sleep at one o'clock, but I knew she wouldn't go off by her face. So I winded her some more and tried again, but I knew she wasn't going to. It's my own fault. If you think your baby's going to cry it cries. But how can you think it's going to go to sleep when it just isn't? So I tried letting her cry. Like people say it's good for their lungs and ... Why shouldn't she be unhappy for a bit? Everyone else is, I am, cry on. She's got no right. You can't make it perfect for them so why ...? But I never can stick her crying. It gets on my stomach.

[*She isn't looking at* ALBERT. *He furtively gets a chocolate biscuit from a packet in the table drawer and quietly and quickly eats it.*]

So I get her up and give her some gripe water. And she likes that. It makes her really good. She lets me put her down and she's not even asleep, just being good. I felt fine. Up till then I was feeling really fine. Quarter to three she starts up again. So this time we both have some gripe water and she won't stop. I give her a shake, Albert. Not hard but ... a shake. She screamed so hard I had to put her down, I didn't know what to do. So after a bit I put the pram on the wheels and rocked it because often she goes off if she's on a walk but it was raining so hard and my shoe's got this great hole so I put the pram on the wheels and pushed her back and forward, you know, rocking her ...

ALBERT: Do stop going on.

SYL: Boring to listen to?

ALBERT: A bit.

SYL: Boring to do.

ALBERT: I don't come home and tell you every boring thing I did all day. 'Then I thought I must have a piss so I walked along to the toilet.'

SYL: I've nothing else but boring things to tell.

ALBERT: Then try saying nothing.

SYL: Did you know a little baby is three times the size of a human being?

ALBERT: Come on, love. Saturday day after tomorrow.

SYL: I've been looking forward to Saturday since Sunday night.

ALBERT: Best I can do.

SYL: Because it's completely impossible for you to give up work and look after her and me go out to work for a bit.

ALBERT: That's right.

SYL: And why?

ALBERT: I'd go mad.

SYL: And me?

ALBERT: I'm not saying it's fair. Just a fact.

SYL: What if I went out? What if I just went out? What if I went?

ALBERT: If you don't want to take care of it, leave it in a church pew. Put it on the steps of the town hall, get taken into care.

SYL: And a great cure for a headache's to cut off your head.

ALBERT: You wouldn't earn as much as I do. There's no work. There's nothing you're trained for. You're lucky I'm still in work so you're getting supported. You've no patience, Syl. She'll grow up in no time. I've seen it with mine. They're at school, they're smoking, they've gone. Enjoy it.

SYL: Something funny happened at quarter to three. I looked at the clock five times and the hands hadn't moved hardly. Got in a panic.

ALBERT: When I get my cards I'll stay home and you can try and get a job, all right? It won't be long. When I talk I can tell from their eyes they're thinking. They're working out what the bastard's after. Ah, got it. Wants us to play darts, does he, bleedin' agitator. It's got so if I go in the canteen and say 'Terrible weather for the time of year,' it's 'Oh, don't talk politics, Albert.'

SYL: I do love her and all that. It's just . . .

[A knock at the door.]
[ALBERT gestures to stop SYL saying 'Come in.']
[REG puts his head round the door.]

REG: Oh. Sorry to bother you. I did knock. I expect you didn't hear.

76

[REG *comes in. He is smartly dressed in a heavy coat and carries a very large box of chocolates.*]

The good lady said the top two floors. I'm looking for Jack Slade.

ALBERT: Nobody answering to that name.

REG: Slade. Jack.

ALBERT: That's right.

REG: He doesn't live here?

ALBERT: I hope very much you're calling me a liar. I've been wanting to hit somebody all day.

REG: Joking apart, the lady downstairs said –

ALBERT: What makes you think you've got the right name?

REG: He's my brother-in-law. Tall scruffy lad.

ALBERT: He never said he'd got a brother-in-law. Why should I believe that?

REG: You don't deny knowing him then?

ALBERT: He didn't leave a forwarding address. Moved to the country for a healthier life.

REG: There hasn't been anyone asking for him?

ALBERT: What's he done?

REG: Has there been a woman asking for him?

ALBERT: That would be his own business, wouldn't it?

[REG *approaches* SYL, *who is doing the jigsaw.*]

REG: I don't mind not seeing Jack. I've no interest at all. The one I'm looking for is the other one ... Who's looking for Jack herself. I believe. I don't want to bother you with the details.

ALBERT: Ask at the pub. He sends postcards to the publican.

REG [*to* SYL]: I do apologise for taking your time. But if someone else turns up looking for Jack, if you tell her Reg was here and I'm in the pub, I'd be very grateful. No need to let her get you into conversation.

SYL: Reg.

REG: Most kind.

ALBERT: Jack isn't married so how could he have a brother-in-law?

REG: I'm the one that's married.

ALBERT: If Jack's got a sister.

REG: If she's here all along, hiding, and doesn't want to see me, it would be a help to know. I haven't got all day.

ALBERT: Turn left out the front door.

REG [*to* SYL]: Tell her Reg came to take her home.

ALBERT: King's Head on the corner.

[*As* REG *is about to go,* JACK *comes in.*]

REG: There seems to be some misunderstanding.

JACK: No. Amazing. Yeah. What about that?

ALBERT: Not everyone in uniform is the gasman and there's all sorts of plain clothes. You don't answer every enquiry made at the door. People asking for you by name could lead anywhere. The details are transferred to a computer.

REG [*to* JACK]: You gave instructions to have me turned away. I know there's no love lost. You must have expected me, that's the item of interest.

JACK: Expected is too much. I haven't the confidence. I still can't believe you're not a figment. Amazing.

REG: I just dropped by to give Christie a lift home.

JACK: Christie's not been here for about a year.

SYL [*to* ALBERT]: You're getting to be impossible to live with.

REG: She said something about paying you a visit. So I drove up.

JACK: Oh yeah.

REG: New Volvo since you saw us.

JACK: Yeah.

REG: So where is she?

JACK: I wonder where she's got to.

REG: I'll be on my way then.

JACK: If you like, yeah.

REG: Frankly, Jack, considering the bizarre way I was received I find it impossible to believe you're telling the truth.

JACK: She'll most likely come.

REG: She phoned you up. I never know when she gets in touch with you. It comes out later.

ALBERT [*to* SYL]: What do you mean by that?

SYL: It's just true.

ALBERT: Is that a threat?

SYL: I didn't think so.

ALBERT: Who do you talk to in the daytime?

JACK: Look, Reg, what I was doing when you came. I was . . . You're not going to believe this.

REG: Yes I am.

JACK: No you're not. No point telling you.

ALBERT [to SYL]: Eh? Who turns you against me?

REG: This is typical of your whole attitude towards me and you must know how I resent it over the years. Totally unjustified scorn bearing no relation to my actual character. You make trouble where there could be normal accord.

[JACK *takes off his socks, which are not a pair, and starts clipping his toenails.*]

SYL: You wouldn't like to do the ironing, Albert?

ALBERT: When have I ever done the ironing?

SYL: You tell me.

ALBERT: I don't think clothes need ironing.

SYL: Right, I won't bother.

ALBERT: Look, I'm getting flu.

SYL: You've a slight snuffle.

ALBERT: I keep shivering. It doesn't show.

JACK: Tell you something though, Reg. Yesterday I spotted a kidnap. I saw this guy sort of shouldered into a car, and as they sped off I was thinking 'Was that a gun?'

REG: Really?

JACK: Did you know I've got a photographic memory? I did an identikit.

REG: Which case would that be?

JACK: No coverage in the media. To bore the villains. You'll read all about it after. I'm right, you see, you don't believe anything.

REG: It wouldn't surprise me. You can't walk down a normal street now or eat dinner in a normal restaurant. There's no such thing as a normal street.

JACK: Another very interesting thing. I saw a flight of geese going south. You don't often.

REG: Have you had any news of Christie?

JACK: You can take off your coat.

REG: No thank you.

JACK: Take off your coat.

REG: I don't want to.

JACK: If you're waiting for Christie –

REG: I want my coat on.

JACK: You must be getting flu.

REG: I'm not staying. I'm going to the pub for a double whisky.

JACK: What I was doing was ... You listening, Syl? I was willing Christie to come. I got you. It's a near miss. And maybe she's on her way.

REG: It is something of a coincidence. Depending how often you think about Christie.

JACK: I was not thinking about Christie. I was bringing her.

REG: Depending how often you try to bring Christie.

JACK: She'll come. You'll see. Even if she doesn't, it still worked.

REG: You haven't had any news from her? When did she last phone you?

JACK: I sometimes get the definite idea something's wrong with her.

REG: Did she phone last night? Or was it this morning?

JACK: We're not on the phone.

REG: I'm afraid I've no time for these religious performances. Nor has Christie.

JACK: It's not religious.

REG: That area. Mumbo jumbo.

JACK: It's fact. It's what happens. It's how it is.

REG: If Christie comes I'd be most grateful if you'd tell her I was here. To collect her. Do explain properly will you? There's no need to listen too much to what she says. Don't let her be an imposition. She might try to stay. It's absolutely unnecessary.

[JACK *locks the door and puts the key in his pocket.*]

[ALBERT *by now has taken some Araldite from the table drawer and is absorbed in mixing the two glues. He mends the broken bowl, joining the pieces precisely.*]

[SYL *by now is ironing.*]

SYL: Have you tried to get her here before, Jack?

JACK: Not very often, no.

REG: Locking the door? What?

JACK: Has she left you?

REG: Are you threatening me?

JACK: Has she left you?

REG: She hasn't left me. She left the house. Purely in the sense went out.

JACK: When?

REG: Last night.

JACK: What time?

REG: Does it matter?

JACK: I wouldn't ask, would I?

REG: During the night.

JACK: What time?

REG: I didn't look at the clock. After midnight.

JACK: Two fifteen?

REG: I didn't look at the clock.

JACK: Maybe she'll know when she comes.

REG: You've some reason for thinking she will come.

JACK: Have a look at the clock another time, will you?

REG: She may have friends. She has, I know for a fact. Or money. She might be at a hotel enjoying herself.

JACK: What did you do to her?

REG: I don't think I got that.

JACK: To make her leave.

REG: Don't you allege I made her leave. You should know your sister.

JACK: She must have left for a reason.

REG: She doesn't have reasons.

JACK: Is she in love?

REG: Nothing like that.

JACK: How would you know?

REG: Why she left is between me and Christie. I don't like the word left.

JACK: If she has left you, that's a big step.

REG: Yes.

JACK: Forward.

REG: In-laws never get on. That's no excuse for trying to cause a tragedy.

JACK: Give her half an hour. I should take off your coat.

REG: Would you mind opening the door, please? I said, Jack would you kindly open the door?

ALBERT: What do you mean I'm impossible to live with?

SYL: I'm thirty next week. I think 'Where am I getting?' I'm not that good a dancer. If I haven't had a child in the next five years, I'm not likely to have one at all. That's okay.

ALBERT: Five years is a long time.

SYL: Yes, it's okay. So long as I'm clear about it.

ALBERT: I'd say you were a very good dancer.

SYL: Not to give up everything else. Not great.

ALBERT: You get work.

SYL: That's all I was saying.

ALBERT: So who do we know that's great?

SYL: It is up to you as well you know.

ALBERT: Great, what a concept. Do you want a mob, or is it posterity?

SYL: I'm talking about if my work's nothing and a child would be something.

ALBERT: Everyone's work is nothing. What do you think? It's profit for the dinosaurs.

SYL: Well then.

ALBERT: Your child too. Tinned dinner for tyrannosaurus rex. There is nothing except make them extinct. I wouldn't want it to spend half its life in prison.

SYL: You're getting paranoid, Albert.

ALBERT: Yes, I know. It doesn't mean they're not after me.

SYL: I wouldn't want its father to be a lunatic.

ALBERT: I'm not doing my flu any good getting cold feet.

SYL: If I make up my mind to come off the pill, I've made up my mind.

ALBERT: Why is it every time I look out of the window there's a policeman riding past on a horse?

SYL: I could switch to the safe period and let it be an accident.

ALBERT: I'm happy to be a father any time. I wouldn't make a very good mother.

SYL: Go and get some dry socks on.

[ALBERT *goes out, taking the pile of ironed clothes. The door's not locked.*]

[SYL *puts the ironing board away.*]

REG: Sorry I can't offer you a chocolate. It's a present for Christie.

[REG *tries the door. It's locked.*]

[JACK *goes to* SYL *and they kiss.*]

Let me out of here. Is it some kind of joke? Christie and I are expected to dinner with our likely future managing director. He has a charming American wife who's going to be most put out. You have to meet expectations. I can't afford to be thought unreliable. I've already been passed over because Christie gave me an air of being . . . of not being . . . some wives are an asset. She has the looks when she wants to but she never. . . . If Christie's not here I must get to a telephone. I could phone from the pub. It's bad enough that I'm going to have to fib. Christie makes it very hard to be straightforward. I was brought up black and white and now I'm always. . . . But if I leave it till the last minute I'll have to think of a really outrageous lie. I'll have to invent a whole car accident with which roads and what kind of vehicle.

JACK [*to* SYL]: When shall we leave?

SYL: Not before the end of next week.

JACK: When are we going to tell him?

SYL: Not yet.

JACK: It was better when we lived in the country. I could read your mind easy in those days.

REG: Jack was an employee of mine. I fired him. He used to steal.

JACK: Paper clips.

REG: Petty cash.

JACK: Now and then.

REG: I bought you a Christmas present last year. A pot of candied ginger from Fortnum's. But Christie and I ate it ourselves since we didn't see you. She didn't ask to see you. She doesn't refer to you by name.

SYL: Jack never talks about Christie.

JACK: If I'm dreaming and there's somebody with me in the dream, it's usually her, that's all. She's not the main subject. What's happening happens to us both. There's nothing to be said.

REG: Christie never dreams about you.

[ALBERT *comes back, wearing the same odd socks as* JACK.]

[REG *gets to the door before* ALBERT *shuts it.*]

I never said a word to the police. We are relations and I've got
standards. It's not my fault we're not friends. Christie needs me.
That's the factor you don't bear in mind.

[REG *goes.*]

[ALBERT *goes to the window.*]

ALBERT: Helicopter. What did I tell you? In the event of a civil
emergency they'd have us rounded up and off into the sky
before we knew what we'd started. They can land troops in your
back garden. Do you realise if I left my job now no one would
employ me? I'm known of. Last Tuesday a helicopter came
down on a waste lot not half a mile from here and arrested a
man.

[JACK *starts shelling peas into the bowl* ALBERT *mended.*]

[SYL *shuffles cards.*]

SYL: Pick a card.

[JACK *picks a card.*]

JACK: You can't do that trick.

SYL: Put it back.

[JACK *puts it back.*]

[SYL *shuffles the pack.*]

SYL: Where in the pack would you like your card to go?

JACK: You're not going to get it right.

SYL: Tell it where to move.

JACK: Tenth from the top.

SYL: We'll just make sure it's not tenth from the top already.

[SYL *deals ten cards, showing* JACK *the tenth.*]

SYL: Come on, look at it.

JACK: Of course it's not.

SYL: Right then. Tell it to move.

[SYL *puts the dealt cards back on top of the pack.*]

JACK: Move, card.

SYL: Right, I felt it go. Here we are then. One. Two. Three. Four.
Five. Six. Seven. Eight. Nine. Ten. Four of hearts.

JACK: Told you.

SYL: Four of hearts.

JACK: Seven of spades.

SYL: Honest? Shit. Look, here it is, the next card.

JACK: You're not magic.

SYL: You still don't know how I did it.

JACK: You didn't do it.

SYL: I can't count, that's all. I did the trick.

    [SYL *deals Patience and plays.*]

    [ALBERT *joins in over her shoulder.*]

ALBERT: You could get a job.

JACK: I'm trying to get a job.

ALBERT: Like hell.

SYL: He is.

ALBERT: What have you signed on as this time? An elephant trainer?

SYL: He went after two jobs this morning and they'd both gone.

ALBERT: I already know you're on his side.

SYL: I start work myself on Monday.

JACK: Albert secretly wants to be rich and famous. He's got a lingering weakness for the work ethic. His grandmother was a lady.

ALBERT: I've given up a wife and children.

JACK: Yes, but why?

ALBERT: For you mainly.

JACK: Before you met me.

ALBERT: I could have gone back if I hadn't met you.

JACK: She wasn't going to have you back once she'd got married.

SYL: Would you rather be living with her?

ALBERT: I've never said that.

SYL: Then what do you keep going on about it for?

ALBERT: It was twelve years –

SYL: It's over.

ALBERT: She's still alive. Our children are still alive.

SYL: You see your children.

ALBERT: I see my children.

SYL: Don't blame Jack.

ALBERT: He could at least believe I love him.

JACK: I don't believe anyone's after you. I don't think you believe it.

ALBERT: I've got nothing. I get frightened. What do I wake up into every morning?

JACK: You don't look at me.

85

ALBERT: I am looking at you.

[DEL *comes in.*]

DEL: Took me two days getting here so I'm not leaving yet.

SYL: Del, come in.

DEL: Come to tell you bastards what I think of you.

JACK: I think we've already some idea of that. Why not have a cup of tea.

[DEL *knocks the cards on to the floor.*]

ALBERT: Sit down, Del.

DEL: You sit down. *Sit down.* Thought you were rid of me. Did you think at all? Did you? Did you think of me? Wonder how old Del is. Hope old Del's making out. *Hell.* Slammed out, what a relief eh? All that trouble gone, stretching your legs, settling your bums deeper in your cushions, clearing your heads. Del's out there some place, he's gone, he's not here thank God, hope he's well. Oh yeah, I do hope he's feeling fine and making out and *fucking derelicts you are, no.* You owe me money too. I paid the milk bill before I left and nobody paid their share. I want thirty pence from each of you for the principle. Let Del do it. I *will not.* Two hours in the rain waiting for my last lift to get here and tell you. Which one of you would wait two hours in the rain for me? Which one of you would sit two hours in a warm room with me? Garbage disposal units. Necrophiliacs. Media substitutes. You have all lied to me. Sometimes together, sometimes separately. You don't correlate. I've made lists.

SYL: Del –

DEL: Who did you last fuck?

JACK: Where have you come from?

SYL: Fucked Jack, okay?

DEL: Coming back down a Mobius strip motorway ever since I left. You thought I was on the other side but all the time I was . . . Mobius strip, right?

ALBERT: Get your wet hat off, Del. You're staying the night, there's time for all of it.

DEL: Paper, scissors, Sellotape.

SYL: I know what a Mobius –

DEL: *Scissors.*

[JACK *puts 30p on the table.*]

[SYL *gets paper, scissors and Sellotape from the drawer.*]

From the middle of July I was squeezed out. There was every kind of alliance. Albert and Jack. Jack and Syl. Syl and Albert, Albert and Jack and Syl. But no Del. Where was Del? When I think what expectations. Never again. Utopia means nowhere, right?

SYL: You weren't asked to go. You were asked to stay.

DEL: Settlers fled to America from persecution. Away from the tyrannies of governments and religions. New World. Think of the longing that got them on to those ships. Brotherhood, vision, pursuit of happiness. And what do they do soon as they get there? Slaughter Indians.

[DEL *starts making a Mobius strip.*]

SYL: I already know what a Mobius strip is.

DEL: And we were the settlers. And we were the Indians. Bloody massacre. And I still get that vision. I get on ships. But now I know at the same time how it ends.

JACK: Paid my debt, okay?

DEL: Mobius strip.

[DEL *holds the strip up and runs his finger round it.*]

You thought you'd get on the other side from me. But I can fly over spaghetti junction and speed up behind blowing my horn and crowd you buggers into the ditch.

JACK: Would you like to try making a specific accusation?

DEL: Everything I ever said to you, Jack, you repeated to Albert. And you got it wrong. I don't mind that, nothing's exclusive. I don't want individuality. But you gave me an individuality and the wrong sodding one. Who was this Del character you talked about? I never met him. You lived with him, not me. You stole his clothes. That's my shirt you're wearing now. Don't let it bother you, I've got a shirt. Just so you know. My books are still here for you to read. I've given up reading. You haven't. You get the benefit. You live off me. I put in far more than anyone. And I want it back. Not just my jacket. Energy. It's my charge running this place and I'm switching off. You can all die of darkness and hypothermia. You think I like being like this? This is what I'm like. My ideal would be for me to feel loving kindness

to you all and harmony with the sodding Way. Look at me.
Shaking. Shouting. See why I hate you.

ALBERT: Think you didn't do any damage?

DEL: Nothing to what I'm going to do, mate.

SYL: Del, what have we done? We didn't.

DEL: You don't remember. I believe that. But I can't continually
wake up every day as if the day before hadn't happened. Sometimes, yes, but not every day. You owe me thirty pence. Thank
you, Jack, it makes a start. I've kept lists, you see. I've got a
diary. Forgetting won't get you out of it. I can put a date and
place to everything. I want an explanation.

ALBERT: We're glad to see you.

  [ALBERT *touches* DEL]

DEL: Sod off.

  [*After a moment* DEL *goes to* JACK *and embraces him.*]

JACK: Get out of that wet coat, will you?

  [SYL *embraces* DEL *and* JACK.]

DEL: Still want a fucking explanation don't I. And apologies.

  [DEL *takes off his coat and* ALBERT *takes it.*]

  [DEL *kisses* ALBERT.]

  [SYL *starts picking cards up off the floor.*]

SYL: Sorry, Del.

  [DEL *starts to cry and stops. He cuts round the middle of the
  Mobius strip so it makes a large one.*]

DEL: Lived with a girl in Sheffield for two months. Beautiful girl.

SYL: What went wrong?

DEL: She got to know me, didn't she.

ALBERT: Why is it every time I look out of the window there's a
policeman walking past?

DEL: You're paranoid, that's why. It brings them. Think of it like
magnetism.

  [DEL *takes the cards and shuffles them.*]

DEL: Pick a card.

SYL: I can do this trick.

  [SYL *picks a card and puts it back.*]

  [DEL *shuffles.*]

DEL: Where in the pack would you like your card to go?

SYL: Say tenth from the top. I know this trick.

[DEL *deals ten cards, showing* SYL *the tenth.*]

DEL: So it's not there yet, right?

SYL: Del –

DEL: Right?

SYL: Right.

[DEL *puts the dealt cards on top of the pack.*]

DEL: Tell it to move. Will it to move. Move it.

SYL: Yup.

DEL: You got beautiful willpower. Move mountains with that. Here we go.

[DEL *counts out ten cards.*]

Queen of spades, right?

SYL: Queen of spades.

ALBERT: How do you do that?

DEL: Magic.

ALBERT: I mean really.

JACK: Magic. A three year old child could tell you that.

[JACK *goes out.*]

ALBERT: Long correspondence with the council. I got quite literate. I speak fluent jargonese like a native of the town hall, but translated we can stay till the builders come in the autumn, right, which further translated means at least two years. I've got all the letters here if you want to see. Copies of my letters. I kept on top of it, it's chronological.

[ALBERT *gets a folder of letters out of the drawer and gives it to* DEL]

DEL: It was better living in the country. All went wrong once we got here.

ALBERT: Away from it all yuk. Back to ugh nature. Saving our pow wham souls zap.

DEL: City's so fucking ugly.

ALBERT: So are you.

DEL: Comes of living in cities.

ALBERT: Somebody has to.

DEL: Changing it are you? Imperceptibly? It didn't strike me the minute I arrived, Albert's pamphlets and meetings are making all the difference. I didn't spot anyone transfigured. But I dare say the membership's rising. Consciousness is raised. Is it?

ALBERT: Yes, it is.

DEL: Cities are fine if you don't look at anything. Just use your eyes for not tripping over.

[JACK *has come back with a tray of mugs.*]

SYL: You made too many.

JACK: One for Christie.

DEL: Is Christie here?

JACK: She will be.

ALBERT: Get away.

[*The dog barks downstairs.*]

[CHRISTIE *calls from downstairs.*]

CHRISTIE: Jack?

SYL: You'd heard her already. You'd seen her from the window.

JACK: No, I'm beginning to frighten myself.

CHRISTIE: Jack?

[JACK *opens the door.*]

JACK: Here.

[CHRISTIE *comes in.*]

CHRISTIE: Sorry turning up.

JACK: We expected you.

CHRISTIE: Don't know why I came. Stupid.

JACK: Doesn't matter.

CHRISTIE: Sorry.

JACK: Albert. Syl. Del.

DEL: We've met.

CHRISTIE: Don't let me interrupt.

SYL: We've even got your cup of tea ready.

JACK: Two sugars already in.

CHRISTIE: Took a long time getting here. Got on the wrong train and had to come back.

SYL: There was someone asking . . .

[*She stops because of* JACK.]

[*During the next speech* ALBERT *goes out.*]

CHRISTIE: I would have phoned if you were on the phone. I wanted to make arrangements. The time has come for decisive . . . There wasn't a train till morning and then I got the wrong one. I could have gone to a doctor if I had one but I can't go to our doctor any more because they play golf. You can't get a

90

strange doctor in the night. I'm straightaway in the category of nuisance. Hospitals never close, but you might never get out. I'm afraid if I handed myself over. Who knows what's wrong with me. What would go wrong with me once I was treated. Bruises are the least part. I don't want bandaids or manipulation. I want to be saved. So I thought it was time I paid you a visit.

JACK: Does Reg hit you?

CHRISTIE: Sometimes.

JACK: Don't you hit him back?

CHRISTIE: He's stronger than me. I don't feel like it.

SYL: Why don't you leave him?

CHRISTIE: Yes, I know, but I'm very comfortable.

JACK: You've left him now.

[ALBERT *comes back with an armful of creased damp clothes identical with the ones* SYL *ironed earlier. He sets up the ironing board and starts ironing them.*]

DEL: Do you still go to evening classes in mending fuses?

CHRISTIE: When did I do that?

DEL: Three years ago?

JACK: When was that?

CHRISTIE: When we lived in Doncaster.

ALBERT: Del's lived with everyone.

DEL: What does that mean?

ALBERT: I don't know anyone you haven't lived with.

DEL: You can't know many people.

ALBERT: That's right.

DEL: Do you want me to stay?

ALBERT: It's pissing down out there.

DEL: Stay on.

ALBERT: See how it goes, shall we?

DEL: Day by day. By day by day.

JACK: Nobody stays except by unanimous agreement of the household.

DEL: But I'm one of the family myself. I've just been away for a short trip.

JACK: That's one way of looking at it.

SYL: Albert's got a real family with children, so he's got an advantage.

CHRISTIE: I'm Jack's family.

SYL: I'm an only child. And an orphan. It's not rare.

[SYL *brings the cake to the table and cuts it. They all have some.*]

ALBERT: It would be nice to have a family. Aunts and grannies and great-aunts and grandpas and babies and second cousins once removed and black sheep and ones you can't remember that suddenly look just like your dad. For Christmas. Nobody's got that nowadays.

SYL: Most people have got relations.

ALBERT: Not relations they like. Not relations they belong with. Imagine a family of relations you liked to be with.

SYL: You belong with them even if you don't like them.

ALBERT: No you don't.

JACK: We don't need any other family. What are you talking about? What's this?

DEL: I've got an auntie somewhere. I haven't seen her since I was six.

JACK: You've got us. Seems to me.

DEL: Even if I'm not liked?

SYL: You belong in a family whether you're liked or not.

ALBERT: I'm still not sure that's right.

SYL: Is Del staying?

ALBERT: I myself don't dislike him so there's no problem.

JACK: Is Christie staying?

CHRISTIE: Are you asking me?

SYL: You don't have to decide. He's putting pressure on. You can stay from day to day till you feel better. See how you feel.

CHRISTIE: I just got here. I can't possibly.

ALBERT: That's all right.

JACK: I only asked.

DEL: Give her time. You always did rush her.

JACK: I've not been in touch for a year.

CHRISTIE: Why was that?

JACK: One bit of news you haven't had, not being in touch, is Syl and I got married.

92

CHRISTIE: White wedding?

JACK: We did the state bit in the morning and then we had a party on a hill up near where we were. It was sunny nearly all day and full moon.

DEL: That was the wedding. That was the celebration.

CHRISTIE: I wouldn't have wanted to miss a white wedding. Nor any wedding of yours really.

JACK: We thought we'd get married, we suddenly thought. Since she's pregnant, we thought why not.

SYL: I want a big family. Thirteen.

JACK: Will you like to be an auntie, Christie?

CHRISTIE: I ought to let Reg know where I am. He'll have the police.

ALBERT: We don't want the police here. We don't want to draw attention. I want to get the place wired up with an alarm bell.

CHRISTIE: Don't want Reg here.

ALBERT: Lie low.

DEL: She does that. She lives under plain cover.

ALBERT: It's only fair to tell you this house is watched. You may notice yourself being followed.

CHRISTIE: I always do.

[DEL *touches the plant.*]

DEL: Hello there, how you keeping? All right? You're looking good. Jack remember to water you, does he? You feel fine. You're a great shade of green these days. It's lovely to see you. You've grown, you know that? You're getting enormous.

SYL: Jack and Del talk to the plant to make it grow.

CHRISTIE: Does it work?

SYL: It grows.

JACK: If you don't understand something, Syl, just leave it alone.

SYL: Fucking animals is bestiality, but I don't know the word for lusting after vegetation. You should see Jack and his plant gazing into each other's eyes.

JACK: It hasn't got your defences.

DEL: It doesn't ask where I was yesterday. Or if I'll be here tomorrow. It doesn't ask if I love it more than Jack does or more than I love Jack or anything. Totally here, every time, all the time.

ALBERT: It's not a great conversationalist, mind you.

JACK: Reg is in the pub.

CHRISTIE: What?

JACK: He came here just before, looking for you. He's waiting in the pub.

CHRISTIE: He doesn't know I'm here?

JACK: He knows you.

CHRISTIE: Nothing ever works out.

ALBERT: You don't have to see him.

SYL: You don't have to go back with him.

CHRISTIE: I'm frightened.

SYL: Of Reg?

CHRISTIE: No.

SYL: What then?

CHRISTIE: Don't know. Sorry.

JACK: What are you frightened of?

CHRISTIE: Being alone.

JACK: Why's that frightening? What are you frightened of?

CHRISTIE: Not knowing what's going to happen.

JACK: What are you frightened of?

CHRISTIE: Time.

JACK: What else?

CHRISTIE: Space.

JACK: What else?

CHRISTIE: Me.

JACK: What else? What are you frightened of?

CHRISTIE: You.

JACK: What are you frightened of?

CHRISTIE: Creeping bloody crawlies and heights, right?

DEL: Too true, she's frightened of earwigs and balconies.

SYL: I'm frightened of blood.

ALBERT: Your own?

SYL: Of course not my own. Other people's.

ALBERT: No, I'm frightened of my own blood.

JACK: Do you know why you're here?

CHRISTIE: You a Christian all of a sudden or what?

JACK: Do you know why you came?

CHRISTIE: I was fed up.

JACK: Reg been hitting you?

CHRISTIE: Bit.

JACK: That's not why.

CHRISTIE: Jack, you give me a headache. I came for a rest.

JACK: I willed you to come.

CHRISTIE: What do you mean?

JACK: What time did you leave last night?

CHRISTIE: I don't know.

JACK: Try.

CHRISTIE: After midnight.

JACK: How long after?

CHRISTIE: Two maybe.

JACK: Two-fifteen.

CHRISTIE: Could have been.

JACK: It was. I'm telling you. I woke up just before two-fifteen and I knew there was something wrong with you.

SYL: You'd just been dreaming about her.

JACK: It doesn't make any difference at all if I'd been dreaming about her or not. If I'd been dreaming about her, that helps. So I sat up in bed and concentrated on you. I felt you'd better come here so I started to bring you. After about quarter of an hour I felt things were better so I went to sleep. Then all day I thought you were coming. But it got a bit faint. I spent another hour on it this morning. Then half the afternoon, it was getting dark. It seemed like a waste of a day, but I couldn't get on with anything else. I could feel you were on your way, I just got into that, you were on your way. Sat there with my eyes shut and ... sat there, you know, with my eyes shut.

SYL: And Reg came.

JACK: Reg is a side effect.

CHRISTIE: You did not bring me.

JACK: Yes I did.

CHRISTIE: It was my own decision.

JACK: It would feel like that to you, yeah.

CHRISTIE: It was me decided to come. And you picked up on that and knew I was coming.

JACK: No.

CHRISTIE: You can read my mind, all right, I'll give you that. You cannot make my mind up.

JACK: Yes I can.

CHRISTIE: No.

JACK: Well, I did, so.

CHRISTIE: You did not.

DEL: Sounds like simple synchronicity. Nothing to get angry about.

SYL: It's just coincidence.

ALBERT: You've got to know what's a coincidence and what isn't. People don't look at you in a funny way unless they've got something on their mind.

DEL: If I go to the pub for some fags, how will I know this Reg?

SYL: Holding a very large box of chocolates.

DEL: And I'll say to him?

CHRISTIE: Tell him I'm here if you like. He'll only find out.

DEL: All right?

[*No one answers.* DEL *puts on his coat and goes.*]

SYL: You'll find it's not bad living alone. I find it okay. I come and go all round the place. It's nice I can come here. But mostly I'm on my own and I can do that. Saves a lot of worry about being left. And no one minds if I'm not here.

JACK: Come and see the plant.

CHRISTIE: Jack, I came here for a rest.

JACK: I'm giving you a rest. I want you to get quiet. Don't think anything and don't worry about trying not to think anything. Just keep coming back to the plant. You're not trying to do anything, you're doing it. If anything starts happening in your head, don't bother, don't wander, don't shy off, don't grab it, just see the plant. You can shut your eyes.

ALBERT: It kills time like a crossword, but you don't have to be so clever. And meanwhile the Special Branch are recruiting men who pretend to be killers to lure other men into killing so the Special Branch have somebody to catch. And then who murders that spy? Mercenaries are recruited here. If there's no police-man riding past the window, it's because they're getting cagey. They know I know. Somewhere I'm on a list. I posted two letters this morning. One to you and one to me. If your letter gets here before mine, it's proof positive my post's being tampered with. The next thing is install the alarm system. Remind me to buy some wire. And all he does is garden in a flower pot. If he thinks his mind beats fertilisers, why doesn't he get down to the Sahel and bloom a few tons of wheat out of the desert?

SYL: He's practising, isn't he.

ALBERT: I'm warning you, Syl. I'm patient to a fault. It's your life. I've no right. I'm not saying this righteously. Possession doesn't come in. There's nothing chauvinistic. You could be a man, I'd say the same. But I can only go so far. I don't take a literal view of marriage. I don't expect forsaking all others. But you and Jack are in danger of making me feel irrelevant. If I was to go, you might not mind. It's not a threat. It's not what I want. It's the direction. So think about it. Think of the babe. I mean not only, not stay together for that, but that as well. I hate to ask. I'd like to do without security. But there's none at work. There's none when I look round the street. I'm trying to build a new world and I can't get the bricks. Or I get the bricks and I don't get the labour. Or I get the labour and they throw the bricks at me. So if you could be clearer.

SYL: What are you asking? Something impossible.

ALBERT: I don't want perfection. Just changes.

[*The dog barks downstairs.*]

CHRISTIE: Jack —

JACK: Shh.

CHRISTIE: Jack —

JACK: No.

CHRISTIE: Jack, before he comes. What shall I say?

[REG *comes in.*]

REG: A young man came up to me in the pub and ... yes. It's satisfying to know one stands where one thought one stood.

JACK: I got her all this way just in my head.

REG: She had arranged with you to come here.

JACK: This is the beginning of my life's work. Like Fleming's bit of mouldy bread. I'm a scientist. Was it Fleming?

REG: All right, Christie?

CHRISTIE: Yes.

REG: I got no sleep last night at all.

CHRISTIE: Sorry.

REG: I'm only telling you so you can see how concerned I was.

CHRISTIE: Yes. I'm sorry.

REG: Don't keep apologising.

CHRISTIE: No. I'm sorry. I can't help it. I'm sorry. I can't help it.

REG: Well, we must apologise for intruding on your hospitality and make our way back. I had to cancel dinner.

CHRISTIE: Yes. I'm sorry.

REG: I'd better take you home and put you to bed.

CHRISTIE: I'm not going home.

REG: What do you mean?

CHRISTIE: I'm sorry.

REG: You want to have a little talk with Jack now you're here. You must have a lot to say to each other. Don't let me stop you, of course.

[Silence.]

Do carry on.

[Silence.]

I'm forgetting to give you these.

[REG gives CHRISTIE the chocolates.]

CHRISTIE: Thank you very much. How delicious. What a big box. Shall I open them now?

REG: Yes, pass them round among your friends.

SYL: I want to work it out on the little chart.

ALBERT: Hard one for me.

JACK: Won't you take off your coat?

REG: Thank you, no, I won't be staying long.

CHRISTIE: I'm not going home, Reg.

REG: You're inviting yourself to stay here the night?

CHRISTIE: Yes.

REG: What am I supposed to do? Stay in a hotel at vast expense? Go home and come back for you tomorrow?

CHRISTIE: No.

REG: What then?

CHRISTIE: I'm sorry.

REG: What are you playing at, Christie?

CHRISTIE: I'm sorry.

JACK: What are you frightened of?

REG: Leave her alone, Jack.

SYL [*to* REG]: Let her speak for herself.

REG [*to* SYL]: Will you kindly mind your own business, young
woman.

ALBERT [*to* REG]: Don't talk to Syl like that.

CHRISTIE [*to* ALBERT]: Shut up and keep out of it.

[SYL *sits down at the table and deals Patience.*]

[ALBERT *joins in over her shoulder.*]

REG: Come along, Christie.

CHRISTIE: No.

REG: I'm leaving now. I'll wait five minutes in the car. It's parked
just round the corner.

CHRISTIE: Please stay.

REG: I've wasted enough time. I've work to do.

CHRISTIE: Stay just a little.

REG: You come now or you don't come at all.

JACK: She's not coming at all. She's staying here.

SYL: Stop telling her, Jack.

JACK: Jealous now?

SYL: I'd like her to stay, but stop telling her.

CHRISTIE: It's my own fault. I'm sorry. I can't do more than not
go.

SYL: Stay here then.

CHRISTIE: Yes, I am.

JACK: Who's telling her?

REG: Christie, I'm leaving now.

CHRISTIE: I'm sorry.

REG: You'll regret this.

CHRISTIE: Yes, I do. I'm sorry. Goodbye.

REG: This is final.

CHRISTIE: All right.

REG: I'm not coming to get you tomorrow.

CHRISTIE: I know that.

REG: If you come home I won't let you in. I'm changing the lock.

[DEL *comes in exactly as before.*]

DEL: Taken me two days getting here, so I'm not leaving yet.

SYL: What are you doing here?

DEL: Come to tell you bastards what I think of you.

JACK: We've some idea of that. I shouldn't bother.

[DEL *knocks the cards on to the floor.*]

ALBERT: Sit down, Del, and shut up.

DEL: You sit down. [*Sit down.*] Thought you were rid of me. Did you think at all? Hope old Del's making out. *Hell.*

SYL: Del, we've got people —

DEL: You've got Christie. I know Christie. Christie knows me. You won't shut me up for Christie. She wouldn't have treated me like you did. And who's this? Your husband, Christie? You won't shut me up for Christie's husband. You owe me money. I paid the milk bill.

JACK: You borrowed fifteen pounds off me, Del.

DEL: Want it back? With interest? What's the rate of interest?

JACK: Just don't talk to me about the milk bill.

DEL: You think you can make me do what you like. I *will not.* Necrophiliacs. But I'm not dead, too bad, I'm alive. You've all lied to me. Media substitutes. You're not real people. You don't correlate.

SYL: Del —

DEL: Who did you last fuck?

SYL: Someone better than you, okay?

ALBERT: If you've come to shout, just go away. We had enough of that.

JACK: There's other things going on here, Del. I'm talking to Christie.

[DEL *knocks the bowl of peas on to the floor, breaking the bowl.*]

DEL: Talk to me. Talk to me.

ALBERT: Stop it.

[ALBERT *grabs* DEL *to contain him.*]

REG: I can't leave you here with this going on.

CHRISTIE: Stay then.

REG: Come along.

[DEL *gets free of* ALBERT *and picks up the plant, tearing the leaves and smashing it on the floor.*]

DEL: Hate you, kill you.

[JACK *throws himself at* DEL *and they roll on the floor.*]

100

[ALBERT *and* JACK *get* DEL *to his feet.*]

ALBERT: We don't want you here, right?

DEL: You can't do this.

SYL: We're sick of you.

JACK: You don't live here any more. Get that straight. You've left us. Go away.

DEL: Why?

CHRISTIE: I don't think they like you.

DEL: Christie, I'll see you sometime.

[DEL *goes.*]

[JACK *starts clearing up the plant, the bowl, the cards.*]

REG: Who was that? Christie? How do you know him?

CHRISTIE: Long time ago.

REG: A friend of Jack's. Typical. Strikes me he should be in hospital under heavy sedation. I shouldn't think he's safe. In his own interest.

[ALBERT *is at the window.*]

ALBERT: There he goes.

SYL: He just uses us.

CHRISTIE: What can we do about the plant, Jack?

REG: We won't be able to eat those peas, you know.

SYL: Christie, where's the baby?

CHRISTIE: In the garden.

ACT TWO

The room is almost exactly as it was, but bright sunlight is shining through the window.

The floor has been cleaned up; the plant is exactly as it was at the beginning of the play; the bowl of peas is unbroken, as it was when Jack finished shelling them; the cards are on the table. The ironing board is folded and the ironed clothes in a pile. REG's *coat is across the back of a chair. The folder of letters is where* DEL *left it. The newspapers are as they were, so is the cake. The guitar and gun are in different places. There is a different picture on the wall. The jigsaw is as it was at the end of Act I. The clock still tells real time.*

*   DEL *and* CHRISTIE *are huddled in the armchair, arms round each other, the box of chocolates on their laps, eating chocolates and talking almost in whispers.*

DEL: Haven't told anybody else.

CHRISTIE: Why tell me?

DEL: You understand anything like that.

CHRISTIE: I don't.

DEL: You're like me in that way.

CHRISTIE: I'm not.

DEL: Always have been. Killer deep down.

CHRISTIE: No one ever suspected you at all?

DEL: No.

CHRISTIE: So you think you got away with it?

DEL: I did.

CHRISTIE: What if I told?

DEL: You're the risk I take. Always have been.

CHRISTIE: I don't want to know what you do.

DEL: But it doesn't surprise you.

CHRISTIE: No.

DEL: See what I mean?

CHRISTIE: Was she a total stranger?

DEL: She looked back at me over her shoulder.

CHRISTIE: Was she what you think of as attractive?

DEL: It was wasted if she was. I just hated her so I couldn't see.

CHRISTIE: What for?

DEL: What for?

CHRISTIE: Yeah.

DEL: Have another strawberry cream.

CHRISTIE: Stop imagining I understand.

DEL: I hated her because I was raping her. You don't think I enjoyed it?

CHRISTIE: Did you stop hating her after?

DEL: I was pissed off with the whole thing, wasn't I. I blamed her.

CHRISTIE: Did you think she wanted you to? Did you kid yourself that?

DEL: Something happens, you don't want to be stuck with it. She didn't have to get herself killed, did she, fighting and that. Look where it puts me. I couldn't consider being locked up and they mess about in your head. It was some time ago. More than enough you messing me about.

CHRISTIE: Do you think you'll do it again?

DEL: I don't enjoy it.

CHRISTIE: Do you think you will?

DEL: I get all this hate. I get locked on.

CHRISTIE: Does it seem likely?

DEL: Doesn't it?

CHRISTIE: How you feeling now?

DEL: How you feeling?

CHRISTIE: Nothing much.

[CHRISTIE *stands up and takes her shirt up over her head so he can see her back, which is badly bruised.*]

Del.

DEL: Yeah. Who did that then?

CHRISTIE: Reg.

DEL: He find you with another guy or what?

CHRISTIE: No, nothing. He seems to need pain or he doesn't know he's alive.

DEL: Yeah. Well. It's wartime isn't it.

[CHRISTIE *puts her shirt down and moves away.*]

CHRISTIE: Shall we go away together?

DEL: Where to?

103

CHRISTIE: It won't last.

DEL: Yes, I'd like that.

CHRISTIE: But you'd want Jack to come.

DEL: Yes.

CHRISTIE: You could just go away with Jack.

DEL: What do you see in Reg?

CHRISTIE: He buys me things.

DEL: Really?

CHRISTIE: He really does buy me things.

DEL: Is that really why?

CHRISTIE: I don't like work. It's only like living on the dole.

DEL: I always paid stamps.

CHRISTIE: I pay stamps.

DEL: But don't you like him?

CHRISTIE: Tell me what you wouldn't do to get free food, housing, clothes, use of car, holidays on hot islands?

DEL: No one's asked me.

CHRISTIE: Surprisingly enough I do like him.

DEL: Yeah?

CHRISTIE: I'm tougher than you.

DEL: You're what?

CHRISTIE: I'll give you an arm wrestle then.

[DEL *and* CHRISTIE *sit at the table to arm wrestle. He gets her arm down easily.*]

My arm's shorter, that's all it is.

[JACK *comes in with some planks and a roll of wire netting.*]

[DEL *soon starts doing the jigsaw.*]

JACK: Mr Fellows came by on a horse. He's lost a cow. What he means is did we leave the gate open.

CHRISTIE: They jump out. He must have seen them in all his life here. I've seen them.

DEL: He doesn't like us.

JACK: You don't expect people to like us?

CHRISTIE: The country's always hard to belong in.

JACK: He thinks we're here just for the summer. I've told him.

CHRISTIE: He doesn't think we'll survive once it snows. With the outside bog and one cold tap. He thinks we won't get the roof mended.

DEL: He could be right.

CHRISTIE: We're staying here the rest of our lives.

JACK: I am, but no one else has to.

DEL: There's nothing else much I want to do. It's all beyond me. I'd sooner leave it behind and grow some potatoes and not smoke so much.

CHRISTIE: Give Mr Fellows ten years. Or his children might like us when we're grey and shaky.

JACK: Leave what behind, Del?

DEL: Whatever.

JACK: Do you think living here is running away?

DEL: No, no, it's running to, I know that.

JACK: We're not on holiday.

DEL: I'm never on holiday.

JACK: The best thing would be for you to leave.

DEL: I do take it all very seriously.

JACK: No, this is basic.

DEL: I do understand.

JACK: What?

DEL: We will be new. The world will catch our perfection like an infection. Contagious joy will cause the entire population to levitate two feet off the ground perceptibly.

CHRISTIE: Jack believes that.

JACK: I believe everything.

DEL: Ghosts?

JACK: Don't you?

DEL: I tried very hard one time to believe in Father Christmas.

JACK: I believe all world religions and minor sects before I even start. All science and superscience. And that every vision can be made real. Before breakfast. That's all possible things. I spend the morning lieving impossible things.

DEL: Like?

JACK: That you love me.

DEL: And the afternoon?

JACK: Being impossible things.

DEL: Like?

JACK: Here. Now.

[CHRISTIE *is at the window. The light has faded and slightly reddened.*]

CHRISTIE: There's Mr Fellows with his cow.

DEL: Shall we get a cow?

JACK: Can we milk a cow?

DEL: It can't be hard to learn. Children do it.

JACK: Children speak Chinese. Chinese children.

DEL: I want a cow.

CHRISTIE: It's going to be sunset. Anyone coming out?

DEL: I've seen the sun set.

JACK: Shall I come?

[REG *comes in.*]

REG: There you are, Christie. Come outside. It's going to be a most beautiful sunset.

CHRISTIE: I can see from here.

DEL: Gardening?

REG: I'm proud to say I've nearly finished the weeding. Two rows of lettuces are nearly ready you know. We'll have to eat salad twice a day all week.

JACK: Go on, Christie.

REG: Don't come outside on my account. I just didn't want you to miss it through failing to notice. It's a mackerel sky in the west tinted pink and a full moon rising on the dark side. The east. I only just begin to appreciate how the sun shines on the moon. I knew it all along. I did diagrams in exercise books as a child. The word 'penumbra' comes to mind. New to me then. Possibly in connection with the eclipse. One knows the theory but when one sees it . . . the sun there and the moon there, full, or the sun there and the moon there, half. I'm always delighted by the neatness. That it all works. And of course the colours.

[REG *goes.*]

DEL: Do you find incest a worry? The fear of the thought of committing incest?

CHRISTIE: We did all that a long time ago. We weren't all that good together.

JACK: We were very young.

CHRISTIE: It turned us off a bit.

JACK: It's not the solution to me and Christie, Del. More something you get out of the way.

CHRISTIE: We're related.

JACK: It's not the problem, Del.

DEL: All right, I believe you.

JACK: Go and watch the moon rise, Christie.

CHRISTIE: Come on then.

[JACK *doesn't go.*]

[CHRISTIE *goes.*]

[JACK *takes from his pocket a book about poultry and reads.*]

[DEL *does the jigsaw.*]

JACK: If each chicken needs six square feet, right, a chicken house twelve feet by six would hold twelve chickens.

Rhode Island Red is the most popular laying breed in this country today. Leghorns . . . they don't put on weight. Do we want to eat the chickens or just the eggs?

North Holland Blue has table qualities. It lays tinted eggs and is very hardy.

DEL: I don't think I could say I love anyone. Not like feel any different than what I do.

JACK: I'd just as soon you left.

DEL: I'd just as soon stick around a bit.

JACK: You're meant to be committed.

DEL: I am.

JACK: One day you'll just go.

DEL: The day I just stop being committed.

JACK: I want you to go.

DEL: You can't get rid of me.

JACK: I refuse –

DEL: What can you do about it?

[DEL *takes from his pocket a book about poultry and reads.*]

[JACK *takes a half-eaten packet of chocolate biscuits from the drawer and eats one while he does the jigsaw.*]

North Holland Blue has table qualities.

Rhode Island Red . . . the most popular laying breed.

Each chicken needs six square feet, right?

[SYL *comes in with a string bag of carrots and potatoes, and a saucepan. She puts them on the table.*]

SYL: Jack, I've decided to call the baby Albert. After Albert. Would you mind that?

JACK: Only if it's a girl.

DEL: I mind.

SYL: All right then, Jack?

DEL: I thought it was going to be a communal baby.

SYL: Then we call it Albert. Because it's a communal baby.

JACK: Del, I do think ... I mean if Albert was alive he'd be with us here, so it is a good idea.

DEL: I don't mind the idea, I mind the name.

SYL: I like the name.

DEL: It's your baby.

SYL: It's certainly not yours.

DEL: I'm not competing.

JACK: I'm just quite certain it's a girl.

DEL: There's something where you swing a thingummy on a string. It goes round in circles if it's a girl and in straight lines if it's a boy. Or the other way round.

SYL: No, I like it whichever it is.

DEL: Would you stop liking it if you knew?

SYL: I don't want to know.

DEL: Why not?

SYL: It isn't either sex until it's born.

DEL: It is in fact.

SYL: I don't want to know. It's part of me.

DEL: You're resisting progress. You'll be evolved out.

SYL: Look, Del, just leave my baby alone.

[CHRISTIE comes in.]

CHRISTIE: I must have left my fags.

JACK: If I want to call my daughter Albert, I'll call her Albert.

CHRISTIE: Seen my fags? I left them somewhere.

DEL: Want one?

CHRISTIE: No, I'll find them.

JACK: What did you come back for?

CHRISTIE: I just said.

JACK: I thought you were looking at the sunset.

CHRISTIE: I am, I want to smoke and enjoy it.

DEL: It won't wait.

[DEL *starts making a roll-up.*]

JACK: You came back because I brought you back.

CHRISTIE: Came back to get my fags.

JACK: I willed you.

CHRISTIE: Don't start that.

JACK: Look in your pocket.

CHRISTIE: I've already looked in my pocket.

[CHRISTIE *takes a cigarette packet out of her pocket.*]
I didn't think they were there.

JACK: Too right you didn't.

CHRISTIE: It's an empty packet. I did leave my others here.

JACK: Where?

CHRISTIE: You've hidden them.

JACK: I'm not interested in tricking you.

CHRISTIE: But anyway I thought I'd left them here, so that's why I came back.

JACK: You thought that was why you came back. You wanted to come back because I was willing it and you found that reason for yourself.

DEL: Before it gets dark.

[DEL *gives* CHRISTIE *the roll-up*]

CHRISTIE: Leave me alone, Jack, will you?

JACK: Believe it? Do you? Do you believe it?

[CHRISTIE *starts to go.*]

SYL: Christie?

CHRISTIE: What?

SYL: Do you believe it?

[CHRISTIE *goes.*]
[DEL *takes a sharp knife from the drawer and starts preparing the vegetables.*]

JACK: Do you believe it?

SYL: Is it only Christie?

JACK: The Russians took new-born rabbits down in a submarine and kept the mother on shore with electrodes in her brain, and every time they killed a baby the mother bunny's brain waves went *vroom*.

SYL: But you're not that close to me.

JACK: Maybe not.

SYL: Have you tried?

JACK: Not very hard.

SYL: And Albert?

JACK: What about Albert?

[DEL *meanwhile cuts his finger, not badly. He gets a plaster from a packet in the drawer and puts it on. He goes on with the vegetables.*]

[*The sunlight has faded.*]

SYL: Did you try to make him do things?

JACK: It's not so much what appeals to a Marxist, is it? Quite wrongly, because Russia's one of the most advanced countries in researching –

SYL: Did you?

JACK: And America to some extent. They think of it as a weapon.

SYL: Did you?

JACK: The results weren't conclusive at all.

SYL: He is dead.

JACK: Are you saying I willed him to die?

SYL: Am I saying that?

JACK: What would I do that for?

SYL: I only said . . . I'm not . . . I don't mean . . .

JACK: What? What?

SYL: To get him out of the way.

JACK: Out of which way?

SYL: Me.

JACK: You've got a very *News of the World* view of how Albert and I felt about you. If I ever felt like killing anyone it certainly wasn't Albert. I'm just staggered at your vanity.

SYL: No, but just . . . you might not have meant to . . . more just to see . . .

JACK: See if I could? No. What, see if I could harm him just a little bit? No.

SYL: No.

JACK: No.

SYL: It was better to say it.

JACK: Sure.

SYL: Than have it on my mind.

JACK: Sure.

SYL: What kind of thing did you make him do then?

JACK: Like look out of the window. Nothing. Things he was doing anyway. I didn't try. I didn't want to touch minds with Albert.

SYL: I wish I wasn't so angry with him. He'd no right to kill himself without telling us. He should have said something. It needn't have been to me.

DEL: Albert was obviously a schizophrenic.

JACK: Oh, for Christ's sake.

DEL: I'm just telling you. If you don't want to know —

JACK: Shut up will you?

SYL: He deceived us the whole evening. He might have been planning it for weeks. It's hard to know how to remember him.

JACK: He might have thought about it a lot without ever believing he'd do it. Then suddenly did it without thinking at all.

SYL: I can't believe he didn't say someting.

JACK: To me?

SYL: Did he?

JACK: No. He said he wanted to have a look at the river.

SYL: I thought you might be trying to protect me . . . if what he said . . .

JACK: Nothing about you.

SYL: But he said something?

JACK: No.

[DEL *goes and sits by* SYL *with his arm round her.*]

SYL: Unless some organisation murdered him. Is that so impossible? Or like the police or . . .

JACK: What had he done then?

[JACK *goes and sits where* DEL *was and goes on with the vegetables.*]

DEL: He was totally paranoid.

JACK: But he might have done something as well.

SYL: Do you really think . . .?

JACK: It's not likely, is it?

SYL: Ought we to . . .?

JACK: What?

SYL: Tell somebody?

JACK: Who?

SYL: The police?

JACK: He used to get very depressed about his wife.

SYL: He could have said.

JACK: He used to get very depressed about his kids.

SYL: I know that.

JACK: Well then.

SYL: I want to tell Albert what it's like without him.

[JACK *meanwhile cuts his finger, not badly. He gets a plaster from a packet in the drawer and puts it on. He goes on with the vegetables.*]

[*It is getting dark.*]

DEL: When I was in Finland it was light all night. I felt quite sick by morning. It was midday before I got to sleep.

JACK: Syl, I ought to tell you.

SYL: What? What, go on.

JACK: I want to go away for a bit.

SYL: Where to?

JACK: Haven't thought exactly where.

SYL: How long for?

JACK: Have to see.

SYL: If you don't know when you're going or where you're going, I don't see why you have to go at all.

JACK: At least I'm telling you. You won't just wake up and find me gone.

SYL: I don't want to have a baby.

JACK: I will be back.

SYL: One day it's going to have to come out of me, alive or dead, either way, that's something there's no way out of.

JACK: I want to have a baby.

DEL: I'd like to go to Finland in the winter.

JACK: If you like, Syl, when she's born . . . see how you feel, but ... I'll take her away.

SYL: What?

JACK: She's my baby just as much. You needn't look after her. I'll keep her with me.

SYL: You serious?

JACK: Why not?

SYL: A newborn baby?

JACK: Tell me why not.

SYL: No, you'd be good at it.

JACK: I know I would, I'd be great.

DEL: In the winter you'd see the sun going round the edge of the horizon.

SYL: But what about me?

DEL: Do you want to come with us, Syl?

SYL: Would you like that?

DEL: Yes of course, it's what I'm after. Can't you tell?

SYL: No, I want Jack to stay here. Jack?:

JACK: There's no hurry.

    [DEL *gets up.*]

    [He and JACK *are looking at each other.*]

    [SYL *starts to cry quietly.*]

    [*The light is now the same as at the beginning of the play.*]

    [CHRISTIE *comes in.*]

CHRISTIE: You're all sitting in the dark. Why haven't you got a light on?

JACK: Yes, and it's bath night tonight.

CHRISTIE: Syl?

DEL: We'd better get some water on to boil.

CHRISTIE: Supper before or after?

SYL: Did you see the badgers?

DEL: Get it all on at once.

CHRISTIE: Just one. Reg saw two.

JACK: Is there anything else except the vegetables?

DEL: There's a bit of cheese left.

SYL: No eggs.

JACK: Better shop tomorrow.

DEL: Plenty of bread.

    [DEL *and* JACK *go out, taking the bowl of peas and the saucepan of chopped vegetables.*]

    [CHRISTIE *lights the oil lamp and brings it to the table.*]

    [SYL *deals Patience.*]

    [CHRISTIE *offers* SYL *a cigarette from the packet in her pocket.* SYL *refuses.*]

    [CHRISTIE *gets a half-eaten packet of chocolate biscuits from the drawer and offers one to* SYL. SYL *refuses.* CHRISTIE *leaves the packet on the table.*]

113

[CHRISTIE *puts a pound note on the table.*]

[SYL *goes on playing Patience while they talk.*]

CHRISTIE: I owe you a pound.

SYL: No.

CHRISTIE: Yes, I do.

SYL: You bought the drinks.

CHRISTIE: Drinks don't count.

[SYL *doesn't take the pound. It stays on the table.*]

Are you cold?

SYL: No.

CHRISTIE: You're shivering.

[CHRISTIE *takes off her jacket and puts it round* SYL's *shoulders.* SYL *goes on playing.*]

Won't you forgive me?

SYL: Where's Reg?

CHRISTIE: I came on ahead.

SYL: Is he happy enough?

CHRISTIE: Do you care?

SYL: If he's to stay.

[CHRISTIE *plays a card* SYL *hasn't noticed.*]

Don't.

CHRISTIE: Why?

SYL: It's my mistake.

CHRISTIE: Sorry.

[SYL *goes on playing.*]

It seems to be working out all right.

[SYL *goes on playing. Suddenly she mixes all the cards up.*]

SYL: No, it's stuck.

[*They stay silent.*]

[CHRISTIE *is about to say something but doesn't. She eats a biscuit.*]

Sorry about yesterday.

CHRISTIE: That's all right.

SYL: No, I'm sorry. I should be better at . . . Anyway.

CHRISTIE: It's difficult.

SYL: But I am glad you came.

CHRISTIE: Are you?

SYL: Yes.

CHRISTIE: So am I.

SYL: There then.

[*Silence.* CHRISTIE *tears off a very small bit of leaf from the plant and rubs it between her fingers.*]

CHRISTIE: Syl, what shall I do?

SYL: About what?

CHRISTIE: Syl, what shall I do?

[SYL *gathers up the cards and deals Patience.*]

It's all very well to talk about the moon. Indoors it's just another bit of scenery. But out there. Oh, I can glance at it. But I can't meet it. Can't rise to it. I'm too partial. I can't.

[SYL *goes on playing. Suddenly she gets up. The jacket falls off her shoulders.*]

SYL: Christie, what shall I do?

CHRISTIE: About what?

SYL: Why can't you help me?

CHRISTIE: I can't.

SYL: Help me.

CHRISTIE: I can't.

[SYL *sits down.*]

[CHRISTIE *picks up the jacket and puts it on.*]

[SYL *eats a biscuit. She doesn't go on playing.*]

SYL: I trained as a dancer. But I'm not good enough.

CHRISTIE: Does it matter?

SYL: I expected to be amazing.

CHRISTIE: I'm clever. But I'm not interested. I was always more clever than Jack. But neither of us was very interested.

SYL: I could emigrate.

CHRISTIE: That gets you nowhere.

SYL: New life. Pursuit of happiness.

CHRISTIE: No.

SYL: This is already a new life.

CHRISTIE: Never knowing what's going to happen.

SYL: It's all right, isn't it?

CHRISTIE: I get frightened. Don't you?

SYL: Yes.

CHRISTIE: But it's all right.

SYL: I don't see why not. What shall we play?

115

CHRISTIE: Snap.

SYL: Snap?

CHRISTIE: I don't play cards.

SYL: Right.

> [*They play Snap.*]
>
> [*Both win fairly equally.*]
>
> [REG *comes in. He puts the lid on the box of chocolates and puts it aside neatly.*]
>
> [*They go on playing without looking at him.*]
>
> [REG *stands behind* CHRISTIE *and watches.*]
>
> [CHRISTIE *loses every time, till* SYL *wins all the cards.*]

REG: Not very good at it, are you?

CHRISTIE: Out of practice.

REG: She never practises anything. Piano the same. She played the piano when we were first married. Not very well, but she played. But she never practises. I tell her to. But she won't. Now she's forgotten all she every knew.

CHRISTIE: I'm sorry.

REG: Perhaps you'll start again.

CHRISTIE: There's no piano.

REG: When we get home.

CHRISTIE: You could learn yourself if you're so keen on music.

REG: There's nothing I'd like better if I had the time. I've too many responsibilities.

SYL: Christie's got nothing better to do.

REG: She's very childish.

SYL: You have to tell her.

REG: She has an immature personality.

SYL: She's a flibbertigibbet.

REG: She tries.

SYL: She does try.

CHRISTIE: Don't describe me.

REG: She doesn't like people describing her.

CHRISTIE: *Stop it.*

REG: It makes her shout.

> [CHRISTIE *starts to cry quietly.*]

SYL: If we go on about her, it makes her cry.

REG: Yes, the more we go on, the more she cries.

SYL: If we stop noticing her, she'll stop crying.

[*They wait in silence, while* CHRISTIE *still cries.*]

REG: We want to help, Christie.

[*They wait in silence, while* CHRISTIE *still cries.*]

SYL: Are you going home soon then?

REG: Sunday afternoon. There's a three forty-nine which gets in nicely. Time to get in the right frame of mind for Monday morning. I don't like getting home too late. Yes, it's been a very pleasant little break.

[CHRISTIE *stops crying.*]

[*The other two exchange pleased nods.*]

If Christie likes, she could stay on a few days.

CHRISTIE: No.

REG: Do.

CHRISTIE: Not worth it.

REG: I want to make you happy.

CHRISTIE: I want to be with you.

REG: Just a few days.

CHRISTIE: I can't stay by myself.

REG: I could come back and get you next weekend.

CHRISTIE: I couldn't sleep.

REG: The fresh air does you good. You get peaky in town. It's not as if you've anything to do.

CHRISTIE: I can't bear to be away from you.

[REG *starts to caress her.*]

REG: Don't you trust me in town by myself?

CHRISTIE: Now you mention it, no.

REG: What do you think I might get up to?

CHRISTIE: I miss the shops.

REG: It's true we have some evening engagements.

CHRISTIE: Unless you want me out of the way.

REG: No, I was thinking of your happiness.

CHRISTIE: I know I can be an embarrassment.

REG: I could never go to a dinner party by myself. People would wonder.

CHRISTIE: It's time we had a party.

REG: Yes, we owe some hospitality.

CHRISTIE: I want to wear a very expensive dress. My nipples

117

must stand out under the fabric. Everyone who sees me must get an erection.

REG: We'll have music.

CHRISTIE: But it's quite safe, because I belong to you.

[REG *starts kissing her neck. Suddenly he stops, conscious of* SYL.]

REG: Would you be able to come to the party?

SYL: Send me an invitation, will you?

[SYL *gets the suitcase and starts to pack the ironed clothes in it.*]

[REG *and* CHRISTIE *kiss and caress, at first passionately, then with increasingly cool and hesitant movements.*]

REG: Bitch.

CHRISTIE: What?

REG: Don't pretend you don't know.

CHRISTIE: What?

REG: You don't want me.

CHRISTIE: I do.

REG: You don't.

CHRISTIE: You don't want me.

REG: You don't want me.

CHRISTIE: I try.

REG: You try!

CHRISTIE: You don't try even.

REG: Things will be better when we get home. Strange places are always very tense. We'll feel better alone. We'll have a party. We'll go to the Canaries in the summer. No, we'll go to the Canaries in the winter. We'll got to the Greek islands in the summer. We'll go to the Canaries in the winter. Or we could go skiing in the winter. And go to the Canaries the following summer.

CHRISTIE: If we can afford it.

REG: What?

CHRISTIE: Inflation.

REG: We still have two cars.

CHRISTIE: Two old cars.

REG: If the flood water reaches our knees, it will be over most people's heads.

CHRISTIE: I find you ugly.

[SYL *has finished packing. She leaves the case where it was before she took it. She is about to say something and doesn't. She goes out.*]

REG: You've heard about the little Dutch boy who puts his finger in the dyke?

CHRISTIE: What?

REG: She didn't like it.

CHRISTIE: I wish we could go home.

REG: No. Not now. Never.

CHRISTIE: I'm sorry.

REG: We must part. It's the only way. I don't want to hurt you.

CHRISTIE: Please —

[REG *hits* CHRISTIE *across the face.*]

Please, Reg, I'm sorry. We'll go to the Canaries —

[*He hits her again and she falls over.*]

REG: I don't want to hurt you. Be sensible.

CHRISTIE: I'll do anything —

[*He starts kicking her. She huddles into a ball. He goes and sits at the table. He cries.*]

[CHRISTIE *gets up slowly and sits in a chair.*]

REG: Why don't you stop me?

CHRISTIE: Sorry.

REG: We'd better part.

CHRISTIE: No.

REG: I'd like to die.

CHRISTIE: Sorry.

REG: We'd better part.

[ALBERT *comes in, his hands dirty from gardening. He takes off his boots, which are caked in mud.*]

ALBERT: Am I late? I haven't missed supper? I went on digging. I dug the whole patch. I went on digging in the dark. I haven't missed supper?

CHRISTIE: No.

ALBERT: That's all right then. I deserve some supper. I could do with a bath too. I'm going to be stiff. It wasn't too dark because of the moon.

REG: What are we planting in that bed?

119

ALBERT: Beans, I think, and peas.

CHRISTIE: And next week we get the chickens. I'm an expert now on chickens.

ALBERT: We're getting on slowly.

CHRISTIE: We're getting on fast.

> [JACK *comes in with a big tin bath.*]
>
> [DEL *and* SYL *come in with big saucepans of hot water, which they pour into the bath.*]

DEL: Mind, don't get splashed.

> [REG *starts doing the jigsaw.*]

ALBERT: Look at that. Can I have first bath?

> [DEL *goes out with the empty saucepans.*]

SYL: No, you're too muddy. You'll have to wait.

JACK: It's only for clean people this bath.

CHRISTIE: I'll go first. I went swimming yesterday.

JACK: Don't get in yet. It's scalding.

SYL: It's not best going first, because it's shallow.

JACK: Clean and shallow or deep and dirty.

ALBERT: Jigsaw's getting on.

> [DEL *comes back with a bucket of cold water and tips half of it into the bath.*]

SYL: Somebody try that.

DEL: I'm going first and then I'll get the supper.

> [DEL *undresses.*]
>
> [ALBERT *hugs* SYL.]

ALBERT: Had a nice day?

SYL: Lovely. Have you?

ALBERT: Lovely.

DEL: Where's the soap?

> [CHRISTIE *gets the soap from the drawer and gives it to* DEL.]
>
> [DEL *gets into the bath.*]

Ooh. Hot.

> [SYL *tips more cold in.*]

Agh. Careful.

> [ALBERT *furtively reaches into the drawer and gets a chocolate biscuit, which he eats quickly.*]

SYL: Mr Fellows came round this morning and gave us some eggs.

JACK: We need a rota for cooking.

ALBERT: And all the jobs.

JACK: When's Reg going to cook a meal?

REG: I have cooked.

JACK: Last Tuesday week?

REG: Just ask me. I'll do whatever I'm asked.

JACK: You should just do what needs to be done.

SYL: It takes time spotting that.

JACK: If you keep your eyes shut.

ALBERT: We'll have a rota. Write it all out.

DEL: Ah. Lovely. Somebody wash my back.

> [SYL *washes* DEL's *back.*]
>
> [JACK *scoops water from the bucket with a mug and waters the plant. He talks to it quietly.*]
>
> [REG *keeps looking up from the jigsaw to see if* CHRISTIE *is watching* DEL.]

That time in Finland I fell asleep in a field. I'd no clothes on and the sun was blazing. When I woke up I didn't know where I was.

ALBERT: Hurry up or the water gets cold.

DEL: The saucepans are hot again by now.

> [ALBERT *passes a towel to* SYL, *who gives it to* DEL *as he gets out of the bath.*]

CHRISTIE: Come on, Jack, help me get the water. Jack.

JACK: You all right?

CHRISTIE: No.

> [JACK *and* CHRISTIE *go out.*]
>
> [DEL *dresses and* SYL *undresses.*]
>
> [REG *is doing the jigsaw.*]

REG: There's such a lot of blue sky, that's the problem.

ALBERT: It's too fiddly for me. Here, what about this? And this, look.

REG: You see, you're good at it.

ALBERT: I like it when it works, but it won't last.

> [*They go on with the jigsaw.*]
>
> [JACK *and* CHRISTIE *come back with the water and pour it into the bath.*]
>
> [SYL *gets into the bath.*]

121

SYL: I'm tired tonight. I've worked hard this week. I'm a bit out of practice is the thing. I danced all right today though I think. It felt all right. Has the baby slept well?

DEL: He cried a bit this afternoon, but no, he's fine. I might make him up an extra couple of ounces tonight, he's getting through it all in no time.

ALBERT: You want a new teat with a smaller hole. His stomach can't take it at that spead.

SYL: Do you think so? I'll get one tomorrow.

[DEL *goes out with the saucepans.*]

[JACK *undresses.* SYL *washes.* REG *glances at her, embarrassed.*]

JACK: Come on, out you get.

SYL: No, it's warm.

JACK: Out.

[JACK *tries to lift* SYL *out. She laughs and splashes.*]

ALBERT: Mind out, you'll have it over.

JACK: Tell your wife to get out of the bath then. I'm freezing.

SYL: Give us a towel then. A dry one.

[ALBERT *gets a towel and wraps her in it as she gets out.*]

[JACK *gets in.*]

[DEL *comes in with plates and forks, which he puts on the table. He openly takes the pound note and puts it in his pocket.*]

JACK: Hey, it's cold. I want some more water. Is there any more water, Del?

DEL: Not boiling yet, but it's hot.

JACK: Let's have it then, quick.

[CHRISTIE *and* ALBERT *go.*]

DEL: Food's ready any minute, okay?

[DEL *goes.*]

JACK: It can't all happen at once. Apple trees take time.

[CHRISTIE *comes back with hot water.*]

CHRISTIE: Mind I don't burn you.

JACK: How hot is it then?

[CHRISTIE *pours water into the bath.*]

I saw a flight of geese this morning going south. you don't often.

CHRISTIE: It's my turn.

JACK: I haven't washed.

CHRISTIE: Wash then. Come on, I'll wash you.

>   [CHRISTIE *washes* JACK.]

>   [REG *stands up and moves about awkwardly.*]

>   [ALBERT *comes in with bread and more hot water.*]

SYL: I'll give Del a hand.

>   [SYL *goes out.*]

ALBERT: Settling down then?

REG: More or less, I think.

ALBERT: It takes getting used to.

REG: Oh, I'll be all right.

CHRISTIE: Come out now.

JACK: I want to wash my hair.

CHRISTIE: You can't wash your hair in that. There's no room.

JACK: I can lean over.

CHRISTIE: It takes too long. You'll make the water too dirty.

JACK: I'll go swimming tomorrow in the river and take some soap.

CHRISTIE: I'd like to go swimming.

ALBERT: Yes, I'd like to have a look at the river.

>   [CHRISTIE *undresses. She no longer has any bruises on her back.*]

>   [ALBERT *puts a towel round* JACK'S *shoulders as he gets out.* JACK *stays in the towel and doesn't get dressed.*]

>   [CHRISTIE *gets in the bath and* ALBERT *washes her.*]

>   [REG *stands by.*]

CHRISTIE: I saw the badgers tonight. Did you notice the sunset at all? Full moon makes me a bit wary. I'd have to let go of so many things to make room. But I suddenly ... I don't know what I did. I just stood there and the moon was up. I saw the first badger come out from behind the gorse. It wasn't dark yet in the west. I didn't fall short of anything. There were three badgers altogether.

>   [*Meanwhile* DEL *and* SYL *bring the food in.*]

>   [CHRISTIE *gets out of the bath.* JACK *tosses her a towel.*]

DEL: Is everyone ready to eat?

JACK: We'll start and they can come when they're ready.

ALBERT: Hurry up, Reg.

REG: Oh, go ahead. After you.

ALBERT: I'm meant to be last because of the mud.

REG: I'm in no hurry.

ALBERT: I am, I want my dinner. I'll go now then.

REG: I'm quite muddy too.

> [JACK *and* SYL *dish up the food.*]
>
> [DEL *sits at the table to eat.*]
>
> [CHRISTIE *comes to the table in the towel.*]
>
> [ALBERT *washes quickly.*]

ALBERT: The reason I'm late is the meeting went on so long. We've never had such a big turnout. things are moving, you know. It won't be the same place in six months. Is there a towel?

JACK: None left?

ALBERT: No towel?

> [JACK *gives him his.*]

Bloody wet.

> [JACK *looks round for something else to wrap himself in and puts on Reg's coat.*]
>
> [ALBERT *dresses quickly.*]

JACK: Hurry up, Reg, bath time.

REG: I'll just have my dinner since it's ready.

ALBERT: He doesn't fancy our dirty water.

SYL: We can't top it up any more, it'll overflow.

REG: I won't bother. I don't need a bath.

JACK: No bath, no dinner.

ALBERT: That looks good.

> [He helps himself to food.]

REG: Come on, Jack, pass a plate.

JACK: I said no bath, no dinner.

CHRISTIE: He thinks he's fat.

SYL: We won't look. We're too hungry.

JACK: If you don't want any dinner, don't have a bath.

> [REG *undresses slowly. He gets into the bath.*]

ALBERT: Warm enough still?

JACK: Here, I'll wash your back.

REG: Don't bother.

> [JACK *washes* REG's *back.*]

When I drove up in the rain looking for Christie I could hardly

124

see the road in front of me. What with crying and the windscreen wipers not working properly. So I could hardly say I knew that road.

[JACK *goes back to the table.*]

JACK: How hungry are you?

REG: Can I have it in the bath? It's nice and warm.

[DEL *takes a plate of food to* REG.]

[REG *eats.*]

That's good.

[*They go on with the meal. Some of them have already finished. They are increasingly happy so that gradually, each separately, they start to smile.*]

[REG *starts to smile too.*]

[He laughs.]

VINEGAR TOM

Vinegar Tom

Early in 1976 I met some of the Monstrous Regiment, who were thinking they would like to do a play about witches; so was I, though it's hard now to remember what ideas I was starting from. I think I had already read *Witches, Midwives and Nurses* by Barbara Ehrenreich and Deirdre English. Certainly it had a strong influence on the play I finally wrote.

Soon I met the whole company to talk about working with them. They gave me a list of books they had read and invited me to a rehearsal of *Scum*. I left the meeting exhilarated. My previous work had been completely solitary – I never discussed my ideas while I was writing or showed anyone anything earlier than a final polished draft. So this was a new way of working, which was one of its attractions. Also a touring company, with a wider audience; also a feminist company – I felt briefly shy and daunted, wondering if I would be acceptable, then happy and stimulated by the discovery of shared ideas and the enormous energy and feeling of possibilities in the still new company.

I was about to do a play for Joint Stock, who excited me for some of the same reasons, some different. There wasn't a lot of time, and the two plays, *Vinegar Tom* and *Light Shining in Buckinghamshire*, overlapped both in time and ideas. All I knew at this point about the Joint Stock project was that it was going to be about the English Revolution in the 1640s, what people had wanted from it, and particularly the millenial expectations of the Ranters. A lot of what I was learning about the period, religion, class, the position of women, was relevant to both plays.

I rapidly left aside the interesting theory that witchcraft had existed as a survival of suppressed pre-Christian religions and went instead for the theory that witchcraft existed in the minds of its persecutors, that 'witches' were a scapegoat in times of stress like Jews and blacks. I discovered for the first time the extent of Christian teaching against women and saw the connections between medieval attitudes to witches and continuing attitudes to women in general. The women accused of witchcraft were often those on the edges of society, old, poor, single, sexually unconventional; the old herbal medical tradition of the cunning woman was suppressed by the rising professionalism of the male doctor. I didn't base the play on any precise historical events, but set it rather loosely in the seventeenth century, partly because it was the time of the last major English witchhunts, and partly because the social upheavals, class changes, rising professionalism and great hardship among the poor were the context of the kind of witchhunt I wanted to write about; partly of course because it was the period I was already reading about for Joint Stock. One of the things that struck me reading the detailed accounts of witch trials in Essex (*Witchcraft in Tudor and Stuart England*, Macfarlane) was how petty and everyday the witches' offences were, and how different the atmosphere of actual English witchhunts seemed to be from my received idea, based on slight knowledge of the European witchhunts and films and fiction, of burnings, hysteria and sexual orgies. I wanted to write a play about witches with no witches in it; a play not about evil, hysteria and possession by the devil but about poverty, humiliation and prejudice, and how the women accused of witchcraft saw themselves.

I met Monstrous Regiment again, talked over the ideas I had so far, and found the same aspects of witchcraft appealed to them too. Then I went off and wrote a first draft of the play, very quickly, in about three days. I may have written one or two songs at this stage but not all of them. The company were happy to accept this first draft and leave rewriting till after my work with Joint Stock, which was lucky as in May I started the Joint Stock workshop. In the autumn I met Monstrous Regiment again. Helen Glavin had been working on the music for the songs during the summer. I worked on the text again, expanding it slightly. It was only at this stage that Josefina Cupido joined the company and I wrote in the character of Betty, who didn't exist before and who filled a need that had come up in discussion for a character under pressure to make a conventional marriage. It was a very enjoyable co-operation with the company. My habit of solitary working and shyness at showing what I wrote at an early stage had been wiped out by the even greater self-exposure in Joint Stock's method of work. And our shared view of what the play was about and our commitment to it made rewriting precise and easy. By the time *Traps* was done in January 1977 it seemed more than a year since I had written it. Though I still wanted to write alone sometimes, my attitude to myself, my work and others had been basically and permanently changed.

C.C. 1982

Characters

ALICE, a village girl, early 20s
SUSAN, her married friend, early 20s
JOAN, Alice's mother, a poor widow, 50
MARGERY, Joan's neighbour, a farmer's wife, 40
JACK, Margery's husband, a tenant farmer, 40
BETTY, the landowner's daughter, 16
ELLEN, a cunning woman, 35
GOODY, Packer's assistant, 45
PACKER, a witchfinder, 35
MAN, a gentleman, 30
DOCTOR, a professional, 50
BELLRINGER, a local, any age
KRAMER and SPRENGER — authors of the *Malleus Maleficarum, The Hammer of Witches*, a book highly thought of in the seventeenth century; they appear in top hat and tails as performers in a music hall.

The play takes place in and around a small village over a period of a few weeks in the seventeenth century. The songs take place in the present.

Vinegar Tom was written for Monstrous Regiment and was first presented at the Humberside Theatre, Hull, on 12 October 1976, then on tour and at the ICA and Half Moon theatres, London, with the following cast:

JOAN	Mary McCusker
SUSAN	Sue Todd
ALICE	Gillian Hanna
GOODY	Helen Glavin
BETTY	Josefina Cupido
MARGERY	Linda Broughton
ELLEN	Chris Bowler
JACK	Ian Blower
MAN	
DOCTOR	
BELLRINGER	Roger Allam
PACKER	
KRAMER and SPRENGER	Chris Bowler and Mary McCusker

Directed by Pam Brighton
Designed by Andrea Montag
Music by Helen Glavin

Production Note

The songs, which are contemporary, should if possible be sung by actors in modern dress. They are not part of the action and not sung by the characters in the scenes before them. In the original company all the actors could sing so it was no problem for some members of the company to be out of costume at any time to be in the band. Obviously this may not always be possible. But it is essential that the actors are not in character when they sing the songs.

The first verse of 'Nobody Sings' was left out in the original production because the song seemed too long. I've put it back because I like the song being about a first period as well as about getting old. It could be left out again in performance, or verse 3 or 4 could be dropped instead.

The pricking scene is one of humiliation rather than torture and Packer is an efficient professional, not a sadistic maniac.

Kramer and Sprenger should be played by women. Originally they were played by Chris Bowler and Mary McCusker who, as Ellen and Joan, had just been hanged, which seems to be an ideal doubling. They played them as Edwardian music hall gents in top hats and tails, and some of the opening rhymes and jokes are theirs. The rest of the scene is genuine Kramer and Sprenger, from their handbook on witches and women, *Malleus Maleficarum, The Hammer of Witches*.

SCENE ONE

Roadside.

MAN: Am I the devil?

ALICE: What, sweet?

MAN: I'm the devil. Man in black, they say, they always say, a man in black met me in the night, took me into the thicket and made me commit uncleanness unspeakable.

ALICE: I've seen men in black that's no devils unless clergy and gentlemen are devils.

MAN: Have I not got great burning eyes then?

ALICE: Bright enough eyes.

MAN: Is my body not rough and hairy?

ALICE: I don't like a man too smooth.

MAN: Am I not ice cold?

ALICE: In a ditch in November.

MAN: Didn't I lie on you so heavy I took your breath? Didn't the enormous size of me terrify you?

ALICE: It seemed a fair size like other men's.

MAN: Didn't it hurt you? Are you saying I didn't hurt you?

ALICE: You don't need be the devil, I been hurt by men. Let me go now, you're hurting my shoulder.

MAN: What it is, you didn't see my feet.

ALICE: You never took off your shoes. Take off your shoes if your feet's cloven.

MAN: If you come with me and give me body and soul, you'll never want in this world.

ALICE: Are you saying that as a man?

MAN: Am I saying it as the devil?

ALICE: If you're saying it as a man I'll go with you. There's no one round here knows me going to marry me. There's no way I'll get money. I've a child, mind, I'll not leave the child.

MAN: Has it a father?

ALICE: No, never had.

MAN: So you think that was no sin we did?

135

ALICE: If it was I don't care.

MAN: Don't say that.

ALICE: You'd say worse living here. Any time I'm happy someone says it's a sin.

MAN: There's some in London say there's no sin. Each man has his own religion nearly, or none at all, and there's women speak out too. They smoke and curse in the tavern and they say flesh is no sin for they are God themselves and can't sin. The men and women lie together and say that's bliss and that's heaven and that's no sin. I believe it for there's such changes.

ALICE: I'd like to go to London and hear them.

MAN: But then I believe with Calvin that few are saved and I am damned utterly. Then I think if I'm damned anyway I might as well sin to make it worthwhile. But I'm afraid to die. I'm afraid of the torture after. One of my family was burnt for a Catholic and they all changed to Protestant and one burnt for that too. I wish I was a Catholic and could confess my sins and burn them away in candles. I believe it all in turn and all at once.

ALICE: Would you take me to London? I've nothing to keep me here except my mother and I'd leave her.

MAN: You don't think I'm sent you by the devil? Sometimes I think the devil has me. And then I think there is no devil. And then I think the devil would make me think there was no devil.

ALICE: I'll never get away from here if you don't take me.

MAN: Will you do everything I say, like a witch with the devil her master?

ALICE: I'll do like a wife with a husband her master and that's enough for man or devil.

MAN: Will you kiss my arse like the devil makes his witches?

ALICE: I'll do what gives us pleasure. Was I good just now?

MAN: In Scotland I saw a witch burnt.

ALICE: Did you? A real witch? Was she a real one?

MAN: She was really burnt for one.

ALICE: Did the spirits fly out of her like black bats? Did the devil make the sky go dark? I've heard plenty tales of witches and I've heard some called witch, there's one in the next village some say and others say not, but she's nothing to see. Did she fly at night on a stick? Did you see her flying?

MAN: I saw her burnt.

ALICE: Tell then. What did she say?

MAN: She couldn't speak, I think. They'd been questioning her. There's wrenching the head with a cord. She came to the stake in a cart and men lifted her out, and the stake held her up when she was tied. She'd been in the boots you see that break the bones.

ALICE: And wood was put round? And a fire lit just like lighting a fire? Oh, I'd have shrieked, I cry the least thing.

MAN: She did shriek.

ALICE: I long to see that. But I might hide my face. Did you hide your face?

MAN: No, I saw it.

ALICE: Did you like seeing it then?

MAN: I may have done.

ALICE: Will you take me with you, to London, to Scotland? Nothing happens here.

MAN: Take you with me?

ALICE: Please, I'd be no trouble . . .

MAN: A whore? Take a whore with me?

ALICE: I'm not that.

MAN: What are you then? What name would you put to yourself? You're not a wife or a widow. You're not a virgin. Tell me a name for what you are.

ALICE: You're not going? Stay a bit.

MAN: I've stayed too long. I'm cold. The devil's cold. Back to my warm fire, eh?

ALICE: Stay with me!

MAN: Get away, will you.

ALICE: Please.

MAN: Get away.

[*He pushes her and she falls.*]

ALICE: Go to hell then, go to the devil, you devil.

MAN: Cursing is it? I can outcurse you.

ALICE: You foul devil, you fool, bastard, damn you, you devil!

MAN: Devil take you, whore, whore, damned strumpet, succubus, witch!

ALICE: But come back. I'll not curse you. Don't you curse. We were friends just now.

MAN: You should have behaved better.

ALICE: Will I see you again?

MAN: Unless I see you first.

ALICE: But will I see you? How can I find you?

MAN: You can call on me.

ALICE: How? Where? How shall I call on you?

MAN: You know how to curse. Just call on the devil.

ALICE: Don't tease me, you're not the devil, what's your name?

MAN: Lucifer, isn't it, and Beelzebub.

ALICE: No, what's your name?

MAN: Darling was my name, and sweeting, till you called me devil.

ALICE: I'll not call you devil, come back, what's your name?

MAN: You won't need to know it. You won't be seeing me.

SCENE TWO

Inside JACK *and* MARGERY's.

JACK: The river meadow is the one to get.

MARGERY: I thought the long field up the hill.

JACK: No, the river meadow for the cattle.

MARGERY: But Jack, for corn. Think of the long field full of wheat.

JACK: He's had a bad crop two years. That's why he can't pay the rent.

MARGERY: No, but he's got no cattle. We'd be all right.

JACK: If we took both fields.

MARGERY: Could we? Both?

JACK: The more we have the more we can afford.

MARGERY: And we'll pray God sends us sunshine.

JACK: Who's that down by the river?

MARGERY: That Alice, is it, wandering about?

JACK: I'm surprised Mother Noakes can pay her rent.

MARGERY: Just a cottage isn't much.

JACK: I've been wondering if we'll see them turned out.

MARGERY: I don't know why she's let stay. If we all lived like her it wouldn't be the fine estate it is. And Alice . . .

JACK: You can't blame Alice.

MARGERY: You can blame her. You can't be surprised. She's just what I'd expect of a girl brought up by Joan Noakes.

JACK: If we rent both fields, we'll have to hire a man to help with the harvest.

MARGERY: Hire a man?

JACK: That's not Alice.

MARGERY: It's not Miss Betty out by herself again?

JACK: I wouldn't be her father, not even to own the land.

MARGERY: That's a fine idea, hire a man.

JACK: She's coming here.

MARGERY: What we going to do?

JACK: Be respectful.

MARGERY: No, but shall we take her home? She's not meant to. She's still shut up in her room, everyone says.

JACK: I won't be sorry to see her.

MARGERY: I love to see her. She was always so soft on your lap, not like ours all hard edges. I could sit all afternoon just to smell her hair. But she's not a child, now, you can have run in and out and touch her. She's in trouble at home and we shouldn't help her do wrong.

JACK: We can't stop her, can we, if she walks in?

[*They wait and in a moment* BETTY *does come in.*]

MARGERY: Miss Betty, how nice.

BETTY: I came to see you milking the cows.

JACK: We finished milking, miss. The cows are in.

BETTY: Is it that late?

MARGERY: You want to get home before dark.

BETTY: No, I don't. I want to be out in the dark. It's not late, it's dark in the day time. I could stay out for hours if it was summer.

JACK: If you want to come and see the farm, Miss Betty, you should ask your father to bring you one morning when he's inspecting the estate.

BETTY: I'm not let go where I like.

JACK: I've business with your father.

139

MARGERY: We're going to take on the river meadow for the cattle.

JACK: And the long field up the hill.

BETTY: I used to play here all day. Nothing's different. Have you still got Betty's mug?

MARGERY: That's right, she had her special mug.

BETTY: I milked the red cow right into it one day. I got milk in my eye.

JACK: She died, that red cow. But we've four new cows you've not seen.

MARGERY: Died last week. There's two or three cows died in the neighbourhood.

BETTY: I wish she hadn't.

JACK: That don't matter, losing one, we're doing well enough.

MARGERY: And you're doing well, I hear, miss.

BETTY: What?

MARGERY: I hear you're leaving us for better things.

BETTY: No.

MARGERY: I was only saying yesterday, our little Miss Betty that was and now to be a lady with her own house and . . .

BETTY: They lock me up. I said I won't marry him so they lock me up. Don't you know that?

MARGERY: I had heard something.

BETTY: I get out the window.

MARGERY: Hadn't you better have him, Betty, and be happy? Everyone hopes so. Everyone loves a wedding.

BETTY: Margery, can I stay here tonight?

MARGERY: They'd worry for you.

BETTY: Can I? Please?

JACK: There's no bed fit for you, miss.

BETTY: On my way here I climbed a tree. I could see the whole estate. I could see the other side of the river. I wanted to jump off. And fly.

MARGERY: Shall Jack walk home with you, miss, now its getting dark?

SCENE THREE

Inside JOAN's.

JOAN: Alice?

ALICE: No need wake up, mum.

JOAN: You'll catch cold out all night in this weather.

ALICE: Don't wake up if it's only to moan at me.

JOAN: Who were you with?

ALICE: Did he wake up?

JOAN: No, not a sound.

ALICE: He's sleeping better. Not so much bad dreams.

JOAN: Come on, child, there's some broth left.

ALICE: I couldn't eat.

JOAN: You stay out half the night, you don't even enjoy it. You stay in with the boy. You sit by the fire with no one to talk to but old Vinegar Tomcat. I'll go out.

ALICE: You go out?

JOAN: Funny, isn't it? What would I do going out?

ALICE: I'll stay in if you like.

JOAN: Where would I go? Who wants an old woman?

ALICE: You want me to stay with you more?

JOAN: An old woman wandering about in the cold.

ALICE: Do you want some broth, mum?

JOAN: Who were you with this time? Anyone I know?

ALICE: Oh mum, I'm sick of myself.

JOAN: If we'd each got a man we'd be better off.

ALICE: You weren't better off, mum. You've told me often you're glad he's dead. Think how he used to beat you.

JOAN: We'd have more to eat, that's one thing.

Nobody Sings

I woke up in the morning,
Blood was on the sheet,
I looked at all the women
When I passed them in the street.
　　Nobody sings about it
　　But it happens all the time.

141

I met an old old woman
Who made my blood run cold.
You don't stop wanting sex, she said,
Just because you're old.
    Oh nobody sings about it,
    but it happens all the time.

I could be glad of the change of life,
But it makes me feel so strange.
If your life is being wanted
Do you want your life to change?
    Oh nobody sings about it,
    but it happens all the time.

Do you want your skin to wrinkle
And your cunt get sore and dry?
And they say it's just your hormones
If you cry and cry and cry.
    Oh nobody sings about it,
    but it happens all the time.

Nobody ever saw me,
She whispered in a rage.
They were blinded by my beauty, now
They're blinded by my age.
    Oh nobody sings about it,
    but it happens all the time.

SCENE FOUR

JACK *and* MARGERY's *barn.*
MARGERY *is churning.*
JACK: Hurry up with that butter, woman.
MARGERY: Butter won't come.
JACK: There's other work to do.
MARGERY: Butter won't come.

JACK: You don't churn. You sit gossiping.

MARGERY: Who would I talk to?

JACK: I heard your voice now.

MARGERY: Mother Noakes.

JACK: Always hanging about.

MARGERY: Her girl's no better.

JACK: Was her girl here? No.

MARGERY: I told her be on her way. Mother Noakes.

JACK: You tell her.

MARGERY: I told her.

JACK: Get on now with the butter and don't be always gossiping.

[JACK *goes.* MARGERY *churns and sings very quietly.*]

MARGERY: Come butter come, come butter come. Johnny's standing at the gate waiting for a butter cake. Come butter come, come butter come. Johnny's standing at the gate waiting for a butter cake. Come butter come, come butter come. Johnny's standing at the gate . . .

[*She stops as she realises* JOAN NOAKES *has come in and is standing behind her.*]

JOAN: Just passing by.

MARGERY: Again.

JOAN: I wonder could you lend me a little yeast? I've no yeast, see. I'm fresh out of yeast. I've no bread in the house and I thought, I thought . . . I'll do a little baking now and brew a little beer maybe . . . and I went to get some yeast and I've no yeast. Who'd have thought it? No yeast at all.

MARGERY: You'd be better without beer.

JOAN: I thought a little yeast as I was passing.

MARGERY: You get drunk. You should be ashamed.

JOAN: To bake a couple of little small loaves.

MARGERY: I've no yeast.

JOAN: A couple of little small loaves wouldn't take much yeast. A woman comfortable off with a fine man and a nice field and five cows and three pigs and plenty of apples that makes a good cider, bless you, Margery, many's the time . . . you'd not grudge a neighbour a little loaf? Many's the good times, eh, Margery? I've my own flour, you know, I'm not asking for flour.

MARGERY: I gave you yeast last week.

143

JOAN: A little small crumb of yeast and God will bless you for kindness to your poor old neighbour.

MARGERY: You're not so badly off, Joan Noakes. You're not on the parish.

JOAN: If I was I'd be fed. I should be on relief, then I'd not trouble you. There's some on relief, better off than me. I get nothing.

MARGERY: What money you get you drink.

JOAN: If you'd my troubles, Margery, you'd be glad of a drink, but as you haven't, thank God, and lend me a little yeast like a good woman.

MARGERY: I've no yeast.

JOAN: I know you, Margery.

MARGERY: What do you know?

JOAN: I know you've got yeast. My eyes are old, but I see through you. You're a cold woman and getting worse and you'll die without a friend in this parish when if you gave yeast to your good neighbours everyone would bless you . . .

MARGERY: I've no yeast.

JOAN: But you don't give and they say what a mean bitter woman and curse you.

MARGERY: There's nobody curses me. Now get out of my dairy. Dirty old woman you are, smelling of drink, come in here day after day begging, and stealing, too, I shouldn't wonder . . .

JOAN: You shouldn't say that.

MARGERY: . . . and your great ugly cat in here stealing the cream. Get out of my dairy.

JOAN: You'll be sorry you spoke to me like that. I've always been your friend, Margery, but now you'll find I'm not.

MARGERY: I've work to do. Now get out. I'm making my butter.

JOAN: Damn your butter to hell.

MARGERY: Will you get out?

JOAN: Devil take you and your man and your fields and your cows and your butter and your yeast and your beer and your bread and your cider and your cold face . . .

MARGERY: Will you go?

[JOAN goes. MARGERY churns.]

MARGERY: Come butter come, come butter come. Johnny's

standing at the gate waiting for a butter cake. Come butter . . .
It's not coming, this butter. I'm sick of it.

[JACK *comes.*]

JACK: What's all this? You're a lazy woman, you know that?
Times are bad enough. The little black calf don't look well.

MARGERY: Butter won't come. Mother Noakes said damn the
butter to hell.

JACK: Lazy slut, get on with it.

MARGERY: Come butter come. Come butter come. Come butter
come. Come butter come. Come butter come. Come butter . . .
Mother Noakes come begging and borrowing. She still got my
big bowl I give her some eggs in that time she was poorly. She
makes out I've treated her bad. I've been a good neighbour to
that woman years out of mind and no return. We'll get that
bowl back off her. Jack, do you hear me? Go over Mother
Noakes and get my bowl. And we'll heat a horseshoe red hot
and put it in the milk to make the butter come.

SCENE FIVE

Outside JOAN's.

SUSAN: Don't always talk of men.

ALICE: He knew what he was doing.

SUSAN: You'll know what he was doing in a few months.

ALICE: No, it never happens. The cunning woman put a charm
inside me.

SUSAN: Take more than a charm to do me good.

ALICE: Not again? Does he know?

SUSAN: He wants it. I know the night it was. He said, 'Let's hope
a fine child comes of it.'

ALICE: And what did you say?

SUSAN: Devil take it.

ALICE: What he say to that?

SUSAN: He don't like me swearing.

ALICE: But the baby's not a year.

SUSAN: Two weeks late, so.

145

ALICE: But the baby's not weaned.

SUSAN: The boy wasn't weaned when I fell for the baby.

ALICE: You could go see the cunning woman.

SUSAN: What for?

ALICE: She's a good midwife.

SUSAN: I don't want a midwife. I got my mother, anyway. I don't want to think about it. Nearly died last time. I was two days.

ALICE: Go and see the cunning woman. Just go see.

SUSAN: What for?

ALICE: She could say for certain.

SUSAN: I'm sure for certain.

ALICE: She could give you a charm.

SUSAN: They do say the pain is what's sent to a woman for her sins. I complained last time after churching, and he said I must think on Eve who brought the sin into the world that got me pregnant. I must think on how woman tempts man, and how she pays God with her pain having the baby. So if we try to get round the pain, we're going against God.

ALICE: I hate my body.

SUSAN: You mustn't say that. God sent his son . . .

ALICE: Blood every month, and no way out of that but to be sick and swell up, and no way out of that but pain. No way out of all that till we're old and that's worse. I can't bear to see my mother if she changes her clothes. If I was a man I'd go to London and Scotland and never come back and take a girl under a bush and on my way.

SUSAN: You could go to the cunning woman.

ALICE: What for?

SUSAN: Charm.

ALICE: What for?

SUSAN: Love charm bring him back.

ALICE: I don't want him back.

SUSAN: Did he look wonderful, more than anyone here, that he's got you so low?

ALICE: It was dark, I wouldn't know him again.

SUSAN: Not so much how he looked as how he felt?

ALICE: I could do with it now, I can tell you. I could do with walking across that field again and finding him there just the same. I want a man I can have when I want, not if I'm lucky to meet some villain one night.

SUSAN: You always say you don't want to be married.

ALICE: I don't want to be married. Look at you. Who'd want to be you?

SUSAN: He doesn't beat me.

ALICE: He doesn't beat you.

SUSAN: What's wrong with me? Better than you.

ALICE: Three babies and what, two, three times miscarried and wonderful he doesn't beat you.

SUSAN: No one's going to marry you because they know you here. That's why you say you don't want to be married – because no one's going to ask you round here, because they know you.

[*They move apart.* JACK *has been lingering in the background a while, and now comes up to* ALICE.]

JACK: It's not you I've come to see.

ALICE: Never thought it was.

JACK: You should have done then.

ALICE: Why?

JACK: You know why.

ALICE: You've come to see my mum, have you?

JACK: I've business with her, yes. That's why I came.

ALICE: She's somewhere around. I'll get her.

JACK: No hurry. Wait a bit. Never seem to talk.

ALICE: Nothing to talk about.

JACK: I'm forgetting. I brought something.

[*He gives her two apples.*]

ALICE: Thank you. What then?

JACK: Am I not handsome enough, is that it?

ALICE: I don't want trouble.

JACK: No one's to know.

ALICE: If I say you're not handsome enough, will you go away?

JACK: Alice, you must. I have dreams.

ALICE: You've a wife.

JACK: I'm no good to my wife. I can't do it. Not these three months. It's only when I dream of you or like now talking to you . . .

ALICE: Mum. There's someone to see you.

147

JACK: Alice, have some pity . . .

ALICE: Do you hear me? Mum? She'll be out to see you.

[*She moves away.* JOAN *comes.*]

JOAN: What's the matter?

JACK: I've come for the bowl.

JOAN: Bowl? Bowl?

JACK: Bowl my wife gave you some eggs in, you ungrateful old hag.

JOAN: You're asking for the bowl? You think I wouldn't give you back your bowl? You think I'm stealing your bowl? When have I ever kept anything? Have your bowl. I'll get your bowl and much good may it do you.

JACK: Then get it, damn you, and quick or you'll feel my hand.

[*She goes.*]

ALICE: Why treat her like that?

JACK: Don't speak to me. Let me get the bowl and go.

ALICE: And don't come back.

JACK: Alice, I'd be good to you. I'm not a poor man. I could give you things for your boy . . .

ALICE: Go away to hell.

[JOAN *comes back.*]

JOAN: Here's your bowl, Jack, and the devil go with it. Get away home and I hope you've more trouble there than I have here.

JACK: I'll break your neck if you speak to me.

JOAN: You lift your hand to me, may it drop off.

ALICE: Go home away to hell, man.

[JACK *goes.*]

JOAN: Away to hell with him. Never liked the man. Never liked the wife.

ALICE: Don't think on them, mum. They're not worth your time. Go in by the fire, go on, go in and be warm.

[JOAN *goes.* SUSAN *approaches.*]

Nobody likes my mother. That's what it is why nobody wants me.

SUSAN: I'm sorry for what I said, Alice.

ALICE: Going to see the cunning woman then?

SUSAN: Are you going for a love charm?

ALICE: It's something to do, isn't it? Better than waiting and waiting for something to happen. If I had a charm I could make him just appear in front of me now, I'd do anything. Will you come?

[ALICE *gives* SUSAN *an apple*.]

SUSAN: I'll keep you company then. Just tell her my trouble. There's no harm.

Oh Doctor

Oh, doctor, tell
me, make me well.
What's wrong with me
the way I am?
I know I'm sad.
I may be sick.
I may be bad.
Please cure me quick,
oh doctor.

SCENE SIX

The landowner's house.

BETTY *tied to a chair. The* DOCTOR *is about to bleed her arm.*

BETTY: Why am I tied? Tied to be bled. Why am I bled? Because I was screaming. Why was I screaming? Because I'm bad. Why was I bad? Because I was happy. Why was I happy? Because I ran out by myself and got away from them and – Why was I screaming? Because I'm bad. Why am I bad? Because I'm tied. Why am I tied? Because I was happy. Why was I happy? Because I was screaming.

DOCTOR: Hysteria is a woman's weakness. Hysteron, Greek, the womb. Excessive blood causes an imbalance in the humours. The noxious gases that form inwardly every month rise to the brain and cause behaviour quite contrary to the patient's real feelings. After bleeding you must be purged. Tonight you shall be blistered. You will soon be well enough to be married.

Oh Doctor

Where are you taking my skin?
Where are you putting my bones?
I shut my eyes and I opened wide,
But why is my heart on the other side?
Why are you putting my brain in my cunt?
You're putting me back all back to front.

Stop looking up me with your metal eye.
Stop cutting me apart before I die.
Stop, put me back.
Stop, put me back.
Put back my body.

Who are you giving my womb?
Who are you showing my breath?
Tell me what you whisper to nurse,
Whatever I've got, you're making it worse.
I'm wide awake, but I still can't shout.
Why can't I see what you're taking out?

Stop looking up me with your metal eye.
Stop cutting me apart before I die.
Stop, put me back.
Stop, put me back.
Put back my body.

Oh, doctor, tell
me, make me well.
What's wrong with me
the way I am?
I know I'm sad
I may be sick.
I may be bad.
Please cure me quick,
oh doctor,
What's wrong with me the way I am?
What's wrong with me?

150

I want to see myself.
I want to see inside myself.
Give me back my head.
I'll put my heart in straight.
Let me out of bed now.
I can't wait
To see myself.
Give me back my body.
I can see myself.
Give me back my body.
I can see myself.

SCENE SEVEN

JACK *and* MARGERY'*s barn.*

MARGERY: Jack, Jack, come quick – Jack.

JACK: What's the matter now?

MARGERY: The calves. Have you seen the calves?

JACK: What's the woman on about?

MARGERY: The calves are shaking and they've a terrible stench, so you can't go near them and their bellies are swollen up. [JACK *goes off.*] There's no good running. There's nothing you can do for them. They'll die like the red cow. You don't love me. Damn this stinking life to hell. Calves stinking and shaking there. No good you going to see, Jack. Better stand and curse. Everything dying on us. Aah. What's that? Who's there? Get out, you beast, get out. [*She throws her shoe.*] Jack, Jack.

JACK: Hold your noise.

MARGERY: That nasty old cat of Mother Noakes. I'll kill that cat if I get it, stinking up my clean dairy, stealing my cream. Where's it gone?

JACK: Let it go.

MARGERY: What you think of those calves then? Nothing to be done is there? What can we do? Nothing. Nothing to be done. Can't do nothing. Oh. Oh.

JACK: Now what is it?

MARGERY: Jack!

JACK: What is it? Don't frighten me, woman.

MARGERY: My head, oh, my stomach. Oh, Jack, I feel ill.

[*She sits on the ground.*]

JACK: Get up, woman. It's no time. There's things to do.

MARGERY: Nothing.

JACK: Lie there a bit then. You'll maybe feel better. I can hardly stir myself. What have I done to deserve it? Why me? Why my calves shaking? Why my wife falling down?

MARGERY: It's passing now.

JACK: Why me?

MARGERY: That was a terrible pain. I still feel it. I'm shaking, look.

JACK: Other people sin and aren't punished so much as we are.

MARGERY: We must pray to God.

JACK: We do pray to God, and he sends afflictions.

MARGERY: It must be we deserve it somehow, but I don't know how. I do my best. I do my best, Jack, God knows, don't I, Jack? God knows I do my best.

JACK: Don't other people sin? Is it just me?

MARGERY: You're not a bad man, Jack.

JACK: I must be the worst man.

MARGERY: No, dear.

JACK: Would God send all this to a good man? Would he? It's my sins those calves shaking and stinking and swelling up their bellies in there.

MARGERY: Don't talk so.

JACK: My sins stinking and swelling up.

MARGERY: Unless it's not God.

JACK: How can I bear it?

MARGERY: If it's not God.

JACK: What?

MARGERY: If it's not God sends the trouble.

JACK: The devil?

MARGERY: One of his servants. If we're bewitched, Jack, that explains all.

JACK: If we're bewitched . . .

MARGERY: Butter not coming. Calves swelling. Me struck in the head.

JACK: Then it's not my sins. Good folk get bewitched.

MARGERY: Good folk like us.

JACK: It can happen to anyone.

MARGERY: Rich folk can have spells against them.

JACK: It's good people the witches want to hurt.

MARGERY: The devil can't bear to see us so good.

JACK: You know who it is?

MARGERY: Who?

JACK: The witch. Who it is.

MARGERY: Who?

JACK: You know who.

MARGERY: She cursed the butter to hell.

JACK: She cursed me when I got the bowl.

MARGERY: She said I'd be sorry I'd spoken to her.

JACK: She wished me trouble at home.

MARGERY: Devil take your man and your cows, she said that, and your butter. She cursed the calves see and she's made them shake. She struck me on the head and in the stomach.

JACK: I'll break her neck.

MARGERY: Be careful now, what she might do.

JACK: I'm not afraid of an old witch.

MARGERY: You should be. She could kill you.

JACK: I'll kill her first.

MARGERY: Wait, Jack. Let's meet cunning with cunning. What we must do is get the spell off.

JACK: She's not going to take it off for asking. She might for a few hard knocks.

MARGERY: No, wait, Jack. We can take the spell off and never go near her. Serve her right.

JACK: What we do then? Burn something?

MARGERY: Burn an animal alive, don't we? Or bury it alive. That takes witchcraft off the rest.

JACK: Burn the black calf then shall we? We'll get some straw and wood and put it in the yard and the calf on top and set it on fire.

MARGERY: Will it walk?

JACK: Or I'll carry it.

153

MARGERY: It stinks terrible.

JACK: Stink of witchcraft it is. Burn it up.

MARGERY: We must pray to God to keep us safe from the devil. Praying's strong against witches.

JACK: We'll pray God help us and help ourselves too.

MARGERY: She'll see the fire and smell it and she'll know we're fighting her back, stinking old witch, can't hurt us.

Something to Burn

What can we do, there's nothing to do,
about sickness and hunger and dying.
What can we do, there's nothing to do,
nothing but cursing and crying.
    Find something to burn.
    Let it go up in smoke.
    Burn your troubles away.

Sometimes it's witches, or what will you choose?
Sometimes it's lunatics, shut them away.
It's blacks and it's women and often it's Jews.
We'd all be quite happy if they'd go away.
    Find something to burn.
    Let it go up in smoke.
    Burn your troubles away.

SCENE EIGHT

ELLEN's *cottage*.

ELLEN: Take it or leave it, my dear, it's one to me. If you want to be rid of your trouble, you'll take it. But only you know what you want.

SUSAN: It's not what I came for.

ALICE: Of course it is.

SUSAN: I wanted to know for certain.

ALICE: You know for certain.

SUSAN: I want a charm against pain.

ELLEN: I'll come as your midwife if you send for me near the time and do what I can, if that's all you want.

ALICE: She wants to be rid of it. Well, do you want it?

SUSAN: I don't want it but I don't want to be rid of it. I want to be rid of it, but not do anything to be rid of it.

ELLEN: If you won't do anything to help yourself you must stay as you are.

SUSAN: I shall pray to God.

ALICE: It's no sin. You just give yourself the drink.

SUSAN: Oh, I don't know.

ELLEN: Let her go home. She can come back. You have your charm safe, Alice? I could do more if you could come at the young man and give him a potion I'd let you have.

ALICE: If I could come at him he wouldn't need potion.

ELLEN: And you're sure you've nothing of his?

ALICE: He gave me nothing.

ELLEN: A few hairs or a drop of blood makes all the difference. It's part of him and the powers can work on it to call him.

ALICE: I'll pull a few hairs out next time I've a lover. Come on, Susan.

ELLEN: For your heartache I'll give you these herbs to boil up in water and drink at night. Give you a sound sleep and think less of him.

ALICE: Don't want to think less of him.

ELLEN: You have your sleep. There'll be other men along if not that one. Clever girl like you could think of other things.

ALICE: Like what?

ELLEN: Learn a trade.

ALICE: Nothing dangerous.

ELLEN: Where's the danger in herbs?

ALICE: Not just herbs.

ELLEN: Where's the danger in healing?

ALICE: Not just healing, is it?

ELLEN: There's powers, and you use them for healing or hurt. You use them how you like. There's no hurt if you're healing so where's the danger? You could use them. Not everyone can.

ALICE: Learn the herbs?

ELLEN: There's all kinds of wisdom. Bit by bit I'd teach you.

155

ALICE: I'd never thought.

ELLEN: There's no hurry. I don't want you unless it's what you want. You'll be coming by to leave a little something for me in a few days, since I have to live and wouldn't charge you. You can tell me how you've got on with your young man and what you're thinking.

ALICE: Yes, I'll be coming by. Goodnight then. What are you standing there for, Susan?

SUSAN: Maybe I'll take some potion with me. And see when I get home whether I take it.

ELLEN: Don't be afraid if it makes you sick. It's to do you good.

SCENE NINE

ELLEN's *cottage*.

BETTY: I don't know what I'm here for. I've had so much treatment already. The doctor comes every day.

ELLEN: You know what you're here for.

BETTY: The doctor says people like you don't know anything. He thinks he's cured me because I said I would get married to stop them locking me up. But I'll never do it.

ELLEN: Do you want a potion to make you love the man?

BETTY: I'd rather have one to make him hate me so he'd leave me alone. Or make him die.

ELLEN: The best I can do for you is help you sleep. I won't harm him for you, so don't ask. Get some sleep and think out what you want.

BETTY: Can I come again sometimes just to be here? I like it here.

ELLEN: Come when you like. I don't charge but you'll bring a little present.

BETTY: I'll give you anything if you can help me.

ELLEN: Come when you like.

156

ELLEN's *cottage.*

ELLEN: I'm not saying I can't do anything. But if I can't, it's because you've left it too late.

JACK: Lift your hand to me, she said, may it drop off. Then next day it went stiff.

MARGERY: We want to be certain. I've talked to others and they've things against her too. She's cursed and scolded two or three, and one's lame and the other lost her hen. And while we were talking we thought of her great cat that's always in my dairy, stinking it up and stealing the cream. Ah what's that, I said crying out, didn't I, and that was the cat, and I was struck down with a blow inside my head. That's her familiar sent her by Satan.

JACK: I've seen a rat run out of her yard into ours and I went for it with a pitchfork and the spikes were turned aside and nearly went in my own foot by her foul magic. And that rat's another of her imps.

MARGERY: But you don't like to think it of your neighbour. Time was she was neighbourly enough. If you could tell us it was true, we could act against her more certain in our minds.

JACK: I shouted at her over the fence, I said I'll have you hanged you old strumpet, burnt and hanged, and she cursed me again.

MARGERY: We burnt a calf alive to save our calves but it was too late. If I knew for certain it was her I'd be easier.

ELLEN: I've a glass here, a cloudy glass. Look in the glass, so, and see if any face comes into it.

 [*She gives them a mirror.*]

MARGERY: Come on, Jack, don't be afraid.

JACK: I don't like it.

MARGERY: Come on, it's good magic to find a witch.

ELLEN: Look in the glass and think on all the misfortunes you've had and see what comes.

MARGERY: Nothing yet. Do you see anything?

JACK: No.

MARGERY: Nothing still.

JACK: Don't keep talking.

MARGERY: Look.

JACK: What?

MARGERY: Did something move in the glass? My heart's beating so.

JACK: It's too dark.

MARGERY: No. Look.

JACK: I did see something.

MARGERY: It's the witch.

JACK: It's her sure enough.

MARGERY: It is, isn't it, Jack? Mother Noakes, isn't it?

JACK: It was Mother Noakes in that glass.

ELLEN: There then. You have what you came for.

MARGERY: Proves she's a witch then?

ELLEN: Not for me to say one's a witch or not a witch. I give you the glass and you see in it what you see in it.

JACK: Saw Mother Noakes.

MARGERY: Proves she's a witch.

ELLEN: Saw what you come to see. Is your mind easy?

SCENE ELEVEN

ELLEN's *cottage.*

JACK: Want to ask you something private. It's about my ... [*He gestures, embarrassed.*] It's gone. I can't do anything with it, haven't for some time. I accepted that. But now it's not even there, it's completely gone. There's a girl bewitched me. She's daughter of that witch. And I've heard how witches sometimes get a whole boxful and they move and stir by themselves like living creatures and the witch feeds them oats and hay. There was one witch told a man in my condition to climb a tree and he'd find a nest with several in it and take which he liked, and when he took the big one she said no, not that one, because that one belongs to the parish priest. I don't want a big one, I want my own back, and this witch has it.

ELLEN: You'd better go and ask her nicely for it.

JACK: Is that all you can say? Can't you force her to give it me?
ELLEN: It's sure to come back. You ask the girl nicely, she'll give it you back. I'll give you a little potion to take.
JACK: Kill her else.

SCENE TWELVE

Outside JACK *and* MARGERY'*s.*

JOAN: That's a foul stink. I don't know how you can stay there. Whatever is it?
MARGERY: Do you know why you've come?
JOAN: I was passing.
MARGERY: Why were you passing?
JOAN: Can't I pass by your door now? Time was it was always open for me.
MARGERY: And what's that?
JOAN: A foul stink. Whatever are you making? I thought I'd come and see you as I was passing. I don't want any trouble between us. I thought, come and see her, make it all right.
MARGERY: You come to see me because of that. That's my piss boiling. And two feathers of your chicken burning. It's a foul stink brings a witch. If you come when I do that, proves you've a spell on me. And now I'll get it off. You know how?
JOAN: Come and see you. Make it all right.
MARGERY: Blood you, that's how.

    [MARGERY *scratches* JOAN'*s head.*]

JOAN: Damn you, get away.
MARGERY: Can't hurt me now. And if that doesn't bring the spell off I'll burn your thatch.

If Everybody Worked as Hard as Me
    If everybody worked as hard as me,
    if our children's shirts are white,
    if their language is polite,
    if nobody stays out late at night,
    Oh, happy family.

Oh, the country's what it is because
the family's what it is because
the wife is what she is
to her man.
Oh I do all I can.
Yes, I do all I can.
I try to do what's right,
so I'll never be alone and afraid in the night.
And nobody comes knocking at my door in the night.
The horrors that are done will not be done to me.

Nobody loves a scold,
nobody loves a slut,
nobody loves you when you're old,
unless you're someone's gran.
Nobody loves you
unless you keep your mouth shut.
Nobody loves you
if you don't support your man.
Oh you can,
oh you can
have a happy family.

If everybody worked as hard as me,
sometimes you'll be bored,
you'll often be ignored,
but in your heart you'll know you are adored.
Oh, happy family.
Your dreams will all come true.
You'll make your country strong.
Oh the country's what it is because
the family's what it is because
the wife is what she is
to her man.
Oh please do all you can.
Yes, please do all you can
Oh, please don't do what's wrong,
so you'll never be alone and afraid in the night.

So nobody comes knocking at your door in the night.
So the horrors that are done will not be done to you.

Yes you can.
Yes you can.
Oh the country's what it is because
the family's what it is because
the wife is what she is
to her man.

SCENE THIRTEEN

Outside JACK *and* MARGERY's.

SUSAN: You're sure it was him? You said you wouldn't know him.

ALICE: I did when I saw him.

SUSAN: Riding? Couldn't see him close.

ALICE: Close enough to be spattered with his mud. He saw me.

SUSAN: But he didn't show he knew you.

ALICE: Pretended not to.

SUSAN: It wasn't him.

ALICE: It was him.

SUSAN: And you don't know the beautiful lady?

ALICE: I'll know her again. Scratch her eyes if I come at her.

SUSAN: What was she wearing?

ALICE: What was she wearing? How should I know? A fine rich dress made her beautiful, I suppose. Are you trying to plague me?

SUSAN: Was he in black still?

ALICE: Blue velvet jacket.

SUSAN: Blue velvet.

ALICE: Yes, damn you, I said that before. Are you stupid? [*Silence.*] For God's sake, now what is it? Are you crying? Shouldn't I be crying?

SUSAN: It's not your fault, Ally. I cry all the time.

ALICE: You're still weak, that's what it is. It's the blood you lost. You should rest more.

SUSAN: I don't want him to know.

ALICE: Doesn't he know?

SUSAN: He may guess but I don't dare ask. He was out all day that day and I said I'd been ill, but not why.

ALICE: It's done anyway.

SUSAN: Can't be undone.

ALICE: You're not sorry now?

SUSAN: I don't know.

ALICE: You'd be a fool to be sorry.

SUSAN: I am sorry. I'm wicked. You're wicked.
    [*She cries.*]

ALICE: Oh, Susan, you're tired out, that's all. You're not wicked. You'd have cried more to have it. All the extra work, another baby.

SUSAN: I like babies.

ALICE: You'll have plenty more, God, you'll have plenty. What's the use of crying?

SUSAN: You were crying for that lover.

ALICE: I'm not now. I'd sooner kill him. If I could get at him. If thoughts could get at him he'd feel it.

SUSAN: I'm so tired, Ally.

ALICE: Do you think it's true thoughts can reach someone?

SUSAN: What are you thinking of?

ALICE: Like if I had something of his, I could bring him. Or harm him.

SUSAN: Don't try that.

ALICE: But I've nothing of his. I'd have to make a puppet.

SUSAN: Don't talk so. Oh, don't, Alice, when I'm so tired.

ALICE: Does it have to be like? Is it like just if you say it's like?

SUSAN: Alice!

ALICE: If I get this wet mud, it's like clay. There should be at least a spider or some ashes of bones, but mud will do. Here's a man's shape, see, that's his head and that's arms and legs.

SUSAN: I'm going home. I'm too tired to move.

ALICE: You stay here and watch. This is the man. We know who though we don't know his name. Now here's a pin, let's prick him. Where shall I prick him? Between the legs first so he can't get on with his lady.

SUSAN: Alice, stop.

ALICE: Once in the head to drive him mad. Shall I give him one in the heart? Do I want him to die yet? Or just waste till I please.

SUSAN: Alice . . .

[SUSAN *tries to get the mud man, it falls on the ground and breaks.*]

ALICE: Now look. You've broken him up. You've killed him.

SUSAN: I haven't.

ALICE: All in pieces. Think of the poor man. Come apart.

SUSAN: I didn't. Alice, I didn't. It was you.

ALICE: If it was me, I don't care.

SUSAN: Alice, what have you done? Oh Alice, Alice.

ALICE: It's not true, stupid. It's not him.

SUSAN: How do you know?

ALICE: It's a bit of mud.

SUSAN: But you said.

ALICE: That's just words.

SUSAN: But . . .

ALICE: No. I did nothing. I never do anything. Might be better if I did. [*They sit in silence.*] You're crying again. Here, don't cry.

[ALICE *holds* SUSAN *while she cries.*]

SUSAN: Little clay puppet like a tiny baby not big enough to live and we crumble it away.

[JACK *comes.*]

JACK: Witch.

ALICE: Are you drunk?

JACK: Give it back.

ALICE: What?

JACK: Give it back.

ALICE: What now, Jack?

JACK: Give it me back. You know. You took it from me these three months. I've not been a man since. You bewitched me. You took it off me.

ALICE: Is he mad?

SUSAN: What is it?

ALICE: Susan's ill, will you leave us alone?

JACK: Everyone comes near you is ill. Give it back, come on, give it back.

163

ALICE: How can I?

JACK: She said speak nicely to you. I would, Alice, if you were good to me. I never wanted this. Please, sweet good Alice, give it back.

ALICE: What? How can I?

JACK: Give it me.

[*He grabs her round the neck.* SUSAN *screams.*]

ALICE: Damn you!

SUSAN: You'll kill her.

JACK: Give it me.

SUSAN: Let her go, she'll give it you whatever it is, you'll kill her Jack.

[JACK *lets go.*]

JACK: Give it me then. Come on.

SUSAN: Wait, she can't move, leave her alone.

JACK: Give it me.

[ALICE *puts her hand between his thighs.*]

ALICE: There. It's back.

JACK: It is. It is back. Thank you, Alice. I wasn't sure you were a witch till then.

[JACK *goes.*]

SUSAN: What you doing Alice? Alice? Alice?

[ALICE *turns to her.*]

ALICE: It's nothing. He's mad. Oh my neck, Susan. Oh, I'd laugh if it didn't hurt.

SUSAN: Don't touch me. I'll not be touched by a witch.

SCENE FOURTEEN

Public square.

BELLRINGER: Whereas if anyone has any complaint against any woman for a witch, let them go to the townhall and lay their complaint. For a man is in town that is a famous finder of witches and has had above thirty hanged in the country round and he will discover if they are or no. Whereas if anyone has any complaint against any woman for a witch, let them go . . .

164

MARGERY: Stopped the butter.

JACK: Killed the calves.

MARGERY: Struck me in the head.

JACK: Lamed my hand.

MARGERY: Struck me in the stomach.

JACK: Bewitched my organ.

MARGERY: When I boiled my urine she came.

JACK: Blooded her and made my hand well.

MARGERY: Burnt her thatch.

JACK: And Susan, her friend, is like possessed screaming and crying and lay two days without speaking.

MARGERY: Susan's baby turned blue and its limbs twisted and it died.

JACK: Boy threw stones and called them witch, and after he vomited pins and straw.

MARGERY: Big nasty cat she has in her bed and sends it to people's dairies.

JACK: A rat's her imp.

MARGERY: And the great storm last night brought a tree down in the lane, who made that out of a clear sky?

PACKER: I thank God that he has brought me again where I am needed. Don't be afraid any more. You have been in great danger but the devil can never overcome the faithful. For God in his mercy has called me and shown me a wonderful way of finding out witches, which is finding the place on the body of the witch made insensitive to pain by the devil. So that if you prick that place with a pin no blood comes out and the witch feels nothing at all.

[PACKER *and* GOODY *take* JOAN, *and* GOODY *holds her, while* PACKER *pulls up her skirts and pricks her legs.* JOAN *curses and screams throughout.* PACKER *and* GOODY *abuse her: a short sharp moment of great noise and confusion.*]

GOODY: Hold still you old witch. Devil not help you now, no good calling him. Strong for your age, that's the devil's strength in her, see. Hold still, you stinking old strumpet.

PACKER: Hold your noise, witch, how can we tell what we're doing? Ah, ah, there's for you devil, there's blood, and there's blood, where's your spot, we'll find you out Satan.

JOAN: Damn you to hell, oh Christ help me! Ah, ah, you're hurting, let go, damn you, oh sweet God, oh you devils, oh devil take you.

PACKER: There, there, no blood here, Goody Haskins. Here's her spot. Hardly a speck here.

GOODY: How she cries the old liar, pretending it hurts her.

PACKER: There's one for hanging, stand aside there. We've others to attend to. Next please, Goody.

[GOODY *takes* ALICE. PACKER *helps, and her skirts are thrown over her head while he pricks her. She tries not to cry out.*]

GOODY: Why so much blood?

PACKER: The devil's cunning here.

GOODY: She's not crying much, she can't feel it.

PACKER: Have I the spot though? Which is the spot? There. There. There. No, I haven't the spot. Oh, it's tiring work. Set this one aside. Maybe there's others will speak against her and let us know more clearly what she is.

[ALICE *is stood aside.*]

PACKER: If anyone here knows anything more of this woman why she might be a witch, I charge them in God's name to speak out, or the guilt of filthy witchcraft will be on you for concealing it.

SUSAN: I know something of her.

PACKER: Don't be shy then girl, speak out.

ALICE: Susan, what you doing? Don't speak against me.

SUSAN: Don't let her at me.

ALICE: You'll have me hanged.

[SUSAN *starts to shriek hysterically.*]

GOODY: Look, she's bewitched.

MARGERY: It's Alice did it to her.

ALICE: Susan, stop.

SUSAN: Alice. Alice. Alice.

PACKER: Take the witch out and the girl may be quiet.

[GOODY *takes* ALICE *off.* SUSAN *stops.*]

MARGERY: See that.

JACK: Praise God I escaped such danger.

SUSAN: She met with the devil, she told me, like a man in black she met him in the night and did uncleanness with him, and ever after she was not herself but wanted to be with the devil again. She took me to a cunning woman and they made me take a foul potion to destroy the baby in my womb and it was destroyed. And the cunning woman said she would teach Alice her wicked magic, and she'd have powers and not everyone could learn that, but Alice could because she's a witch, and the cunning woman gave her something to call the devil, and she tried to call him, and she made a puppet, and stuck pins in, and tried to make me believe that was the devil, but that was my baby girl, and next day she was sick and her face blue and limbs all twisted up and she died. And I don't want to see her.

PACKER: These cunning women are worst of all. Everyone hates witches who do harm but good witches they go to for help and come into the devil's power without knowing it. The infection will spread through the whole country if we don't stop it. Yes, all witches deserve death, and the good witch even more than the bad one. Oh God, do not let your kingdom be overrun by the devil. And you, girl, you went to this good witch, and you destroyed the child in your womb by witchcraft, which is a grievous offence. And you were there when this puppet was stuck with pins, and consented to the death of your own baby daughter?

SUSAN: No, I didn't. I didn't consent. I never wished her harm. Oh if I was angry sometimes or cursed her for crying, I never meant it. I'd take it back if I could have her back. I never meant to harm her.

PACKER: You can't take your curses back, you cursed her to death. That's two of your children you killed. And what other harm have you done? Don't look amazed, you'll speak soon enough. We'll prick you as you pricked your babies.

Public square.
GOODY *takes* SUSAN *and* PACKER *pulls up her skirt.*
GOODY: There's no man finds more witches than Henry Packer.

He can tell by their look, he says, but of course he has more ways than that. He's read all the books and he's travelled. He says the reason there's so much witchcraft in England is England is too soft with its witches, for in Europe and Scotland they are hanged and burned and if they are not penitent they are burnt alive, but in England they are only hanged. And the ways of discovering witches are not so good here, for in other countries they have thumbscrews and racks and the bootikens which is said to be the worst pain in the world, for it fits tight over the legs from ankle to knee and is driven tighter and tighter till the legs are crushed as small as might be and the blood and marrow spout out and the bones crushed and the legs made unserviceable forever. And very few continue their lies and denials then. In England we haven't got such thorough ways, our ways are slower but they get the truth in the end when a fine skilful man like Henry Packer is onto them. He's well worth the twenty shillings a time, and I get the same, which is very good of him to insist on and well worth it though some folk complain and say, 'what, the price of a cow, just to have a witch hanged?' But I say to them think of the expense a witch is to you in the damage she does to property, such as a cow killed one or two pounds, a horse maybe four pounds, besides all the pigs and sheep at a few shillings a time, and chickens at sixpence all adds up. For two pounds and our expenses at the inn, you have all that saving, besides knowing you're free of the threat of sudden illness and death. Yes, it's interesting work being a searcher and nice to do good at the same time as earning a living. Better than staying home a widow. I'd end up like the old women you see, soft in the head and full of spite with their muttering and spells. I keep healthy keeping the country healthy. It's an honour to work with a great professional.

SCENE SIXTEEN

ELLEN's *cottage.*

BETTY: I'm frightened to come any more. They'll say I'm a witch.

ELLEN: Are they saying I'm a witch?

BETTY: They say because I screamed that was the devil in me. And when I ran out of the house they say where was I going if not to meet other witches. And some know I come to see you.

ELLEN: Nobody's said it yet to my face.

BETTY: But the doctor says he'll save me. He says I'm not a witch, he says I'm ill. He says I'm his patient so I can't be a witch. He says he's making me better. I hope I can be better.

ELLEN: You get married, Betty, that's safest.

BETTY: But I want to be left alone. You know I do.

ELLEN: Left alone for what? To be like me? There's no doctor going to save me from being called a witch. Your best chance of being left alone is marry a rich man, because it's part of his honour to have a wife who does nothing. He has his big house and rose garden and trout stream, he just needs a fine lady to make it complete and you can be that. You can sing and sit on the lawn and change your dresses and order the dinner. That's the best you can do. What would you rather? Marry a poor man and work all day? Or go on as you're going, go on strange? That's not safe. Plenty of girls feel like you've been feeling, just for a bit. But you're not one to go on with it.

BETTY: If it's true there's witches, maybe I've been bewitched. If the witches are stopped, maybe I'll get well.

ELLEN: You'll get well, my dear, and you'll get married, and you'll tell your children about the witches.

BETTY: What's going to happen? Will you be all right?

ELLEN: You go home now. You don't want them finding you here.

[BETTY *goes.*]

I could ask to be swum. They think the water won't keep a witch in, for Christ's baptism sake, so if a woman floats she's a witch. And if she sinks they have to let her go. I could sink. Any fool can sink. It's how to sink without drowning. It's whether they get you out. No, why should I ask to be half drowned? I've

169

done nothing. I'll explain to them what I do. It's healing, not harm. There's no devil in it. If I keep calm and explain it, they can't hurt me.

If You Float

If you float you're a witch.
If you scream you're a witch
If you sink, then you're dead anyway.
If you cure you're a witch
Or impure you're a witch
Whatever you do, you must pay.
Fingers are pointed, a knock at the door,
You may be a mother, a child or a whore.
If you complain you're a witch
Or you're lame you're a witch
Any marks or deviations count for more.
Got big tits you're a witch
Fall to bits you're a witch
He likes them young, concupiscent and poor.
Fingers are pointed, a knock at the door,
They're coming to get you, do you know what for?
So don't drop a stitch
My poor little bitch
If you're making a spell
Do it well
Deny it you're bad
Admit it you're mad
Say nothing at all
They'll damn you to hell.

SCENE SEVENTEEN

A prison.

ALICE *is tied up, sitting on the floor,* GOODY *is eating and yawning.*

GOODY: You'd better confess, my dear, for he'll have you watched night and day and there's nothing makes a body so wretched as not sleeping. I'm tired myself. It's for your own good, you know, to save you from the devil. If we let you stay as you are, you'd be damned eternally and better a little pain now than eternal ... [*She realises* ALICE *is nodding to sleep and picks up a drum and bangs it loudly. She gives it several bangs to keep* ALICE *awake.* PACKER *comes in.*] She's an obstinate young witch, this one, on her second night. She tires a body out.

PACKER: Go and sleep, Goody, I'll watch her a while.

GOODY: You're a considerate man, Mr Packer. We earn our money.

[GOODY *goes.*]

PACKER: I'm not a hard man. I like to have my confession so I'm easy in my mind I've done right.

ALICE: Where's my boy?

PACKER: Safe with good people.

ALICE: He wants me.

PACKER: He's safe from the devil, where you'll never come.

ALICE: I want him.

PACKER: Why won't you confess and make this shorter?

ALICE: It isn't true.

PACKER: Tell me your familiars. Tell me your imps' names. I won't let them plague you for telling. God will protect you if you repent.

ALICE: I haven't any. [PACKER *drums.*] I want my boy.

PACKER: Then you should have stayed home at night with him and not gone out after the devil.

ALICE: I want him.

PACKER: How could a mother be a filthy witch and put her child in danger?

ALICE: I didn't.

PACKER: Night after night, it's well known.

ALICE: But what's going to happen to him? He's only got me.

PACKER: He should have a father. Who's his father? Speak up, who's his father?

ALICE: I don't know.

PACKER: You must speak.

ALICE: I don't know.

PACKER: You must confess.

[PACKER *drums*.]

ALICE: Oh my head. Please don't. Everything's drumming.

PACKER: I'll watch. Your imps will come to see you.

ALICE: Drumming.

[PACKER *suddenly stops*.]

PACKER: Ah. Ah. What's this? A spider. A huge black one. And it ran off when it saw a godly man. Deny if you can that spider's one of your imps.

ALICE: No.

PACKER: Then why should it come? Tell me that.

ALICE: I want my boy.

PACKER: Why? Why do you keep on about the boy? Who's his father? Is the devil his father?

ALICE: No, no, no.

PACKER: I'll have the boy to see me in the morning. If he's not the devil's child he'll speak against you. [ALICE *cries*.] I'll watch you. I've watched plenty of witches and hanged them all. I'll get that spider too if it comes back.

SCENE EIGHTEEN

A prison.

GOODY *is shaving* SUSAN *under the arm.*

GOODY: There, that's the second arm done, and no mark yet. Devil hides his marks all kinds of places. The more secret the better he likes it. Though I knew one witch had a great pink mark on her shoulder and neck so everyone could see. And a woman last week with a big lump in her breast like another whole teat where she sucked her imps, a little black one she had and a little white one and kept them in wool in a bottle. And when I squeezed it first white stuff came out like milk and then blood, for she fed those horrid creatures on milk and blood and they sucked her secret parts in the night too. Now let's see your secret parts and see what the devil does there.

[*She makes* SUSAN *lie down, and pulls up her skirt to shave her.* PACKER *comes in.*]

PACKER: What devil's marks?

GOODY: No need to shave the other for she has three bigs in her privates almost an inch long like great teats where the devil sucks her and a bloody place on her side where she can't deny she cut a lump off herself so I wouldn't find it.

PACKER: Such a stinking old witch I won't look myself. Is there nothing here?

GOODY: She's clean yet but we'll shave her and see what shameful thing's hidden.

PACKER: Though a mark is a sure sign of a witch's guilt having no mark is no sign of innoccence for the devil can take marks off.

JOAN: And the devil take you.

PACKER: You'll be with the devil soon enough.

JOAN: And I'll be glad to see him. I been a witch these ten years. Boys was always calling after me and one day I said to a boy, 'Boy boy you call me witch but when did I make your arse to itch.' And he ran off and I met a little grey kitling and the kitling said, 'you must go with me' and I said, 'Avoid, Satan.' And he said, 'You must give me your body and soul and you'll have all happiness.' And I did. And I gave him my blood every day, and that's my old cat Vinegar Tom. And he lamed John Peter's son that's a cripple this day, that was ten years ago. And I had two more imps sent me, crept in my bed in the night, sucked my privy parts so sore they hurt me and wouldn't leave me. And I asked them to kill Mary Johnson who crossed me and she wasted after. And everyone knows Anne that had fits and would gnash her teeth and took six strong men to hold her. That was me sent those fits to her. My little imps are like moles with four feet but no tails and a black colour. And I'd send them off and they'd come back in the night and say they did what I said. Jack is lucky I didn't bewitch him to death and Margery, but she was kind to me long ago. But I killed their cows like I killed ten cows last year. And the great storm and tempest comes when I call it and strikes down trees. But now I'm in prison my power's all gone or I'd call down thunder and twist your guts.

PACKER: Is there any reason you shouldn't be hanged?

JOAN: I'm with child.

GOODY: Who'd believe that?

SCENE NINETEEN

Public square.

JOAN *and* ELLEN *are hanged while* MARGERY *prays.*

MARGERY: Dear God, thank you for saving us. Let us live safe now. I have scrubbed the dairy out. You have shown your power in destroying the wicked, and you show it in blessing the good. You have helped me in my struggle against the witches, help me in my daily struggle. Help me work harder and our good harvests will be to your glory. Bless Miss Betty's marriage and let her live happy. Bless Jack and keep him safe from evil and let him love me and give us the land, amen.

SCENE TWENTY

Public square.

JOAN *and* ELLEN *hanging.*

SUSAN: Alice, how can you look? Your poor mother. You're not even crying.

ALICE: She wasn't a witch. She wouldn't know how.

SUSAN: Alice, she was.

ALICE: The cunning woman was, I think. That's why I was frightened of her.

SUSAN: I was a witch and never knew it. I killed my babies. I never meant it. I didn't know I was so wicked. I didn't know I had that mark on me. I'm so wicked. Alice, let's pray to God we won't be damned. If we're hanged, we're saved, Alice, so we mustn't be frightened. It's done to help us. Oh God, I know now

I'm loathsome and a sinner and Mr Packer has shown me how bad I am and I repent I never knew that but now I know and please forgive me and don't make me go to hell and be burnt forever –

ALICE: I'm not a witch.

SUSAN: Alice, you know you are. God, don't hear her say that.

ALICE: I'm not a witch. But I wish I was. If I could live I'd be a witch now after what they've done. I'd make wax men and melt them on a slow fire. I'd kill their animals and blast their crops and make such storms, I'd wreck their ships all over the world. I shouldn't have been frightened of Ellen, I should have learnt. Oh if I could meet with the devil now I'd give him anything if he'd give me power. There's no way for us except by the devil. If I only did have magic, I'd make them feel it.

Lament for the Witches

Where have the witches gone?
Who are the witches now?
Here we are.

All the gentle witches' spells
blast the doctors' sleeping pills.
The witches hanging in the sky
haunt the courts where lawyers lie.
Here we are.

They were gentle witches
with healing spells
They were desperate witches
with no way out but the other side of hell.

A witch's crying in the night
switches out your children's light.
All your houses safe and warm
are struck at by the witches' storm.
Here we are.

Where have the witches gone?
Who are the witches now?
Here we are.

They were gentle witches
with healing spells.
They were desperate witches
with no way out but the other side of hell.
Here we are.

Look in the mirror tonight.
Would they have hanged you then?
Ask how they're stopping you now.
Where have the witches gone?
Who are the witches now?
Ask how they're stopping you now.
Here we are.

SCENE TWENTY-ONE

SPRENGER: He's Kramer.
KRAMER: He's Sprenger.
KRAMER/SPRENGER: Professors of Theology
KRAMER: delegated by letters apostolic
SPRENGER: (here's a toast, non-alcoholic).
KRAMER: Inquisitors of heretical pravities
SPRENGER: we must fill those moral cavities
KRAMER: so we've written a book
SPRENGER: *Malleus Maleficarum*
KRAMER: *The Hammer of Witches*.
SPRENGER: It works like a charm
KRAMER: to discover witches
SPRENGER: and torture with no hitches.
KRAMER: Why is a greater number of witches found in the fragile
   feminine sex than in men?

176

SPRENGER: Why is a greater number of witches found in the fragile feminine sex than in men?

KRAMER: 'All wickedness is but little to the wickedness of a woman.' Ecclesiastes.

SPRENGER: Here are three reasons, first because

KRAMER: woman is more credulous and since the aim of the devil is to corrupt faith he attacks them. Second because

SPRENGER: women are more impressionable. Third because

KRAMER: women have slippery tongues and cannot conceal from other women what by their evil art they know.

SPRENGER: Women are feebler in both body and mind so it's not surprising.

KRAMER: In intellect they seem to be of a different nature from men –

SPRENGER: like children.

KRAMER: Yes.

SPRENGER: But the main reason is

KRAMER/SPRENGER: she is more carnal than a man

KRAMER: as may be seen from her many carnal abominations.

SPRENGER: She was formed from a bent rib

KRAMER: and so is an imperfect animal.

SPRENGER: Fe mina, female, that is fe faith minus without

KRAMER: so cannot keep faith.

SPRENGER: A defect of intelligence.

KRAMER: A defect of inordinate passions.

SPRENGER: They brood on vengeance.

KRAMER/SPRENGER: Wherefore it is no wonder they are witches.

KRAMER: Women have weak memories.

SPRENGER: Follow their own impulses.

KRAMER: Nearly all the kingdoms of the worlds have been overthrown by women.

SPRENGER: as Troy, etc.

KRAMER: She's a liar by nature

SPRENGER: vain

KRAMER: more bitter than death

SPRENGER: contaminating to touch

KRAMER: their carnal desires

SPRENGER: their insatiable malice

KRAMER: their hands are as bands for binding when they place their hands on a creature to bewitch it with the help of the devil.

SPRENGER: To conclude.

KRAMER: All witchcraft

SPRENGER: comes from carnal lust

KRAMER: which is in woman

KRAMER/SPRENGER: insatiable.

KRAMER: It is no wonder there are more women than men found infected with the heresy of witchcraft.

SPRENGER: And blessed be the Most High, which has so far preserved the male sex from so great a crime.

Evil Women

Evil women
Is that what you want?
Is that what you want to see?
On the movie screen
Of your own wet dream
Evil women.

If you like sex sinful, what you want is us.
You can be sucked off by a succubus.
We had this man, and afterwards he died.

Does she do what she's told or does she nag?
Are you cornered in the kitchen by a bitching hag?
Satan's lady, Satan's pride.
Satan's baby, Satan's bride,
A devil woman's not easily satisfied.

Do you ever get afraid
You don't do it right?
Does your lady demand it
Three times a night?
If we don't say you're big
Do you start to shrink?

We earn our own money
And buy our own drink.

Did you learn you were dirty boys, did you learn
Women were wicked to make you burn?

Satan's lady, Satan's pride,
Satan's baby, Satan's bride,
Witches were wicked and had to burn.

Evil women
Is that what you want?
Is that what you want to see?
In your movie dream
Do they scream and scream?
Evil women
Evil women
Women.

LIGHT SHINING IN
BUCKINGHAMSHIRE

Light Shining in Buckinghamshire

You great Curmudgeons, you hang a man for stealing, when you yourselves have stolen from your brethren all land and creatures.

More Light Shining in Buckinghamshire, a Digger pamphlet 1649

A revolutionary belief in the millenium went through the middle ages and broke out strongly in England at the time of the civil war. Soldiers fought the king in the belief that Christ would come and establish heaven on earth. What was established instead was an authoritarian parliament, the massacre of the Irish, the development of capitalism.

For a short time when the king had been defeated anything seemed possible, and the play shows the amazed excitement of people taking hold of their own lives, and their gradual betrayal as those who led them realised that freedom could not be had without property being destroyed. At the Putney debates Cromwell and Ireton argued for property; Gerrard Winstanley led Diggers to take over the common land: 'There can be no universal liberty till this universal community be established.' The Levellers and Diggers were crushed by the Army, and many turned in desperation to the remaining belief in the millenium, that Christ would come to do what they had failed in. The last long scene of the play is a meeting of Ranters, whose ecstatic and anarchic belief in economic and sexual freedom was the last desperate burst of revolutionary feeling before the restoration.

The simple 'Cavaliers and Roundheads' history taught at school hides the complexity of the aims and conflicts of those to the left of Parliament. We are told of a step forward to today's democracy but not of a revolution that didn't happen; we are told of Charles and Cromwell but not of the thousands of men and women who tried to change their lives. Though nobody now expects Christ to make heaven on earth, their voices are surprisingly close to us.

C.C. 1978

A Note on the Production

First of all, Max Stafford-Clark and I read and talked till we had found a subject in the millenial movement in the civil war. There was then a three-week workshop with the actors in which, through talk, reading, games and improvisation, we tried to get closer to the issues and the people. During the next nine weeks I wrote a script, and went on working on it with the company during the six-week rehearsal period.

It is hard to explain exactly the relationship between the workshop and the text. The play is not improvised: it is a written text and the actors did not make up its lines. But many of the characters and scenes were based on ideas that came from improvisation at the workshop and during rehearsal. I could give endless examples of how something said or done by one of the actors is directly connected to something in the text. Just as important, though harder to define, was the effect on the writing of the way the actors worked, their accuracy and commitment. I worked very closely with Max, and though I wrote the text the play is something we both imagined.

The characters Claxton and Cobbe are loosely based on Laurence Clarkson, or Claxton, and Abiezer Coppe, or Cobbe, two Ranters whose writings have survived; the others are fictional, except for those in the Putney debates, which is a much-condensed transcript of three days of debate among Army officers and soldiers' delegates which took place in 1647.

The characters are not played by the same actors each time they appear. The audience should not have to worry exactly which character they are seeing. Each scene can be taken as a separate event rather than part of a story. This seems to reflect better the reality of large events like war and revolution where many people share the same kind of experience. I recommend other productions to distribute parts in the same way, since the play was constructed with this in mind; and there would be difficulties if each character was played by one actor – for instance, Brigg's friend in the recruiting scene is by implication Claxton, from the reference to the baby, yet in the last scene Briggs and Claxton meet as strangers. When different actors play the parts what comes over is a large event involving many people, whose characters resonate in a way they wouldn't if they were more clearly defined.

The play was performed with a table and six chairs, which were used as needed in each scene. When any chairs were not used they were put on either side of the stage, and actors who were not in a scene sat at the side and watched the action. They moved the furniture themselves. Props were carefully chosen and minimal.

Light Shining in Buckinghamshire opened at the Traverse Theatre, Edinburgh, in September 1976, and was then on tour and at the Royal Court Theatre Upstairs.

Actors in the workshop:
Ian Charleson
Jenny Cryst
Linda Goddard
Carole Hayman
Will Knightley
Colin McCormack
Anne Raitt
David Rintoul

Actors in the play:
Janet Chappell
Linda Goddard
Bob Hamilton
Will Knightley
Colin McCormack
Nigel Terry

When Janet Chappell had to leave the cast her parts were played by Carole Hayman.

Directed by Max Stafford-Clark
Designed by Sue Plummer
Lighting by Steve Whitson
Music by Colin Sell

Scenes;	Parts played by:
COBBE PRAYS	Nigel
THE VICAR TALKS TO HIS SERVANT	Colin and Bob
MARGARET BROTHERTON IS TRIED	Janet, Colin and Will
STAR RECRUITS	Bob as Star, Will as Briggs, Colin as Friend, and the rest
BROTHERTON MEETS THE MAN	Janet and Bob
HOSKIN INTERRUPTS THE PREACHER	Nigel, Linda, and the rest
CLAXTON BRINGS HOSKINS HOME	Linda as Wife, Janet as Hoskins, Will
COBBE'S VISION	Bob announcing, Colin as Cobbe
TWO WOMEN LOOK IN A MIRROR	Janet and Linda
BRIGGS RECALLS A BATTLE	Nigel
THE PUTNEY DEBATES	Nigel as Rainborough, Bob as Sexby, Linda as Rich, Janet as Wildman, Colin as Cromwell, Will as Ireton
DIGGERS	All
CLAXTON EXPLAINS	Will

Documentary material:

Fear, and the pit . . . Isaiah 24, xvii-xx
A Fiery Flying Roll Abiezer Coppe 1649
All Seems Beautiful . . . Song of Myself Walt Whitman
The Putney Debates 1647
The True Levellers Standard Advanced Gerrard Winstanley, 1649
The English Soldier's Standard to Repair to 1649
The Moderate, a Leveller newspaper, 1649
The sleep of the labouring man . . . Ecclesiastes 5

List of characters in order of appearance:
COBBE, a gentleman
VICAR, an Anglican
SERVANT
1ST JP
2ND JP
MARGARET BROTHERTON, a vagrant
STAR, a corn merchant
BRIGGS, a working man
FRIEND, a working man
MAN, a vagrant
PREACHER, a Calvinist
HOSKINS, a vagrant preacher
CLAXTON, a working man
CLAXTON'S WIFE
1ST WOMAN
2ND WOMAN
COLONEL THOMAS RAINBOROUGH, a Leveller, from Cromwell's army
EDWARD SEXBY, an elected representative from Cromwell's army
COLONEL NATHANIEL RICH
JOHN WILDMAN, a gentleman
OLIVER CROMWELL
GENERAL IRETON
WINSTANLEY
BUTCHER
DRUNK, a poor man

ACT ONE

ALL [*Sing Isaiah 24 xvii-xx.*]

Fear, and the pit, and the snare are upon thee, O inhabitant of the earth.

And it shall come to pass that he who fleeth from the noise of the fear shall fall into the pit; and he that cometh out of the midst of the pit shall be taken in the snare; for the windows from on high are open, and the foundations of the earth do shake.

The earth is utterly broken down, the earth is clean dissolved, the earth is moved exceedingly.

The earth shall reel to and fro like a drunkard, and shall be removed like a cottage; and the transgression thereof shall be heavy upon it; and it shall fall and not rise again.

COBBE PRAYS

COBBE: Forgive my sins of the night and already this new day. Oh prevent me today from all the sins I will note – action, word, thought or faint motion less than any of these – or commit unknowing despite my strict guard set. Sloth not rising when mother called, the air so cold, lay five minutes of sin till she called again. Break me, God, to welcome your cold. Lust when the girl gave meat last night, not keeping my eyes on my plate but followed her hand. Repented last night with groans to you, O God, and still dreamt. Guard me today. Let me not go to hell, hot nor cold hell, let me be one of your elect. What is worst, I am not praying to you about the worst sin. I sin in my fear of praying about that sin, I sin in denying my fear. But you cut through that mesh, knowing. Why is it not enough to use your name in prayer, oh God, oh Lord Jesus Christ, amen, this is prayer, oh God, no swearing. Rich men of Antichrist on horses swear, king's officers say 'dammee' laughing. The beggar swore when they whipped him through the street and my heart leapt at each curse, a curse for each lash. Is he damned? Would I be? At table last night when father said grace I wanted to seize the

191

table and turn it over so the white cloth slid, silver, glass, capon, claret, comfits overturned. I wanted to shout your name and damn my family and myself eating so quietly when what is going on outside our gate? Words come out of my mouth like toads, I swear toads, toads will sit on me in hell. And what light on my father, still no light? Not to honour my father is sin, and sin to honour a greedy, cruel, hypocritical − Is it sin to kneel here till he leave the house? I cannot go down to him. It is sin to go down. I will wait till I hear the door. To avoid his blessing.

THE VICAR TALKS TO HIS SERVANT (CLAXTON)

The VICAR *sits at table, with wine and oranges.*

VICAR: How's the baby today? Any better?

SERVANT: No, sir.

VICAR: You saw who were missing again from morning service.

SERVANT: Sir.

VICAR: No better − no worse, I hope?

SERVANT: Yes, sir.

VICAR: Good, good. The sermon would have done them good. It wasn't my own, you could probably tell. The Bishop's naturally more gifted. But it's no good having it read in every parish if nobody compels the tenants to hear it. It's the ones who weren't there that I was talking to. 'From whence come wars and fightings among you?' From their lusts, from greed and envy and pride, which are from the devil, that's where the wars come from. When you said yes, you meant no worse?

SERVANT: No sir.

VICAR: Worse.

SERVANT: Sir.

VICAR: God tries you severely in your children. It must have been a comfort this morning to have the Bishop himself encourage you to suffer. 'Be afflicted and mourn and weep.' That is the way to heaven.

SERVANT: Sir.

[*He pours more wine.*]

VICAR: Why we have this war is because men want heaven now. If God meant us to have heaven on earth, why did he throw us out of paradise? They're fighting God himself, do they know that? They must be brought before the magistrates and forced to come next Sunday, and I'll tell them in my own words. Thank you, a little. This a godly estate and they will be evicted if they don't submit.

[*He gives* SERVANT *an orange.*]

Still we must pray your baby is spared this time. Take it an orange.

[*He drinks and takes an orange.*]

VICAR: Thank you, sir.

SERVANT: And if it is not spared, we must submit. We all have to suffer in this life.

[*He drinks.*]

MARGARET BROTHERTON IS TRIED

She is barely audible.

1ST JP: Is this the last?

2ND JP: One more.

1ST JP: It's a long list.

2ND JP: Hard times.

1ST JP: Soft hearts. Yours.

2ND JP: Step forward please.

1ST JP: I still say he should have been hanged.

2ND JP: He'll die in jail. Name?

BROTHERTON: Margaret Brotherton.

1ST JP: That's no example, nobody sees it.

2ND JP: Margaret Brotherton. Begging. Guilty or not guilty?

BROTHERTON: I don't know what you mean . . .

1ST JP: You're not of this parish?

2ND JP: Where do you come from?

BROTHERTON: Last week I was at Aston Clinton, and before that from Northampton.

1ST JP: I don't want to be told every place you've ever been. Where were you born?

BROTHERTON: Long Buckby.

1ST JP: If you belong fifty miles away what are you doing here?

2ND JP: Have you relations here? Friends you could stay with?

1ST JP: Tell us about your third cousin's wife's brother who has work for you. No? Or have you been told you get something for nothing here?

2ND JP: It's only our own poor who get help from this parish.

1ST JP: And we don't give money. So you can't drink it. It's your system of poor relief that brings them — they hear there's free bread and cheese, free fuel, there's no parish for miles that does that.

2ND JP: We can't help every vagrant in the country.

1ST JP: You must go back to where you were born.

2ND JP: If her parents didn't come from there they won't take her.

1ST JP: Her father's parish.

2ND JP: She's never been there.

1ST JP: The parish she last lived in.

2ND JP: They turned her out for begging.

1ST JP: Exactly, and so do we.

2ND JP: Why aren't you married?

BROTHERTON: . . .

1ST JP: Can we please agree on a sentence.

2ND JP: First offence. Let's be lenient.

1ST JP: It's only fair to warn you in advance that the next council meeting may reconsider the whole question of poor relief.

2ND JP: Margaret Brotherton, we find you guilty of vagrancy and sentence you to be stripped to the waist and beaten to the bounds of this parish and returned parish by parish to . . .

1ST JP: Where she was born.

2ND JP: To the parish where you were born. Next please.

STAR RECRUITS

A prayer meeting.

STAR: Christ watch over this meeting and grant that your kingdom will come, amen.

ALL: Amen.

STAR: Life is hard, brothers, and how will it get better? I tell you, life in Babylon is hard and Babylon must be destroyed. In Babylon you are slaves. Babylon is the kingdom of Antichrist. The kingdom of popery. The kingdom of the king. And it must be destroyed. Because then will come the kingdom of Jerusalem. And in Jerusalem you will be free. That is why you will join as soldiers. To destroy Antichrist. To fight with parliament for Jerusalem. To fight with Christ's saints for Christ's kingdom. Because when parliament has defeated Antichrist then Christ will come. Christ will come in person, God and man, and will rule over England for one thousand years. And the saints will reign with him. And who are the saints? You are. The poor people of this country. When Christ came, did he come to the rich? No. He came to the poor. He is coming to you again. If you prepare for him by defeating Antichrist which is the royalists. If you join in the army now you will be one of the saints. You will rule with Jesus a thousand years. We have just had another bad harvest.* But, it is written, when Jesus comes 'the floors shall be full of wheat and the vats overflow with wine'. Why did Jesus Christ purchase the earth with his blood? He purchased it for the saints. For you. It will all be yours. You are poor now. You are despised now. But the gentlemen who look down on you will soon find out that the inhabitants of Jerusalem are commonwealth men. Now is the moment. It will be too late when Christ comes to say you want to be saved. Some will be cast into the pit, into the burning lake, into the unquenchable fire. And some will be clothed in white linen and ride white horses and rule with King Jesus in Jerusalem shining with jasper and chrysolite. So give now, give what you can to Christ now to pay his soldiers. Christ will pay you back in diamonds. Join now for a soldier of Christ and you will march out of this town to Jerusalem. Who are you? What are you? I know you all and you know me. You are nobody here. You have nothing. But the moment you join the army you will have everything. You will be as important as anybody in England. You will be Christ's Saints.

[BRIGGS: Going for a soldier?
FRIEND: What soldier? What side?

*BRIGGS and FRIEND speak their next speeches (indicated in square brackets) at the same time as the rest of STAR's speech from this point on.

195

BRIGGS: Parliament, inne, Mr Star?

FRIEND: He's a gentleman, inne, Mr Star?

BRIGGS: Parliament's gentlemen. But parliament's for us.

FRIEND: What's the pay?

BRIGGS: More than I'm getting now. And they give you a musket.

FRIEND: For yourself?

BRIGGS: To use it. Heard about the baby.

FRIEND: Ah.

BRIGGS: Wife all right? Thinking of going.

FRIEND: What about . . ?

BRIGGS: Send them money. And where I am now, I'll be out again in the winter like last year. I'm not having that. You keep an eye on them. Won't be long.

FRIEND: Christ's coming anyway.

BRIGGS: You reckon?

FRIEND: Something's going on.]

A LISTENER: And when will Christ come?

STAR: When will Christ come? 'From the abomination that maketh desolate, there shall be one thousand, two hundred and ninety days.' Now a day is taken for a year. And that brings us to sixteen hundred and fifty. Yes, sixteen hundred and fifty. So we haven't much time. Jerusalem in England in sixteen fifty. Don't leave it too late. Join the army today and be sure of your place in Jerusalem.

Now I've a list here of names that have joined already. Twenty-three saints that live in this town. Whose name is next on the list of saints?

BRIGGS: What's the pay?

STAR: The pay is eightpence a day. Better than labouring. And it's every day. Not day labour. Not just the days you fight. Every day.

BRIGGS: And keep?

STAR: Keep is taken out. But you're given a musket. Shall I take your name?

[*Three* LISTENERS *speak out.*]

1ST: I won't go to fight. But there's three of us could pay for a musket among the three.

2ND: I've got four silver spoons. They'd pay for something.

3RD: You can have a buckle I was given.

BRIGGS: I'll give my name. Briggs. Thomas Briggs.

BROTHERTON MEETS THE MAN

She has several bags. He has a bottle.

BROTHERTON: Went up the road about a mile then I come back. There's a dog not tied up. So I started back where I slept last night. But that was into the wind. So I'm stopping here. It's not my shoes. I've got better shoes for walking in my bag. My sister's shoes that's dead. They wouldn't fit you. How much you got?

MAN: Drunk it all.

BROTHERTON: I'm not asking.

   [*He gives her the bottle.*]

MAN: It doesn't matter not eating if you can drink. Doesn't matter not drinking if you can sleep. But you can't sleep in this wind.

   [*He takes the bottle back.*]

BROTHERTON: What you got there?

MAN: I thought my hands were cold but they're warm to yours.

BROTHERTON: What you got?

MAN: Look, here, that's my Bible. That's my father's name, that's my name. Two and a half acres. I had to sell my knife. I sold my knife.

BROTHERTON: How much you got now then?

MAN: Tenpence.

BROTHERTON: That's a long time till you got nothing. Then you can sell the Bible.

MAN: No, I need that.

BROTHERTON: What I've got, look. The shoes. A bottle, that's a good bottle. I had another one that was no good. I don't often throw something out but I won't carry anything I don't like. A piece of cloth. You can wrap it round. It's got lots of uses. I could sell you that. You can't see what's in here. That's more of my sister's things that's dead. There's a piece of rope. You could have that for a halfpenny.

MAN: Your face is cold. Your neck's cold. Your back's no warmer. The wind goes right through.

BROTHERTON: You can have the rope and the cloth both for a halfpenny.

MAN: Come and lie down. Out of the wind. I'll give you a half-penny after.

BROTHERTON: No. With tenpence, we can get indoors for that.

MAN: Wouldn't last long.

BROTHERTON: Last more than one day. Even one day's good.

MAN: If only I knew when Christ was coming.

BROTHERTON: You think he's coming?

MAN: He must. If only the money would last till the world ends then it would be all right. It's warm in heaven.

BROTHERTON: If he comes tomorrow and you've not drunk your money. Sitting here with tenpence in the cold. Christ laugh at you for that.

BRIGGS JOINS UP

STAR *eats.*

STAR: You keep your hat on. New style catching on.

BRIGGS: Yes sir. I mean, yes, I do.

STAR: As a sign you're as good as me?

BRIGGS: Yes. Nothing personal, Mr Star. Before God only.

STAR: Parson seen you like that?

BRIGGS: He said I was a scorpion, sir. Mr Star. I mean, he said I was a scorpion.

STAR: A hat's all right for a soldier. It shows courage.

[*Pause, while* STAR *eats.*]

You know what I'm eating?

BRIGGS: Your dinner?

STAR: What it is.

BRIGGS: Meat?

STAR: The name of it.

BRIGGS: Beef? Mutton? I can't tell from here.

STAR: Sheep. Or, if it was, cow, but it's sheep. Now what language is that, beef, mutton?

BRIGGS: It's not language –

STAR: Beef and mutton is Norman words. The Saxon raised the animal. Sheep. Cow. The Norman ate the meat. Boeuf, mouton.

Even the laws of this country aren't written in English.

BRIGGS: So I've come.

STAR: You haven't got a horse, I know, so I can't put you in the horse, though there's more thinking men there with hats on and writing their grievances down on paper. But you'll find plenty to talk about in the foot. Eight-pence a day and we deduct food and clothing. Cheese and hard biscuit. Anything else?

BRIGGS: You don't know how long it's going to be?

STAR: Till we win.

BRIGGS: That's what I mean. How long till we win?

STAR: What we're fighting for . . . We've known each other all our lives. Our paths never cross. But you know me as an honest dealer. I've been leant on many times to keep up the price of corn when it could be down. And I'd be a richer man. The hunger now is no fault of mine. You're a Saxon. I'm a Saxon. Our fathers were conquered six hundred years ago by William the Norman. His colonels are our lords. His cavalry are our knights. His common foot soldiers are our squires. When you join this army you are fighting a foreign enemy. You are fighting an invasion of your own soil. Parliament is Saxon. The Army is Saxon. Jesus Christ is Saxon. The Royalists are Normans and the Normans are Antichrist. We are fighting to be free men and own our own land. So we fight as long as it takes. In the meantime there's no looting. No raping. No driving off of cattle or firing ricks. We're not antichristian royalists. We're Christ's saints. It's an army that values godliness. There's no swearing. The men don't like swearing. They like reading their Bibles. They like singing hymns. They like talk. We don't discourage talk. Your officers are not all gentlemen, they're men like you.

BRIGGS: Bacon. Is bacon Norman?

STAR: Pork, Briggs. Pig. Very good.

BRIGGS: And Jacob the younger brother is the Saxon herds the pigs. And Esau the older brother is the Norman eats the pork.

STAR: Very good, Briggs. Excellent. Now one thing. You wear your hat. Will you take orders?

BRIGGS: If they're not against God.

STAR: They can't be against God in God's army.

HOSKINS INTERRUPTS THE PREACHER

PREACHER: My text today is from Psalm one hundred and forty-nine.

'Sing unto the Lord a new song and his praise in the congregation of saints.

Let the high praises of God be in their mouth and a two-edged sword in their hand.

To bind their kings with chains and their nobles with fetters of iron.'

ALL AND HOSKINS: Amen, amen.

PREACHER: It is no sin to take up arms against the king. It is no sin if we fight singing praises to God, if we fight to bind an unjust king with chains.

ALL: Amen.

PREACHER: For it is written: 'The saints of the most High shall take the kingdom and possess the kingdom forever, even forever and ever.'

HOSKINS: Forever and ever, amen.

ALL: Amen.

PREACHER: The saints will take the kingdom. And who are the saints?

HOSKINS: We all are.

PREACHER: The saints are those whom God has chosen from all eternity to be his people. For he has chosen a certain number of particular men to be his elect. None can be added to them and none can be taken away. And others he has chosen to be eternally damned. As John tells us in Revelation: 'Whosoever was not written in the book of life was cast into the lake of fire.' So it is God's saints, chosen before their birth, written in the book of life, who will bind the king and the nobles and take the kingdom which will last forever.

ALL: Amen.

HOSKINS: But no one is damned. We can all bind the king.

PREACHER: Who are the saints? They are not the same people who rule in this world.

HOSKINS: Amen to that.

ALL: Amen.

PREACHER: When Christ first came to earth he came to the poor. And it is to the poor, to you, to tailors, cobblers, chapmen, ploughmen, that he is coming again. He will not set up a kingdom like we have now, a kingdom of Antichrist, a kingdom of a king, nobles and gentry. In Christ's kingdom no worldly honour counts. A noble can be damned and a beggar saved.

ALL: Amen.

PREACHER: All that counts is whether God has chosen you. Look into your hearts and see whether God has chosen you or –

HOSKINS: He's chosen me. He's chosen everyone.

PREACHER: Or whether you are given over to the devil. For those that are not saved will be cast into the pit. 'And he that cometh out of the midst of the pit shall be taken in the snare.'

HOSKINS: There is no pit, there is no snare.

PREACHER: For now is the time spoken of in Isaiah, 'the earth is utterly broken down, the earth is clean dissolved'.

HOSKINS: God would not send us into the pit. Christ saves us from that.

PREACHER: 'And it shall come to pass in that day, that the Lord shall punish the host of the high ones that are on high, and the kings of the earth upon the earth.'

HOSKINS: Yes he will cast them down but he will not damn them eternally.

PREACHER: Why are you speaking? I let it pass but you are too loud. Women can't speak in church.

HOSKINS: God speaks in me.

PREACHER: For St Paul says, 'I suffer not a woman to teach, nor to usurp authority over the man, but to be in silence.'

HOSKINS: A text? a text is it? do you want a text?

PREACHER: 'For Adam was first formed then Eve. And Adam was not deceived but the woman being deceived was in the transgression.

HOSKINS: Joel. Chapter two. Verse twenty-eight. 'And it shall come to pass that I will pour out my spirit upon all flesh; and your sons and your daughters shall prophecy, and your old men shall dream dreams and your young men shall see visions. And also upon the servants and upon the handmaids in those days will I pour out my spirit.'

PREACHER: It has got about that I allow answers to my sermons. But this is taking the freedom to speak too far. If anyone can call out whenever they like it will be complete confusion. I allow answers to my sermon if they are sober and godly and if the speaker has the courtesy to wait –

HOSKINS: You say most of us are damned. You say we are chosen to be damned before we are born.

PREACHER: I said to wait till the end of the sermon, and I do not allow women to speak at all since it is forbidden.

HOSKINS: How can God choose us from all eternity to be saved or damned when there's nothing we've done?

PREACHER: I will answer this question because it is a common one and others, who have the grace to wait, may be asking it within themselves. But I am not answering you. How can some people be damned before they are born? Sin is the cause of damnation, but the reason God does not choose to save some people from sin and damnation is his free will and pleasure, not our own.

ALL: Amen.

HOSKINS: God's pleasure? that we burn? what sort of God takes pleasure in pain?

PREACHER: And those few that are saved are saved not by their own virtue though if they are the elect they will by their very nature try to live virtuously, but by God's grace and mercy –

HOSKINS: No, it's not just a few. Not just a few elect go to heaven. He thinks most people are bad. The king thinks most people are bad. He's against the king but he's saying the same.

PREACHER: Get her out.

[*Two of the congregation throw* HOSKINS *out.*]

HOSKINS: In his kingdom of heaven there's going to be a few in bliss and the rest of us in hell. What's the difference from what we've got now? You are all saved. Yes, you are all saved. Not one of you is damned –

PREACHER: Woman, you are certainly damned.

202

CLAXTON BRINGS HOSKINS HOME

WIFE *is bathing* HOSKINS's *bruised head.*

WIFE: What you go there for?

CLAXTON: When they beat her, you know . . . I couldn't . . .

WIFE: But who did it?

CLAXTON: They chased her down the hill from the church and
    when she fell over . . . I couldn't stop them. I came up after.

WIFE: But what you go there for?

CLAXTON: Just to see.

WIFE: It's not proper church.

CLAXTON: Just to see.

WIFE: Parson won't like it.

CLAXTON: Parson needn't.

WIFE: I'm not going there if they beat women.

CLAXTON: No but they let you speak.

WIFE: No but they beat her.

CLAXTON: No but men. They let men speak.

WIFE: Did you speak?

CLAXTON: Don't want to work for parson.

WIFE: What then?

CLAXTON: I don't know, I don't know.

[WIFE *finishes bathing* HOSKINS's *head.*]

HOSKINS: Thank you.

WIFE: Better?

HOSKINS: Yes thank you.

WIFE: Where you from?

HOSKINS: Near Leicester.

WIFE: What are you doing here then?

HOSKINS: Travelling.

WIFE: Are you married? Or are you on your own?

HOSKINS: No, I'm never on my own.

CLAXTON: Who are you with then?

HOSKINS: Different men sometimes. But it's not like you think.
    Well it is like you think. But then nothing's like you think. Who
    I'm with is Jesus Christ.

CLAXTON: How do you live?

203

HOSKINS: Sometimes people give me money. They give me for preaching. I'm not a beggar.

CLAXTON: Didn't say that.

HOSKINS: Steal though if I can. It's only the rich go to hell. Did you know that?

CLAXTON: I think they do.

HOSKINS: And we don't, did you know that?

WIFE: You don't live anywhere?

HOSKINS: I'm not the only one.

WIFE: No one look after you?

HOSKINS: Jesus God.

WIFE: Are your parents living?

HOSKINS: You know how Jesus says forsake your parents. Anyone who hath forsaken houses, or brethren, or sisters, or father, or mother, or wife . . . or children, or lands, for my sake. See.

CLAXTON: No need to go that far.

HOSKINS: Well, it's the times. Christ will be here soon so what's it matter.

CLAXTON: Do you believe that?

HOSKINS: I do.

WIFE: But women can't preach. We bear children in pain, that's why. And they die. For our sin, Eve's sin. That's why we have pain. We're not clean. We have to obey. The man, whatever he's like. If he beat us that's why. We have blood, we're shameful, our bodies are worse than a man's. All bodies are evil but ours is worst. That's why we can't speak.

HOSKINS: Well I can.

WIFE: You haven't had children.

HOSKINS: That's all wrong what you said. We're not –

WIFE: Have you had a child?

HOSKINS: No but –

WIFE: Then you don't know. We wouldn't be punished if it wasn't for something.

HOSKINS: We're not –

WIFE: And then they die. You don't know.

HOSKINS: They die because how we live. My brothers did. Died

of hunger more than fever. My mother kept boiling up the same
bones.

WIFE: Go home. Go home.

HOSKINS: No, I'm out with God. You want to get out too.

WIFE: No. No we don't.

CLAXTON: Sometimes I read in Revelation. Because people say
now is the last days. 'And I saw a new heaven and a new earth;
for the first heaven and the first earth were passed away. And
there was no more sea.' Why no more sea? I never seen the sea.
But England's got a fine navy and we trade by sea and go to
new countries, so why no more sea? Now I think this is why. I
can explain this. I see into it. I have something from God. The
sea is water. And salt water, not like a stream or a well, you
can't drink it. And you can't breathe it. Because it's water. But
fish can breathe it. But men can't live in it.

WIFE: What are you talking about?

CLAXTON: What it's saying, seems to me. Fish can live in it. Men
can't. Now men can't live here either. How we live is like the
sea. We can't breathe. Our squire, he's like a fish. Looks like a
fish too, if you saw him. And parson. Parson can breathe. He
swims about, waggles his tail. Bitter water and he lives in it.
Bailiff. Justices, Hangman. Lawyer. Mayor. All the gentry.
Swimming about. We can't live in it. We drown. I'm a drowned
man.

WIFE: Stop it, you can't do it, you're making a fool –

HOSKINS: No, it's good.

CLAXTON: Octopus is a kind of fish with lots of arms grasping
and full of black stink. Sharks eat you. Whales, you're lost
inside them, they're so big, they swallow you up and never
notice. They live in it.

WIFE: Stop it.

CLAXTON: We can't live. We are dead. Bitter water. There shall
be a new heaven. And a new earth. And no more sea.

WIFE: No, don't start. Don't speak. I can't.

COBBE'S VISION

ONE OF THE ACTORS [*announces a pamphlet by Abiezer
Coppe*.]: A fiery flying roll: being a word from the Lord to all

the great ones of the earth, whom this may concern: being the last warning piece at the dreadful day of Judgement. For now the Lord is come to first, warn, second, advise and warn, third, charge, fourth, judge and sentence the great ones. As also most compassionately informing, and most lovingly and pathetically advising and-warning London. And all by his most excellent majesty, dwelling in and shining through Auxilium Patris, alias Coppe. Imprinted in London, at the beginning of that notable day, wherein the secrets of all hearts are laid open.

COBBE: All my strength, my forces, were utterly routed, my house I dwelt in fired, my father and mother forsook me, and the wife of my bosom loathed me, and I was utterly plagued and sunk into nothing, into the bowels of the still Eternity (my mother's womb) out of which I came naked, and whereto I returned again naked. And lying a while there, rapt up in silence, at length (the body's outward form being all this while awake) I heard with my outward ear (to my apprehension) a most terrible thunderclap, and after that a second. And upon the second, which was exceeding terrible, I saw a great body of light like the light of the sun, and red as fire, in the form (as it were) of a drum, whereupon with exceeding trembling and amazement on the flesh, and with joy unspeakable in the spirit, I clapped my hands, and cried out, Amen, Halelujah, Halelujah, Amen. And so lay trembling sweating and smoking (for the space of half an hour). At length with a loud voice I (inwardly) cried out, Lord what wilt thou do with me? My most excellent majesty and eternal glory in me answered and said, fear not. I will take thee up into my everlasting kingdom. But first you must drink a bitter cup, a bitter cup, a bitter cup. Whereupon I was thrown into the belly of hell (and take what you can of it in these expressions, though the matter is beyond expression) I was among all the devils in hell, even in their most hideous crew.

And under all this terror and amazement, a tiny spark of transcendent, unspeakable glory, survived, and sustained itself, triumphing, exulting and exalting itself above all the fiends. And I heard a voice saying, 'Go to London, to London, that great city, and tell them I am coming.'

ACT ONE

TWO WOMEN LOOK IN A MIRROR

1ST WOMAN *comes in with a broken mirror.* 2ND WOMAN *is mending.*

1ST WOMAN: Look, look, you must come quick.

2ND WOMAN: What you got there?

1ST WOMAN: Look. Who's that? That's you. That's you and me.

2ND WOMAN: Is that me? Where you get it?

1ST WOMAN: Up the house.

2ND WOMAN: What? with him away? It's all locked up.

1ST WOMAN: I went in the front door.

2ND WOMAN: The front door?

1ST WOMAN: Nothing happened to me. You can take things –

2ND WOMAN: That's his things. That's stealing. You'll be killed for that.

1ST WOMAN: No, not any more, it's all ours now, so we won't burn the corn because that's our corn now and we're not going to let the cattle out because they're ours too.

2ND WOMAN: You been in his rooms?

1ST WOMAN: I been upstairs. In the bedrooms.

2ND WOMAN: I been in the kitchen.

1ST WOMAN: I lay on the bed. White linen sheets. Three wool blankets.

2ND WOMAN: Did you take one?

1ST WOMAN: I didn't know what to take, there's so much.

2ND WOMAN: Oh if everyone's taking someting I want a blanket. But what when he comes back?

1ST WOMAN: He'll never come back. We're burning his papers, that's the Norman papers that give him his lands. That's like him burnt. There's no one over us. There's pictures of him and his grandfather and his great great – a long row of pictures and we pulled them down.

2ND WOMAN: But he won't miss a blanket.

1ST WOMAN: There's an even bigger mirror that we didn't break. I'll show you where. You see your whole body at once. You see yourself standing in that room. They must know what they look like all the time. And now we do.

BRIGGS RECALLS A BATTLE

BRIGGS: The noise was very loud, the shouting and the cannon behind us, and it was dark from the clouds of smoke blowing over so you couldn't see more than a few yards, so that when I hit this boy across the face with my musket I was suddenly frightened as he went under that he was on my own side; but another man was on me and I hit at him and I didn't know who I was fighting till the smoke cleared and I saw men I knew and a tree I'd stood under before the shooting began. But after I was wounded, lying with my head downhill, watching men take bodies off the field, I didn't know which was our side and which was them, but then I saw it didn't matter because what we were fighting was not each other but Antichrist and even the soldiers on the other side would be made free and be glad when they saw the paradise we'd won, so that the dead on both sides died for that, to free us of that darkness and confusion we'd lived in and brings us all into the quiet and sunlight. And even when they moved me the pain was less than the joy.

[ALL *sing from 'Song of the Open Road' by Walt Whitman.*]
ALL: All seems beautiful to me.

I can repeat over to men and women, You have done such good to me,

I would do the same to you,

I will recruit for myself and you as I go,

I will scatter myself among men and women as I go,

I will toss a new gladness and roughness among them.

Whoever denies me it shall not trouble me,

Whoever accepts me he or she shall be blessed and shall bless me.

THE PUTNEY DEBATES

RAINBOROUGH: The Putney debates, October the twenty-eighth, sixteen forty-seven. I am Colonel Thomas Rainborough, a Leveller.

SEXBY: Edward Sexby, private soldier, elected representative or agitator from Fairfax's regiment of horse.

RICH: Colonel Nathaniel Rich.

WILDMAN: John Wildman, civilian, writer of Leveller pamphlets who has assisted the agitators in drawing up their proposals.

CROMWELL: Oliver Cromwell.

IRETON: Commissary General Henry Ireton.

CROMWELL: If anyone has anything to say concerning the public business, he has liberty to speak.

SEXBY: Lieutenant General Cromwell, Commissary General Ireton, we have been by providence put upon strange things, such as the ancientist here doth scarce remember. And yet we have found little fruit of our endeavours. Truly our miseries and our fellow soldiers' cry out for present help. We, the agents of the common soldiers, have drawn up an Agreement of the People. We declare:

First: That the people of England being very unequally distributed for the election of their deputies in parliament ought to be proportioned according to the number of inhabitants.

Second: That this present parliament be dissolved.

Third: That the people choose a parliament once in two years.

Fourth: That the power of representatives of this nation is inferior only to theirs who choose them, and the people make the following reservations:

First: That matters of religion are not at all entrusted by us to any human power.

Second: That impressing us to serve in wars is against our freedom.

Third: That no person be at any time questioned for anything said or done in the late wars.

These things we declare to be our native rights and are resolved to maintain them with our utmost possibilities.

CROMWELL: These things you have offered, they are new to us. This is the first time we have had a view of them. Truly this paper does contain very great alterations of the very government of the kingdom. If we could leap out of one condition into another, I suppose there would not be much dispute. But how do we know another company of men shall not put out a paper as plausible as this? And not only another, and another, but many of this kind. And what do you think the consequence of that would be? Would it not be confusion? Would it not be utter confusion? As well as the consequences we must consider the ways and means: whether the people are prepared to go along with it and whether the great difficulties in our way are likely to be overcome. But I shall speak to nothing but that that tends to uniting us in one. And I am confident you do not bring this paper in peremptoriness of mind, but to receive amendments. First there is the question what commitments lie upon us. We have in time of danger issued several declarations; we have been required by parliament to declare particularly what we meant, and have done so in proposals drawn up by Commissary General Ireton. So before we consider this paper we must consider how far we are free.

WILDMAN: I was yesterday at a meeting with divers country gentlemen and soldiers and the agitators of the regiments and I declared my agreement with them. They believe that if an obligation is not just, then it is an act of honesty not to keep it.

IRETON: If anyone is free to break any obligation he has entered into, this is a principle that would take away all government. Men would think themselves not obliged by any law they thought not a good law. They would not think themselves obliged to stand by the authority of your paper. There are plausible things in the paper and things very good in it. If we were free from all other commitments I should concur with it further than I can.

RAINBOROUGH: Every honest man is bound in duty to God to decline an obligation when he sees it to be evil: he is obliged to discharge his duty to God. There are two other objections: one is division: I think we are utterly undone if we divide. Another thing is difficulties. Truly I think parliament were very indiscreet to contest with the king if they did not consider first that they should go through difficulties; and I think there was no man that entered into this war that did not engage to go through difficulties. Truly I think let the difficulties be round about you, death before you, the sea behind you, and you are convinced the thing is just, you are bound in conscience to carry it on, and I think at the last day it can never be answered to God that you did not do it.

CROMWELL: Truly I am very glad that this gentleman is here.

We shall enjoy his company longer than I thought we should have done –

RAINBOROUGH: If I should not be kicked out.

CROMWELL: – And it shall not be long enough. We are almost all soldiers. All considerations of not fearing difficulties do wonderfully please us. I do not think any man here wants courage to do that which becomes an honest man and an Englishman to do. And I do not think it was offered by anyone that though a commitment were never so unrighteous it ought to be kept. But perhaps we are upon commitments here that we cannot with honesty break.

WILDMAN: There is a principle much spreading and much to my trouble: that though a commitment appear to be unjust, yet a person must sit down and suffer under it. To me this is very dangerous, and I see it spreading in the army again. The chief thing in the agreement is to secure the rights and freedoms of the people, which was declared by the army to be absolutely insisted on.

IRETON: I am far from holding that if a man have committed himself to a thing that is evil, that he is bound to perform what he hath promised. But convenants freely made must be kept. Take away that, I do not know what ground there is of anything you call any man's right. I would know what you gentlemen account the right to anything you have in England; anything of estate, land or goods, what right you have to it. If you resort only to the Law of Nature, I have as much right to take hold of anything I desire as you. Therefore when I hear men speak of laying aside all commitments I tremble at the boundless and endless consequences of it.

WILDMAN: You take away the substance of the question. Our sense was that an unjust commitment is rather to be broken than kept.

IRETON: But this leads to the end of all government: if you think something is unjust you are not to obey; and if it tends to your loss it is no doubt unjust and you are to oppose it!

RAINBOROUGH: One word, here is the consideration now: do we not engage for the parliament and for the liberties of the people of England? That which is dear to me is my freedom, it is that I would enjoy and I will enjoy it if I can.

IRETON: These gentlemen think their own agreement is so infallibly just and right, that anyone who doesn't agree to it is about a thing unlawful.

RICH: If we do not set upon the work presently we are undone. Since the agreement is ready to our hands, I desire that you would read it and debate it.

IRETON: I think because it is so much insisted on we should read the paper.

WILDMAN: Twenty-ninth of October.

IRETON: Let us hear the first article again.

SEXBY: That the people of England being very unequally distributed for the election of their deputies –

IRETON: 'The people of England.' This makes me think that the meaning is that every man that is an inhabitant is to have an equal vote in the election. But if it only means the people that had the election before, I have nothing to say against it. Do those that brought it know whether they mean all that had a former right, or those that had no right before are to come in?

RAINBOROUGH: All inhabitants that have not lost their birth-right should have an equal vote in elections. For really I think that the poorest he in England hath a life to live as the greatest he; therefore truly sir, I think it's clear, that every man that is to live under a government ought first by his own consent to put himself under it.

IRETON: I think no person hath a right to an interest in the disposing of the affairs of this kingdom that hath not a permanent fixed interest in this kingdom. We talk of birthright. Men may justly have by their birthright, by their being born in England, that we should not seclude them out of England, that we should not refuse to give them air and place and ground and the freedom of the highways. That I think is due to a man by birth. But that by a man's being born here he shall have a share in that power that shall dispose of the lands here, I do not think it sufficient ground.

RAINBOROUGH: Truly sir, I am of the same opinion I was. I do not find anything in the law of God that a lord shall choose twenty members, and a gentleman but two, or a poor man shall choose none. I find no such thing in the law of nature or the law of nations. But I do find that all Englishmen must be subject to English law, and the foundation of the law lies in the people. Every man in England ought not to be exempted from the choice of those who are to make laws for him to live under, and for him, for aught I know, to lose his life by.

IRETON: All the main thing that I speak for is because I would have an eye to property. Let every man consider that he do not go that way to take away all property. Now I wish we may consider of what right you will claim that all the people should have a right to elections. Is it by right of nature? Then I think you must deny all property too. If you say one man hath an equal right with another to the choosing of him that will govern him, by the same right of nature he hath the same right in any goods he sees — he hath a freedom to the land, to take the ground, to till it. I would fain have any man show me their bounds, where you will end.

RAINBOROUGH: Sir, to say that because a man pleads that every man hath a voice, that it destroys all property — this is to forget the law of God. That there's property, the law of God says it, else why hath God made that law, Thou shalt not steal? I am a poor man, therefore I must be oppressed: if I have no interest in the kingdom, I must suffer all their laws be they right or wrong. Nay thus: a gentleman lives in a country and hath three or four lordships, as some men have (God knows how they got them); and when a parliament is called he must be a parliament man; and it may be he sees some poor men, they live near this man, he can crush them — I have known an invasion to turn poor men out of doors; and I would know whether rich men do not do this, and keep them under the greatest tyranny that was ever thought of in the world. And I wish you would not make the world believe we are for anarchy.

CROMWELL: Really, sir, this is not right. No man says you have a mind to anarchy, but that the consequence of this rule tends to anarchy. I am confident on 't, we should not be so hot with one another.

RAINBOROUGH: I know that some particular men we debate with believe we are for anarchy.

IRETON: I must clear myself as to that point. I cannot allow myself to lay the least scandal upon anyone. And I don't know why the gentleman should take so much offence. We speak to the paper not to persons. Now the main answer against my objection was that there was a divine law, Thou shalt not steal. But we cannot prove property in a thing by divine law any more than prove we have an interest in choosing members for parliament by divine law. Our right of sending members to parliament descends from other things and so does our right to property.

RAINBOROUGH: I would fain know what we have fought for. For our laws and liberties? And this is the old law of England – and that which enslaves the people of England – that they should be bound by laws in which they have no voice! And for my part, I look upon the people of England so, that wherein they have not voices in the choosing of their governors they are not bound to obey them.

IRETON: I did not say we should not have any enlargement at all of those who are to be the electors. But if you admit any man that hath breath and being, it may come to destroy property thus: you may have such men chosen as have no local or permanent interest. Why may not those men vote against all property? Show me what you will stop at.

RICH: There is weight in the objection, for you have five to one in this kingdom that have no permanent interest. Some men have ten, some twenty servants. If the master and servant be equal electors, the majority may by law destroy property. But certainly there may be some other way thought of, that there may be a representative of the poor as well as the rich.

RAINBOROUGH: I think it is a fine gilded pill.

WILDMAN: Our case is that we have been under slavery. That's acknowledged by all. Our very laws were made by our conquerors. We are now engaged for our freedom. The question is: Whether any person can justly be bound by law, who doth not give his consent?

IRETON: Yes, and I will make it clear. If a foreigner will have

214

liberty to dwell here, he may very well be content to submit to the law of the land. If any man will receive protection from this people, he ought to be subject to those laws. If this man do think himself unsatisfied to be subject to this law, he may go into another kingdom.

WILDMAN: The gentleman here said five parts of the nation are now excluded and would then have a voice in elections. At present one part makes hewers of wood and drawers of water of the other five, so the greater part of the nation is enslaved. I do not hear any justification given but that it is the present law of the kingdom.

RAINBOROUGH: What shall become of those men that have laid themselves out for the parliament in this present war, that have ruined themselves by fighting? They are Englishmen. They have now no voice in elections.

RICH: All I urged was that I think it worthy consideration whether they should have an equal voice. However, I think we have been a great while upon this point. If we stay but three days until you satisfy one another the king will come and decide who will be hanged first.

SEXBY: October the thirtieth.

RAINBOROUGH: If we can agree where the liberty of the people lies, that will do all.

IRETON: I cannot consent so far. When I see the hand of God destroying king, and lords, and commons too, when I see God had done it, I shall, I hope, comfortably acquiesce in it. But before that, I cannot give my consent to it because it is not good. The law of God doth not give me property, nor the law of nature, but property is of human constitution. I have a property and this I shall enjoy.

SEXBY: I see that though liberty was our end, there is a degeneration from it. We have ventured our lives and it was all for this: to recover our birthrights as Englishmen; and by the arguments urged there is none. There are many thousands of us soldiers that have ventured our lives; we have had little property in the kingdom, yet we have had a birthright. But it seems now, except a man hath a fixed estate in the kingdom, he hath no right in this kingdom. I wonder we were so much deceived. If we had

215

not a right to the kingdom, we were mere mercenary soldiers. I shall tell you in a word my resolution. I am resolved to give my birthright to none. If this thing be denied the poor, that with so much pressing after they have sought, it will be the greatest scandal. It was said that if those in low condition were given their birthright it would be the destruction of this kingdom. I think the poor and meaner of this kingdom have been the means of preservation of this kingdom. Their lives have not been held dear for purchasing the good of the kingdom. And now they demand the birthright for which they fought. They are as free from anarchy and confusion as any, and they have the law of God and the law of their conscience with them. When men come to understand these things, they will not lose that which they have contended for.

IRETON: I am very sorry we are come to this point, that from reasoning one to another we should come to express our resolutions. Now let us consider where our difference lies. We all agree you should be governed by elected representatives. But I think we ought to keep to that constitution which we have now, because there is so much justice and reason and prudence in it. And if you merely on pretence of your birthright pretend that this constitution shall not stand in your way, it is the same principle to me, say I, as if for your better satisfaction you shall take hold of anything that another man calls his own.

RAINBOROUGH: Sir, I see it is impossible to have liberty without all property being taken away. If you will say it, it must be so. But I would fain know what the soldier hath fought for all this while.

IRETON: I will tell you —

RAINBOROUGH: He hath fought to enslave himself, to give power to men of riches, men of estates, to make himself a perpetual slave. We find none must be pressed for the army that have property. When these gentlemen fall out among themselves, they shall press the poor scrubs to come and kill one another for them.

IRETON: I will tell you what the soldier of this kingdom hath fought for. The danger that we stood in was that one man's will must be a law. The people have this right, that they should not be governed but by the representative of those that have the interest of the kingdom. In this way liberty may be had and property not be destroyed.

RICH: I hope it is not denied that any wise discreet man that hath preserved England is worthy of a voice in the government of it. The electorate should be amended in that sense and I think they will desire no more liberty.

CROMWELL: I confess I was most dissatisfied with that I heard Mr Sexby speak of any man here, because it did savour so much of will. But let us not spend so much time in debates. Everyone here would be willing that the representation be made better than it is. If we may but resolve on a committee, things may be done.

WILDMAN: I wonder that should be thought wilfulness in one man that is reason in another. I have not heard anything that doth satisfy me. I am not at all against a committee's meeting. But I think it is no fault in any man to refuse to sell his birthright.

SEXBY: I am sorry that my zeal to what I apprehend is good should be so ill resented. Do you not think it were a sad and miserable condition that we have fought all this time for nothing? All here, both great and small, do think that we fought for something. Many of us fought for those ends which, we since saw, were not those which caused us to venture all in the ship with you. It had been good in you to have advertised us of it, and I believe you would have had fewer under your command to have commanded. Concerning my making rents and divisions in this way. As an individual I could lie down and be trodden there; but truly I am sent by a regiment, and if I should not speak, guilt shall lie upon me. I shall be loath to make a rent and division, but unless I see this put to a vote, I despair of an issue.

RICH: I see you have a long dispute. I see both parties at a stand; and if we dispute here, both are lost.

CROMWELL: If you put this paper to the vote without any qualifications it will not pass freely. If we would have no

217

difference when we vote on the paper, it must be put with due qualifications. I have not heard Commissary General Ireton answered, not in a tittle. To bring this paper nearer a general satisfaction and bring us all to an understanding, I move for a committee.

INTERVAL

ACT TWO

DIGGERS

ONE OF THE ACTORS [*announces*]: Information of Henry Sanders, Walton-upon-Thames, April the sixteenth, sixteen hundred and forty-nine.

One Everard, Gerrard Winstanley, and three more, all living at Cobham, came to St George's Hill in Surrey and began to dig, and sowed the ground with parsnips and carrots and beans. By Friday last they were increased in number to twenty or thirty. They invite all to come in and help them, and promise them meat, drink and clothes.

WINSTANLEY [*announces*]: The true Levellers' standard advanced, sixteen hundred and forty-nine:

A declaration to the powers of England and to all the powers of the world, showing the cause why the common people of England have begun to dig up, manure and sow corn upon George Hill in Surrey. Take notice that England is not a free people till the poor that have no land have a free allowance to dig and labour the commons. It is the sword that brought in property and holds it up, and everyone upon recovery of the conquest ought to return into freedom again, or what benefit have the common people got by the victory over the king?

All men have stood for freedom; and now the common enemy has gone you are all like men in a mist, seeking for freedom, and know not where it is: and those of the richer sort of you that see it are afraid to own it. For freedom is the man that will turn the world upside down, therefore no wonder he hath enemies.

True freedom lies where a man receives his nourishment and that is in the use of the earth. A man had better have no body than have no food for it. True freedom lies in the true enjoyment of the earth. True religion and undefiled is to let every one quietly have earth to manure. There can be no universal liberty till this universal community be established.

1ST ACTOR [*announces*]: A Bill of Account of the most remarkable sufferings that the Diggers have met with since they began to dig the commons for the poor on George Hill in Surrey.

2ND ACTOR: We were fetched by above a hundred people who took away our spades, and some of them we never had again, and taken to prison at Walton.

3RD ACTOR: The dragonly enemy pulled down a house we had built and cut our spades to pieces.

4TH ACTOR: One of us had his head sore wounded, and a boy beaten. Some of us were beaten by the gentlemen, the sheriff looking on, and afterwards five were taken to White Lion prison and kept there about five weeks.

5TH ACTOR: We had all our corn spoilt, for the enemy was so mad that they tumbled the earth up and down and would suffer no corn to grow.

6TH ACTOR: Next day two soldiers and two or three men sent by the parson pulled down another house and turned an old man and his wife out of doors to lie in the field on a cold night.

1ST ACTOR: It is understood the General gave his consent that the soldiers should come to help beat off the Diggers, and it is true the soldiers came with the gentlemen and caused others to pull down our houses; but I think the soldiers were sorry to see what was done.

CLAXTON EXPLAINS

CLAXTON: Wherever I go I leave men behind surprised I no longer agree with them. But I can't stop. Ever since the day I walked over the hill to Wendover to hear the new preacher for the first time. And though I'd thought of going for weeks, the day I went I didn't think at all, I just put on my coat and started walking. I felt quite calm, as if nothing was happening, as if it was an easy thing to do, not something I'd laid awake over all night, so that I wondered if it even mattered to me. But as I walked I found my heart was pounding and my breath got short going up the hill. My body knew I was doing something amazing. I knew I was in the midst of something, I was doing it, not standing still worrying about it, I was simply walking over the hill to another preacher. I'd found everything in my life hard. But now it seemed everything must be this simple. I felt alone. I felt certain. I felt myself moving faster and faster, more and more certainly towards God. And I am alone, because my wife can't follow me. I send her money when I can. But my body is given to other women now for I have come to see that there is no sin but what man thinks is sin. So we can't be free from sin till we can commit it purely, as if it were no sin. Sometimes I lie or steal to show myself there is no lie or theft but in the mind, and I find it all so easy that I am called the Captain of the Rant, and still my heart pounds and my mouth is dry and I rush on towards the infinite nothing that is God.

BRIGGS WRITES A LETTER

STAR: Writing more letters? Our children grow up without us. Is there still no news of your wife? Do you think of leaving the army to look for her? Because if you don't go to Ireland, there's not much to do in the army now.

BRIGGS: Enough.

STAR: You make a mistake about Ireland. I understood two years ago, when the men didn't have their back pay, I was with you then. But now it's different. You were agitator of the regiment then and you still –

BRIGGS: I still am agitator of the regiment.

STAR: – Still think you're agitator of the regiment. I know that was a remarkable time for you. To be chosen out of so many. To stand up before the greatest in the country and be heard out. It's a council of officers now, you know that. You know an agitator means nothing. But you won't let it go. You keep on and on. The other men don't admire you for it.

BRIGGS: We're demanding the council be set up like before. You know that. With two agitators from each regiment.

STAR: I know you won't get it. Everyone knows. The other men laugh. You'd far better go home. Or if you still want to serve the cause of the saints, sign for Ireland. Cromwell himself is going, that says something. It's the same war we fought here. We'll be united again. We'll crush the papists just as we did in England. Antichrist will be exterminated.

BRIGGS: But don't you see, the Irish –

STAR: What, Briggs?

BRIGGS: The Irish are fighting the same —

STAR: The Irish are traitors. What?

BRIGGS: Nothing.

STAR: Show me the letter.

BRIGGS: What?

STAR: Show me the letter.

BRIGGS: Can't we even write a letter now without an officer looking it over?

STAR: It's not to your family.

BRIGGS: No. What then?

STAR: It's a plot.

BRIGGS: It's a list of proposals.

STAR: It's mutiny.

BRIGGS: It's a list of proposals. I've made them often enough.

STAR: You have, yes, and nobody reads them now. You draw up a third agreement of the people, and a fourth, and a tenth. It's a waste of time.

BRIGGS: I waste a few hours then. A few days. If I don't get what I fought for, the whole seven years has been wasted. What's a few weeks.

STAR: Show me the letter.

BRIGGS: No.

STAR: It wasn't an order. You have not refused to obey my order. But I won't be able to save you from mutiny if that's what you're set on.

BRIGGS: So we can't write now. We can't speak.

STAR: There's officers above me. Some of them think free talk doesn't go with discipline. I've always liked talk. I'd be sad to see us lose that privilege.

BRIGGS: It's not a privilege. It's a right.

STAR: If it's a right, Briggs, why was Arnold shot at Ware? Why were five troopers cashiered for petitioning the council of officers?

BRIGGS: Shall I tell you why?

STAR: It's not because I knew you before. The whole company is my friends. My rank leaves us equal before God. And yet my orders have been obeyed, because they have been seen for what

222

they are, good orders. But lately I am talked of by my superiors –

BRIGGS: Shall I tell you why the Levellers have been shot? Because now the officers have all the power, the army is as great a tyrant as the king was.

STAR: I can choose to act as if no one is below me. I hope I do. But I can't pretend no one is above me. I have superior officers and I must obey. I don't think you want me removed.

BRIGGS: You should join us against them.

STAR: If everyone says and does what he likes, what army is it? What discipline is there? In army or government. There must be some obedience. With consent, I would say, yes, but then you must consent, or – what? If every man is his own commander? There was a time when we all wanted the same. The army was united. I gave orders from God and you all heard the same orders from God in you. We fought as one man. But now we begin to be thousands of separate men.

BRIGGS: God is not with this army.

STAR: It is the army of saints.

BRIGGS: And God's saints shot Robert Lockyer for mutiny. By martial law. In time of peace. For demanding what God demanded we fight for.

STAR: If the army splits up –

BRIGGS: It has done.

STAR: If you Levellers split off into conspiracies away from the main army –

BRIGGS: It's you who've split off.

STAR: You risk the King's party getting back again.

BRIGGS: Would that be worse?

STAR: Briggs. We can still be a united army. Remember how we marched on London, singing the fall of Babylon?

BRIGGS: It's you who mutiny. Against God. Against the people.

STAR: Briggs.

BRIGGS: It's Cromwell mutinies.

STAR: Briggs.

BRIGGS: If I was Irish I'd be your enemy. And I am.

STAR: Briggs.

BRIGGS: Sir.

THE WAR IN IRELAND

ONE OF THE ACTORS [*announces*]: Soldier's standard to repair to, addressed to the army, April sixteen hundred and forty-nine.

Whatever they may tell you or however they may flatter you, there's danger lies at the bottom of this business for Ireland. Consider to what end you should hazard your lives against the Irish: have you not been fighting in England these seven years for rights and liberties you are yet deluded of? and will you go on to kill, slay and murder men, to make your officers as absolute lords and masters over Ireland as you have made them over England? If you intend not this, it concerns you in the first place to see that evil reformed here. Sending forces into Ireland is for nothing else but to make way by the blood of the army to extending their territories of power and tyranny. For the cause of the Irish natives in seeking their just freedoms, immunities and liberties is exactly the same with our cause here.

THE VICAR WELCOMES THE NEW LANDLORD

VICAR: Mr Star. I wonder if I am the first to welcome you as the new squire.

STAR: And the last I hope. I'm no squire.

VICAR: You've bought the land, that's all I meant.

STAR: I have bought the land, yes. Parliament is selling the confiscated land to parliament men. That does not make me the squire. Just as the country is better run by parliament than by the King, so estates will be better managed by parliament men than by royalists. You don't agree.

VICAR: It's not for a parson to say about running an estate.

STAR: No, but you bury the tenants when they starve. You'll have fewer to bury. This country can grow enough to feed every single person. Instead of importing corn we could grow enough to export it if all the land was efficiently made profitable. The price of corn will come down in a few years. Agricultural writers recommend growing clover on barren land. I will have the common ploughed and planted with clover.

VICAR: An excellent idea.

STAR: Nettles and thistles cleared, and a great crop.

VICAR: And the little huts cleared, the squatters' huts.

STAR: Squatters?

VICAR: On the common. These last two years. Everyone hopes that now the estate is properly managed again they will be moved on. They are not local people.

STAR: I haven't been down to the common. Well I'll speak to them. All over England waste land is being reclaimed. Even the fens. Many years ago before the war, Oliver Cromwell himself led tenants in protest against enclosing the fens. But now he sees, now we all see, that it is more important to provide corn for the nation than for a few tenants to fish and trap water-birds.

VICAR: Yes indeed. Yes indeed.

STAR: When I say enclose the commons, I don't mean in the old sense, as the old squire did. I mean to grow corn. To make efficient use of the land. To bring down the price of corn. I'm sure the tenants will understand when I explain it to them.

VICAR: They will do as they're told. I'm sure you'll have no trouble collecting the arrears of rent.

STAR: I know one of the reasons they haven't paid is because they've had soldiers billetted in every cottage. So of course I'll give them time to pay. There is some talk of landlords reducing rents by as much as the tenants have paid out on the soldiers.

VICAR: I have heard talk of that.

STAR: I hope very much they're not counting on it. It would make me responsible for the keep for six years of twenty men and would beggar the estate.

VICAR: I told them that. I told them the new squire wouldn't hear of it.

STAR: In their own interests. I couldn't afford seed corn. I need two new ploughs.

VICAR: I'm sure they know their own interest. They'll pay.

STAR: I don't want to evict anyone.

VICAR: No, indeed, give them time. Three months would be ample.

STAR: I thought six.

VICAR: That's very generous. The tenants will certainly bless you.

STAR: I thought I would send for them all to drink my health and I'll drink theirs.

VICAR: That is the custom with a new squire. It is what they expect.

STAR: Is it? It's what I thought I would do.

VICAR: Well, I can only say I welcome all the changes you are making. And I hope you won't make a change so unwelcome to the whole parish as to turn me away after so many years. I know the tenants here are as good and peace-loving as any in England, and I know they'll join me in supporting you in your plans to make this estate prosperous. It's been an unhappy time but the war is over. We are all glad to be at peace and back to normal.

STAR: It will be hard work. For the tenants and for me. I don't shrink from that. It is to God's glory that this land will make a profit.

VICAR: I'm sure it will.

STAR: Don't misunderstand me, Parson. Times have changed.

VICAR: I'm not against change, Mr Star. So long as there's no harm done.

A WOMAN LEAVES HER BABY

Two women. 1ST WOMAN *is carrying a baby.*

1ST WOMAN: You'll laugh.

2ND WOMAN: No?

1ST WOMAN: Now I'm here I can't do it.

2ND WOMAN: Waiting for that.

1ST WOMAN: Don't. Don't go. Don't be angry.

2ND WOMAN: We come all this way.

1ST WOMAN: We go back.

2ND WOMAN: Why we bother?

1ST WOMAN: We go back, quick, never mind.

2ND WOMAN: We come so they look after her.

1ST WOMAN: I can't.

2ND WOMAN: I know but just put her down.

1ST WOMAN: Too soon.

2ND WOMAN: Put her down. Just . . .

[*Silence.*]

2ND WOMAN: She die if you keep her.

1ST WOMAN: I can't.

[*Silence.*]

2ND WOMAN: What you do then? You got no milk. She not even crying now, see. That's not good. You en had one, I'm telling you, she dying.

[*Silence.*]

1ST WOMAN: If I drunk more water. Make more milk.

2ND WOMAN: Not without food. Not how ill you are.

[*Silence.*]

1ST WOMAN: What if nobody . . .?

2ND WOMAN: They will. It's a special house. It's a good town. The mayor himself. Picture inside on the wall with his chain. Mayor himself see her all right.

1ST WOMAN: Another day.

2ND WOMAN: She'll be dead.

1ST WOMAN: If she was bigger.

2ND WOMAN: You're not doing it for you. Do it for her. Wouldn't you die to have her live happy? Won't even put her down. It's for her.

1ST WOMAN: Could die. Can't put her down.

2ND WOMAN: Don't talk. Do it. Do it.

1ST WOMAN: If she was still inside me.

A BUTCHER TALKS TO HIS CUSTOMERS

BUTCHER: Two rabbits, madam, is two shillings, thank you. And sir? A capon? Was yesterday's veal good? Was it? Good. Tender was it? Juicy? Plenty of it? Fill your belly did it? Fill your belly? It can't have done, can it, or you wouldn't want a capon today. Nice capon here, make a fine dinner for half a dozen people. Giving your friends dinner tonight, sir? And another night they give you dinner. You're very generous and christian to each other. There's never a night you don't have dinner. Or do you eat it all yourself, sir? No? You look as if you do. You don't look hungry. You don't look as if you need a dinner. You look less like a man needing a dinner than anyone I've ever seen. What do you need it for? No, tell me. To stuff yourself, that's what

227

for. To make fat. And shit. When it could put a little good flesh on children's bones. It could be the food of life. If it goes into you, it's stink and death. So you can't have it. No, I said you can't have it, take your money back. You're not having meat again this week. You had your meat yesterday. Bacon on Monday. Beef on Sunday. Mutton chops on Saturday. There's no more meat for you. Porridge. Bread. Turnips. No meat for you this week. Not this year. You've had your lifetime's meat. All of you. All of you that can buy meat. You've had your meat. You've had their meat. You've had their meat that can't buy any meat. You've stolen their meat. Are you going to give it back? Are you going to put your hand in your pocket and give them back the price of their meat? I said give them back their meat. You cram yourselves with their children's meat. You cram yourselves with their dead children.

LOCKYER'S FUNERAL

ONE OF THE ACTORS: From *The Moderate*, a Leveller newspaper, April the twenty-ninth, sixteen forty-nine.

Mr Robert Lockyer, a Leveller leader, that was shot Friday last was this day brought through the heart of the city. The manner of his funeral was most remarkable, considering the person to be in no higher quality than a private trooper. The body was accompanied with many thousand citizens, who seemed much dejected. The trooper's horse was clothed all over with mourning and led by a footman (a funeral honour equal to a chief commander). The corpse was adorned with bundles of rosemary stained in blood, and the sword of the deceased with them. Most of this great number that attended the corpse had sea-green and black ribbons in their hat. By the time the corpse came to the new churchyard, some thousands of the higher sort, that said they would not endanger themselves to be publicly seen marching through the city, were there ready to attend it with the same colours of sea-green and black. Some people derided them with the name of Levellers. Others said that King Charles had not had half so many mourners to attend his corpse when interred, as this trooper.

A few weeks later at Burford, the Levellers were finally crushed.

THE MEETING

A drinking place. The DRUNK *sits apart from the rest.*

HOSKINS [*to* BRIGGS]: Come on, plenty to drink. Can't you smile? He wasn't like this last night.

BROTHERTON: What do I do?

COBBE: Anything you like. I worship you, more than the Virgin Mary.

HOSKINS: She was no virgin.

CLAXTON: Christ was a bastard.

HOSKINS: Still is a bastard.

BROTHERTON: I thought you said this was a prayer meeting.

CLAXTON: This is it. This is my one flesh.

COBBE [*to the* DRUNK]: Drinking by yourself? Move in with us, come on. Yes, we need you. Get out there when I tell you or I'll break your arm. That was God telling you.

CLAXTON: God's a great bully, I've noticed that. Do this. Do that. Shalt not. Drop you in the burning lake.

HOSKINS: Give us a sip. He won't give us a sip.

CLAXTON: He's not very godly. He needs praying.

HOSKINS: Let us pray. Or whatever.
   [*Silence.*]

BROTHERTON: When's he coming?

COBBE: Who?

BROTHERTON: The preacher.

COBBE: You're the preacher.

BROTHERTON: What? No. I can't.

HOSKINS: Don't frighten her.

CLAXTON: Anyone has anything to say from God, just say it.
   [*Silence.*]

HOSKINS: There was a preacher. But his head fell off.
   [*Silence.*]

CLAXTON: It's a fine shining day. Whatever troubles we have, the sky's not touched. A clear day. Let us not lose it. Let us remember the Levellers shot. Those at Burford. Will Thompson and his brother. Private Arnold shot at Ware.

HOSKINS: And the four prisoners in the tower just for writing . . .

BRIGGS: Avenge Robert Lockyer.

COBBE: Lockyer's blood. Robert Lockyer's blood. Lockyer's wounds.

BROTHERTON: I don't know these gentlemen. If they have money. Well if you haven't and you're in the common gaol, you're lucky if you don't die. But if they have money for the jailor he gives you a room. With a bed and a window. I was told by a man who'd spent all his money. If you've got money . . .

COBBE: Damn. Damn. Damn. Damn. Damn.

There's angels swear, angels with flowing hair, you'd think they were men, I've seen them. They say damn the churches, the bloody black clergy with their fat guts, damn their white hands. Damn the hellfire presbyterian hypocrites that call a thief a sinner, rot them in hell's jail. They say Christ's wounds, wounds, wounds, wounds. Stick your fingers in. Christ's arsehole. He had an arsehole. Christ shits on you rich. Christ shits. Shitting pissing spewing puking fucking Jesus Christ. Jesus fucking –

BROTHERTON: Is that from God?

COBBE: What did you say?

BROTHERTON: Is that from God?

COBBE: It is, yes. What does he say to you? Does he speak to you? What do you answer? He'll come and speak to you soon enough. The day he comes he'll speak to all of us. He'll come right up to you like this. He wants an answer. What do you say? Nothing? He'll damn and ram you down in the black pit. Is there nothing in you? What are you? Nothing? [*To* BRIGGS.] Is it nothing but a lifetime of false words, little games, devil's tricks, ways to get by in the world and keep safe? You're plastered over, thick shit mucky lies all over, and what's underneath? Where's your true word? Is there anyone left inside or are you shrivelled away to nothing? [*To each.*] What will you say? Speak up. What do you answer God? What do you answer? Answer. What do you answer?

HOSKINS: I love you.

COBBE: There. There.

[*He sits down.* BROTHERTON *laughs. Silence.*]

CLAXTON: I tell you justice. If every judge was hanged.

HOSKINS: I steal all I can. Rich steal from us. Everything they got's stolen. What's it mean 'Thou shalt not steal'? Not steal stolen goods?

COBBE: Riches is the cause of all wickeness. From the blood of Abel to those last Levellers shot. But God is coming, the mighty Leveller, Christ the chief of Levellers is at the door, and then we'll see levelling. Not sword levelling. Not man levelling. And they feared that. Now God is coming to level the hills and the valleys. Christ break the mountains.

[*Silence.* HOSKINS *holds out an apple.*]

HOSKINS: This is something by a farmer. Then by a stallholder. Then by me. It comes to me God's in it. If a man could be so perfect. Look at it.

[*She gives it to* BRIGGS, *who looks at it, then passes it back to her. She gives it to* BROTHERTON.]

BROTHERTON: I always like an apple if I can get it. I haven't been to church for a long time. I don't know if this is a church. It's a drinking place. I always hide on Sunday. They notice you in the street if everyone's in church so I go in the woods on Sunday. I can't see God in this. If God was in it, he'd have us whipped.

CLAXTON: It wouldn't have you whipped, it would bless you. It does bless you. Touch it again. It blesses you. And my hand. Touch my hand. What's the matter?

BROTHERTON: Nobody touches me.

CLAXTON: Why not?

BROTHERTON: They don't touch, I don't know why, nobody touches. I don't count hitting. Nobody's touched me since . . .

CLAXTON: Since what?

BROTHERTON: You don't want to touch me. Don't bother. Pass it on. Pass it on.

HOSKINS: Nobody's touched you since what?

BROTHERTON: It's not right.

CLAXTON: What's not right? Touching or not touching?

BROTHERTON: Both are not right. Pass it on.

CLAXTON: They are, they're both, whichever you want, when you want, is right. Do you want me to touch your hand?

BROTHERTON: No.

CLAXTON: That's right. God's in that too. God's in us. This form that I am is the representative of the whole creation. You are the representative of the whole creation. God's in this apple. He's nowhere else but in the creation. This is where he is.

[*He gives it to* COBBE.]

COBBE: I charge at coaches in the street. I shout at the great ones with my hat on. I proclaim the day of the Lord throughout Southwark. And what do they hear? If they could see God in this apple as I do now, God in the bread that they will not give to the poor who cry out day and night, Bread, bread, bread for the Lord's sake, if they could see it they would rush to the prisons, and they would bow to the poor wretches that are their own flesh, and say, 'Your humble servants, we set you free.'

[COBBE *gives it to the* DRUNK, *who eats it.*]

HOSKINS: There's a man eats God. There's a communion.

BROTHERTON: You don't often see someone eat. They eat when you're not looking.

BRIGGS: Friends. I have nothing from God. I'm sitting here. Nothing. If anyone can speak to my condition.

CLAXTON: You're a soldier?

BRIGGS: I was.

COBBE: A Leveller?

BRIGGS: I was.

CLAXTON: And now?

HOSKINS: Well, a drink would be best.

CLAXTON: You'll find something. I've been different things. When I was first a Seeker, everything shone. I thought the third age was coming, age of the spirit, age of the lily, everything shining, raindrops on the hedges shining in the sun, worlds of light. Well, we know how parliament betrayed us. Then how the army betrayed us. It was all a cheat.

HOSKINS: Preaching itself is a cheat.

CLAXTON: And then I saw even the Seekers were wrong. Because while I was waiting for God, he was here already. So God was first in the king. Then in parliament. Then in the army. And now he has left all government. And shows himself naked. In us.

BRIGGS: We were the army of saints.

CLAXTON: Let it go. Move on. God moves so fast now.

HOSKINS: I try to be sad with you but I can't. King Jesus is coming in clouds of glory in a garment dyed red with blood, and the saints in white linen riding on white horses. It's for next year. Now is just a strange time between Antichrist going and Christ coming, so what do you expect in a time like this? There's been nothing like it before and there never will be again. So what's it matter now if we've no work and no food or can't get parliament like we want? It's only till next year. Then Christ will be here in his body like a man and he'll be like a king only you can talk to him. And he's a spirit too and that's in us and it's getting stronger and stronger. And that's why you see men and women shining now, everything sparkles because God's not far above us like he used to be when preachers stood in the way, he's started some great happening and we're in it now.

CLAXTON: St Paul to Timothy, 'Let the woman learn in silence.'

HOSKINS: Jone Hoskins to St Paul, fuck off you silly old bugger.

> [*They laugh and start getting food out.* CLAXTON *holds out food.*]

CLAXTON: Christ's body.

BROTHERTON: I'm afraid I haven't anything.

CLAXTON: There's plenty.

> [HOSKINS *holds out wine.*]

HOSKINS: This is Christ's blood.

CLAXTON [*to* BROTHERTON]: When did you last eat? Eat slowly now.

BRIGGS: Christ will not come. I don't believe it. Everything I've learnt these seven years. He will not come in some bloody red robe and you all put on white frocks, that will not happen. All I've learnt, how to get things done, that wasn't for nothing. I don't believe this is the last days. England will still be here in hundreds of years. And people working so hard they can't grasp how it happens and can't take hold of their own lives, like us till we had this chance, and we're losing it now, as we sit here, every minute. Jesus Christ isn't going to change it.

CLAXTON: He may not be coming in red.

BRIGGS: He's not coming at all.

CLAXTON: But in us –

233

BRIGGS: No, not at all.

HOSKINS: He's coming in clouds of glory and the saints –

BRIGGS: No, no, no.

COBBE: Do you think God would do all this for nothing? Think of the dead. For nothing? Why did he call me to warn London? What sort of God would he be if he didn't come now?

BRIGGS: No God at all.

CLAXTON: But in us. In us. I know there's no heaven or hell, not places to go, but in us. I know the Bible was written by man and most of it to trick us. I know there's no God or devil outside what's in creation. But in us. I know we can be perfect.

BRIGGS: Then we must do it.

[COBBE *takes off his coat and throws it at* BRIGGS's *feet.*]

COBBE: My coat's yours. And I hope yours is mine. We'll all live together, one family, one marriage, one flesh in God. That's what we do.

HOSKINS: Yes, everything in common.

COBBE: All things common. Or the plague of God will consume whatever you have.

CLAXTON: All goods in common, yes, and our bodies in common –

BRIGGS: No.

HOSKINS: Yes, we'll have no property in the flesh. My wife, that's property. My husband, that's property. All men are one flesh and I can lie with any man as my husband and that's no sin because all men are one man, all my husband's one flesh.

COBBE: I, the Lord, say once more, deliver deliver my money which you have to cripples, thieves, whores, or I will torment you day and night, saith the Lord.

CLAXTON: We'll take the land, all the land, and Christ will come, wait, I have something from God, Christ will come in this sense. He will come in everyone becoming perfect so the landlords all repent stealing the land. Sin is only the dark side of God. So when his light blazes everywhere, their greed will vanish – and that's how evil will go into the pit. Nobody damned, nobody lost, nobody cast out. But Antichrist cast out of us so that we become perfect Christ.

HOSKINS: Perfect men, perfect Christ in the street, I've seen them.

CLAXTON: The rich will be broken out of the hell they are, however they howl to stay there, and when they're out in the light they'll be glad. They'll join us pulling down the hedges.

BRIGGS: The landlords where they were digging at Cobham called the army in. And the soldiers stood by while the diggers' houses were pulled down, their tools destroyed, the corn tramped so it won't grow, men beaten and dragged off to prison. The landlords gave the soldiers ten shillings for drink. Does that sound like the landlords joining us? Does that sound like heaven on earth? I've a friend wounded in Ireland and nearly mad. When they burned the church at Drogheda he heard a man inside crying out, 'God damn me, I burn, I burn.' Is that heaven on earth? Or is it hell?

BROTHERTON: It's hell, life is hell, my life is hell. I can't get out but I'll pull them all in with me.

HOSKINS: No, wait, just wait, you'll see when Christ comes –

BRIGGS: He's never coming, damn him.

COBBE: How we know for certain that God is coming is because of the strange work he has set us on. Who can live through one day the way he used to? I've seen poor men all my life. Last week I met a poor man, the ugliest man I've ever seen, he had two little holes where his nose should be. I said to him, 'Are you poor?' And he said, 'Yes sir, very poor.' I began to shake and I said to him again, 'Are you poor?' 'Yes, very poor.' And a voice spoke inside me and said, 'It's a poor wretch, give him twopence.' But that was the voice of the whore of Babylon and I would not listen. And again, 'It's a poor wretch, give him sixpence, and that's enough for a knight to give one poor man and you a preacher without tithes and never know when you'll get a penny; think of your children; true love begins at home.' So I put my hand in my pocket and took out a shilling, and said, 'Give me sixpence and here's a shilling for you.' He said, 'I can't, I haven't a penny.' And I said, 'I'm sorry to hear that. I would have given you something if you could have changed my money.' And he said, 'God bless you.' So I was riding on when the voice spoke in me again, so that I rode back and told him I would leave sixpence for him in the next town at a house I thought he might know. But then, suddenly, the plague of God fell into my pocket and the rust of my silver rose against me, and I was cast into the lake of fire and brimstone. And all the money I had, every penny, I took out of my pocket and thrust into his hands. I hadn't eaten all day, I had nine more miles to ride, it was raining, the horse was lame, I was sure to need money before the night. And I rode away full of trembling joy, feeling the sparkles of a great glory round me. And then God made me turn my horse's head and I saw the poor wretch staring after me, and I was made to take off my hat and bow to him seven times. And I rode back to him again and said, 'Because I am a king I have done this, but you need not tell anyone.'

HOSKINS, CLAXTON: Amen.

BRIGGS: That man will die without his birthright. I've done all I can and it's not enough.

CLAXTON: It's not over, there's more, God hasn't finished.

BRIGGS: I'll tell you who's with God.

[*He nods at the* DRUNK. HOSKINS *laughs, kisses him, gives him drink.*]

BROTHERTON: No I can't. I'm not one of you, I try, you're very kind, I'm not one of you, I'm not one flesh. I'm damned, I know it.

COBBE: You're in hell now but you can come out. Suddenly, suddenly you are out.

BROTHERTON: I mustn't come in a place where God is. It's your fault bringing me here, I'm no good here, I can't be here –

COBBE: We don't want any filthy plaguey holiness. We want base things. And the baseness confounds the false holiness into nothing. And then, only then, you're like a new-born child in the hands of eternity, picked up, put down, not knowing if you're clean or dirty, good or evil.

BROTHERTON: No, I'm wicked, all women are wicked, and I'm –

HOSKINS: It's a man wrote the Bible.

CLAXTON: All damnation is, listen, all it is. Sin is not cast out but cast in, cast deep into God.

BROTHERTON: No I don't want to.

236

CLAXTON: As cloth is dyed in a vat to a new colour, the sin is changed in God's light into light itself.

BROTHERTON: No.

CLAXTON: That's all damnation is.

BROTHERTON: Let me go.

CLAXTON: It's only God.

BROTHERTON: I must be punished.

HOSKINS: What have you done?

BROTHERTON: Let me go.

COBBE: No, what did you do? God is in me, asking you, God is asking, I am perfect Christ asking why you damn yourself, why you hold yourself back from me?

BROTHERTON: Don't touch me. I'm evil.

BRIGGS: There's nothing you can have done.

CLAXTON: There's no sin except what you think is sin.

HOSKINS: God makes it all, he makes us do it all, he can't make us sin. The men that crucified Christ, Christ made them do it.

BROTHERTON: The devil, the devil's got me.

COBBE: A fart for the devil.

HOSKINS: Don't be frightened. We've got you.

CLAXTON: Sin again, do the same sin as if it were no sin –

HOSKINS: Sin to God's glory.

CLAXTON: Then you'll be free from sin.

COBBE: You're in heaven, look, you're shining.

BROTHERTON: No, how can I do it again? I did it then when I did it. It was a sin. I knew it was. I killed my baby. The same day it was born. I had a bag. I put it in the ditch. There wasn't any noise. The bag moved. I never went back that way.

BRIGGS: That's not your sin. It's one more of theirs. Damn them.

COBBE: God bows to you. God worships you. Who did he come to earth for? For you. That's everyone's grief, we take it.

BROTHERTON: He wasn't baptised. He's lost. I lost him.

CLAXTON: Baptism is over.

HOSKINS: No, wait, sit down, listen –

CLAXTON: A baby doesn't need baptism to make him God, he is God. He's not born evil. He's born good. He's born God. When he died it was like a pail of water poured back in the ocean. He's lost to himself but all the water's God.

237

COBBE: Believe us.

HOSKINS: He's our fellow creature, and you're our fellow creature.

CLAXTON: You're God, you, you're God, no one's more God than you if you could know it yourself, you're lovely, you're perfect –

BROTHERTON: No, I'm nobody's fellow creature.

HOSKINS: God now.

COBBE: Behold, I come quickly, saith the Lord.

CLAXTON: God's going through everything.

BRIGGS: Christ, don't waste those seven years we fought.

CLAXTON: Everything's changing. Everything's moving. God's going right through everything.

COBBE: And God for your sin confounds you into unspeakable glory, your life, your self.

HOSKINS: God has you now.

CLAXTON: Nothing we know will be the same.

BRIGGS: Christ, help her.

CLAXTON: We won't know our own faces. We won't know the words we speak. New words –

COBBE: Believe us.

BRIGGS: Be safe.

HOSKINS: God has you now.

CLAXTON: Everything new, everything for the first time, everything starting –

BROTHERTON: Yes.

BRIGGS: Be safe.

BROTHERTON: Yes.

BRIGGS: So it's over.

BROTHERTON: Yes.

HOSKINS: There.

BRIGGS: You can be touched. It's not so terrible. I'll tell you what I'll do. Avenge your baby and Robert Lockyer. I'll make Cromwell set England free. And how? Easy. Kill him. Killing's no murder. He wanted to free England. That's how he'll do it. Dead.

COBBE: God won't be stopped.

DRUNK: I'm God. I'm God.

BRIGGS: Yes, amen, look who's God now.

DRUNK: I'm God. And I'm the devil. I'm the serpent. I'm in heaven now and I'm in hell.

CLAXTON: Amen.

COBBE: You are God. Every poor man.

DRUNK: I'm in hell, I'm not afraid. I seen worse things. If the devil come at me I kick him up the arse.

CLAXTON: And that's the devil gone.

HOSKINS: Amen, no devil.

DRUNK: I'm in heaven. And I go up to God. And I say, You great tosspot, I'm as good a man as you, as good a God as you.

CLAXTON: And so are we all.

HOSKINS: And so is everyone in England.

DRUNK: Plenty of beer in heaven. Angels all drunk. Devils drunk. Devils and angels all fornicating.

COBBE: You are God, I am God, and I love you, God loves God.

CLAXTON: Oh God, let me be God, be clear in me –

HOSKINS: All the light now –

COBBE: Sparks of glory under these ashes –

HOSKINS: Light shining from us –

DRUNK: And I say to God, get down below on to earth. Live in my cottage. Pay my rent. Look after my children, mind, they're hungry. And don't ever beat my wife or I'll strike you down.

[BROTHERTON *gets out some food.*]

BROTHERTON: I didn't give you – I kept it back – let me give you –

CLAXTON: Yes, yes, God's here, look, God now –

DRUNK: And I say to God, Wait here in my house. You can have a drink while you're waiting. But wait. Wait. Wait till I come.

ALL [*sing Ecclesiastes 5, vii–x, xii.*]:

If thou seest the oppression of the poor, and violent perverting of judgement and justice in a province, marvel not at the matter: for he that is higher than the highest regardeth; and there be higher than they.

Moreover the profit of the earth is for all: the king himself is served by the field.

He that loveth silver shan't be satisfied with silver; nor he that loveth abundance with increase: this is also vanity.

The sleep of the labouring man is sweet, whether he eat little or much; but the abundance of the rich will not suffer him to sleep.

AFTER

HOSKINS: I think what happened was, Jesus Christ did come and nobody noticed. It was time but we somehow missed it. I don't see how.

COBBE: It was for me, to stop me, they passed the Blasphemy Act. I was never God in the sense they asked me at my trial did I claim to be God. I could have answered no quite truthfully but I threw apples and pears round the council chamber, that seemed a good answer. Dr Higham. I changed my name after the restoration.

BROTHERTON: Stole two loaves yesterday. They caught another woman. They thought she did it, took her away. Bastards won't catch me.

DRUNK: The day the king came back there was bread and cheese and beer given free. I went twice. Nobody noticed. Everyone was drunk the day the king came back.

BRIGGS: I worked all right in a shop for a while. The mercer had been in the army, he put up with me. Then I started giving things away. If a boy stole, I couldn't say anything. So when I left I thought I must do something practical. I decided to bring the price of corn down. A few people eat far too much. So if a few people ate far too little that might balance. Then there would be enough corn and the price would come down. I gave up meat first, then cheese and eggs. I lived on a little porridge and vegetables, then I gave up the porridge and stopped cooking the vegetables. It was easier because I was living out. I ate what I could find but not berries and nuts because so many people want those and I do well with sorrell leaves and dandelion. But grass. It was hard to get my body to take grass. It got very ill. It wouldn't give in to grass. But I forced it on. And now it will. There's many kinds, rye grass, meadow grass, fescue. These two years I've been able to eat grass. Very sweet. People come to watch. They can, I can't stop them. I'm living in a field that belongs to a gentleman that comes sometimes, and sometimes he brings a friend to show. He's not unkind but I don't like to see him. I stand where I am stock still and wait till he's gone.

CLAXTON: There's an end of outward preaching now. An end of perfection. There may be a time. I went to the Barbados. I sometimes hear from the world that I have forsaken. I see it fraught with tidings of the same clamour, strife and contention that abounded when I left it. I give it the hearing and that's all. My great desire is to see and say nothing.

CLOUD NINE

Cloud Nine

Cloud Nine was written for Joint Stock Theatre Group in 1978-79. The company's usual work method is to set up a workshop in which the writer, director and actors research a particular subject. The writer then goes away to write the play, before returning to the company for a rehearsal and rewrite period. In the case of *Cloud Nine* the workshop lasted for three weeks, the writing period for twelve, and the rehearsal for six.

The workshop for *Cloud Nine* was about sexual politics. This meant that the starting point for our research was to talk about ourselves and share our very different attitudes and experiences. We also explored stereotypes and role reversals in games and improvisations, read books and talked to other people. Though the play's situations and characters were not developed in the workshop, it draws deeply on this material, and I wouldn't have written the same play without it.

When I came to write the play, I returned to an idea that had been touched on briefly in the workshop – the parallel between colonial and sexual oppression, which Genet calls 'the colonial or feminine mentality of interiorised repression'. So the first act of *Cloud Nine* takes place in Victorian Africa, where Clive, the white man, imposes his ideals on his family and the natives. Betty, Clive's wife, is played by a man because she wants to be what men want her to be, and, in the same way, Joshua, the black servant, is played by a white man because he wants to be what whites want him to be. Betty does not value herself as a woman, nor does Joshua value himself as a black. Edward, Clive's son, is played by a woman for a different reason – partly to do with the stage convention of having boys played by women (Peter Pan, radio plays, etc.) and partly with highlighting the way Clive tries to impose traditional male behaviour on him. Clive struggles throughout the act to maintain the world he wants to see – a faithful wife, a manly son. Harry's homosexuality is reviled, Ellen's is invisible. Rehearsing the play for the first time, we were initially taken by how funny the first act was and then by the painfulness of the relationships – which then became more funny than when they had seemed purely farcical.

The second act is set in London in 1979 – this is where I wanted the play to end up, in the changing sexuality of our own time. Betty is middle-aged, Edward and Victoria have grown up. A hundred years have passed, but for the characters only twenty-five years. There were two reasons for this. I felt the first act would be stronger set in Victorian times, at the height of colonialism, rather than in Africa during the 1950s. And when the company talked about their childhoods and the attitudes to sex and marriage that they had been given when they were young, everyone felt that they had received very conventional, almost Victorian expectations and that they had made great changes and discoveries in their lifetimes.

The first act, like the society it shows, is male dominated and firmly structured. In the second act, more energy comes from the women and the gays. The uncertainties and changes of society, and a more feminine and less authoritarian feeling, are reflected in the looser structure of the act. Betty, Edward and Victoria all change from the rigid positions they had been left in by the first act, partly because of their encounters with Gerry and Lin.

In fact, all the characters in this act change a little for the better. If men are finding it hard to keep control in the first act, they are finding it hard to let go in the second: Martin dominates Victoria, despite his declarations of sympathy for feminism, and the bitter end of colonialism is apparent in Lin's soldier brother, who dies in Northern Ireland. Betty is now played by a woman, as she gradually becomes real to herself. Cathy is played by a man, partly as a simple reversal of Edward being played by a woman, partly because the size and presence of a man on stage seemed appropriate to the emotional force of young children, and partly, as with Edward, to show more clearly the issues involved in learning what is considered correct behaviour for a girl.

It is essential for Joshua to be played by a white, Betty (I) by a man, Edward (I) by a woman, and Cathy by a man. The soldier should be played by the actor who plays Cathy. The doubling of Mrs Saunders and Ellen is not intended to make a point so much as for sheer fun – and of course to keep the company to seven in each act. The doubling can be done in any way that seems right for any particular production. The first production went Clive-Cathy, Betty-Edward, Edward-Betty, Maud-Victoria, Mrs Saunders/Ellen-Lin, Joshua-Gerry, Harry-Martin. When we did the play again, at the Royal Court in 1980, we decided to try a different doubling: Clive-Edward, Betty-Gerry, Edward-Victoria, Maud-Lin, Mrs Saunders/Ellen-Betty, Joshua-Cathy, Harry-Martin. I've a slight preference for the first way because I like seeing Clive become Cathy, and enjoy the Edward-Betty connections. Some doublings aren't practicable, but any way of doing the doubling seems to set up some interesting resonances between the two acts.

C.C. 1983

Characters

ACT ONE

CLIVE, a colonial administrator
BETTY, his wife, played by a man
JOSHUA, his black servant, played by a white
EDWARD, his son, played by a woman
VICTORIA, his daughter, a dummy
MAUD, his mother-in-law
ELLEN, Edward's governess
HARRY BAGLEY, an explorer
MRS SAUNDERS, a widow

ACT TWO

BETTY
EDWARD, her son
VICTORIA, her daughter
MARTIN, Victoria's husband
LIN
CATHY, Lin's daughter age 5, played by a man
GERRY, Edward's lover

Except for Cathy, characters in Act II are played by actors of their own sex.

Act One takes place in a British colony in Africa in Victorian times.
Act Two takes place in London in 1979. But for the characters it is twenty-five years later.

Cloud Nine was first performed at Dartington College of Arts on Wednesday 14 February 1979 by the Joint Stock Theatre Group, then on tour and at the Royal Court Theatre, London, with the following cast:

ACT ONE

CLIVE	Anthony Sher
BETTY	Jim Hooper
JOSHUA	Tony Rohr
EDWARD	Julie Covington
MAUD	Miriam Margolyes
ELLEN/MRS SAUNDERS	Carole Hayman
HARRY BAGLEY	William Hoyland

ACT TWO

BETTY	Julie Covington
EDWARD	Jim Hooper
VICTORIA	Miriam Margolyes
MARTIN	William Hoyland
LIN	Carole Hayman
CATHY	Anthony Sher
GERRY	Tony Rohr
Director	Max Stafford-Clark
Assistant Director	Les Waters
Designer	Peter Hartwell
Musical Director	Andy Roberts
Lighting Designer	Robin Myerscough-Walker

The text

The first edition of *Cloud Nine* (Pluto/Joint Stock 1979) went to press before the end of rehearsal. Further changes were made within the first week or two of production, and these were incorporated in the Pluto/Joint Stock/Royal Court edition 1980. This edition also went to press during rehearsal, so although it may include some small changes made for that production, others don't turn up till the Pluto Plays edition 1983, which also includes a few changes from the American production, a few lines cut here or reinstated there. Other changes for the American production can be found in French's American acting edition – the main ones are the position of Betty's monologue and some lines of the 'ghosts'. For the Fireside Bookclub and Methuen Inc (1984) in America I did another brushing up, not very different from Pluto '83, and I have kept almost the same text for this edition. The scenes I tinker with most are the flogging scene and Edward's and Gerry's last scene – I no longer know what's the final version except by looking at the text.

There's a problem with the Maud and Ellen reappearances in Act Two. If Ellen is doubled with Betty, obviously only Maud can appear. Equally Maud-Betty would mean only Ellen could, though that seems a dull doubling. This text gives both Maud and Ellen. In the production at the Court in 1981 only Maud appeared and she has some extra lines so she can talk about sex as well as work; they can be found in Pluto 1983.

C.C. 1984

ACT ONE

SCENE ONE

Low bright sun. Verandah. Flagpole with union jack. The Family — CLIVE, BETTY, EDWARD, VICTORIA, MAUD, ELLEN, JOSHUA

ALL [*sing.*]:
Come gather, sons of England, come gather in your pride.
Now meet the world united, now face it side by side;
Ye who the earth's wide corners, from veldt to prairie, roam.
From bush and jungle muster all who call old England 'home'.
Then gather round for England,
Rally to the flag,
From North and South and East and West
Come one and all for England!

CLIVE:
This is my family. Though far from home
We serve the Queen wherever we may roam
I am a father to the natives here,
And father to my family so dear.
    [*He presents* BETTY. *She is played by a man.*]
My wife is all I dreamt a wife should be,
And everything she is she owes to me.

BETTY:
I live for Clive. The whole aim of my life
Is to be what he looks for in a wife.
I am a man's creation as you see,
And what men want is what I want to be.
    [CLIVE *presents* JOSHUA. *He is played by a white.*]

CLIVE:
My boy's a jewel. Really has the knack.
You'd hardly notice that the fellow's black.

JOSHUA:
My skin is black but oh my soul is white.
I hate my tribe. My master is my light.

251

I only live for him. As you can see,
What white men want is what I want to be.

[CLIVE *presents* EDWARD. *He is played by a woman.*]

CLIVE:

My son is young. I'm doing all I can
To teach him to grow up to be a man.

EDWARD:

What father wants I'd dearly like to be.
I find it rather hard as you can see.

[CLIVE *presents* VICTORIA, *who is a dummy,* MAUD, *and* ELLEN.]

CLIVE:

No need for any speeches by the rest.
My daughter, mother-in-law, and governess.

ALL [*sing.*]:

O'er countless numbers she, our Queen,
Victoria reigns supreme;
O'er Afric's sunny plains, and o'er
Canadian frozen stream;
The forge of war shall weld the chains of brotherhood secure;
So to all time in ev'ry clime our Empire shall endure.

Then gather round for England,
Rally to the flag,
From North and South and East and West
Come one and all for England!

[*All go except* BETTY. CLIVE *comes.*]

BETTY: Clive?

CLIVE: Betty. Joshua!

[JOSHUA *comes with a drink for* CLIVE.]

BETTY: I thought you would never come. The day's so long without you.

CLIVE: Long ride in the bush.

BETTY: Is anything wrong? I heard drums.

CLIVE: Nothing serious. Beauty is a damned good mare. I must get some new boots sent from home. These ones have never been right. I have a blister.

BETTY: My poor dear foot.

CLIVE: It's nothing.

BETTY: Oh but it's sore.

CLIVE: We are not in this country to enjoy ourselves. Must have ridden fifty miles. Spoke to three different headmen who would all gladly chop off each other's heads and wear them round their waists.

BETTY: Clive!

CLIVE: Don't be squeamish, Betty, let me have my joke. And what has my little dove done today?

BETTY: I've read a little.

CLIVE: Good. Is it good?

BETTY: It's poetry.

CLIVE: You're so delicate and sensitive.

BETTY: And I played the piano. Shall I send for the children?

CLIVE: Yes, in a minute. I've a piece of news for you.

BETTY: Good news?

CLIVE: You'll certainly think it's good. A visitor.

BETTY: From home?

CLIVE: No. Well of course originally from home.

BETTY: Man or woman?

CLIVE: Man.

BETTY: I can't imagine.

CLIVE: Something of an explorer. Bit of a poet. Odd chap but brave as a lion. And a great admirer of yours.

BETTY: What do you mean? Whoever can it be?

CLIVE: With an H and a B. And does conjuring tricks for little Edward.

BETTY: That sounds like Mr Bagley.

CLIVE: Harry Bagley.

BETTY: He certainly doesn't admire me, Clive, what a thing to say. How could I possibly guess from that. He's hardly explored anything at all, he's just been up a river, he's done nothing at all compared to what you do. You should have said a heavy drinker and a bit of a bore.

CLIVE: But you like him well enough. You don't mind him coming?

BETTY: Anyone at all to break the monotony.

CLIVE: But you have your mother. You have Ellen.

BETTY: Ellen is a governess. My mother is my mother.

CLIVE: I hoped when she came to visit she would be company for you.

BETTY: I don't think mother is on a visit. I think she lives with us.

CLIVE: I think she does.

BETTY: Clive you are so good.

CLIVE: But are you bored my love?

BETTY: It's just that I miss you when you're away. We're not in this country to enjoy ourselves. If I lack society that is my form of service.

CLIVE: That's a brave girl. So today has been all right? No fainting? No hysteria?

BETTY: I have been very tranquil.

CLIVE: Ah what a haven of peace to come home to. The coolth, the calm, the beauty.

BETTY: There is one thing, Clive, if you don't mind.

CLIVE: What can I do for you, my dear?

BETTY: It's about Joshua.

CLIVE: I wouldn't leave you alone here with a quiet mind if it weren't for Joshua.

BETTY: Joshua doesn't like me.

CLIVE: Joshua has been my boy for eight years. He has saved my life. I have saved his life. He is devoted to me and to mine. I have said this before.

BETTY: He is rude to me. He doesn't do what I say. Speak to him.

CLIVE: Tell me what happened.

BETTY: He said something improper.

CLIVE: Well, what?

BETTY: I don't like to repeat it.

CLIVE: I must insist.

BETTY: I had left my book inside on the piano. I was in the hammock. I asked him to fetch it.

CLIVE: And did he not fetch it?

BETTY: Yes, he did eventually.

CLIVE: And what did he say?

BETTY: Clive –

CLIVE: Betty.

BETTY: He said Fetch it yourself. You've got legs under that dress.

CLIVE: Joshua!

[JOSHUA *comes*.]

Joshua, madam says you spoke impolitely to her this afternoon.

JOSHUA: Sir?

CLIVE: When she asked you to pass her book from the piano.

JOSHUA: She has the book, sir.

BETTY: I have the book now, but when I told you –

CLIVE: Betty, please, let me handle this. You didn't pass it at once?

JOSHUA: No sir, I made a joke first.

CLIVE: What was that?

JOSHUA: I said my legs were tired, sir. That was funny because the book was very near, it would not make my legs tired to get it.

BETTY: That's not true.

JOSHUA: Did madam hear me wrong?

CLIVE: She heard something else.

JOSHUA: What was that, madam?

BETTY: Never mind.

CLIVE: Now Joshua, it won't do you know. Madam doesn't like that kind of joke. You must do what madam says, just do what she says and don't answer back. You know your place, Joshua. I don't have to say any more.

JOSHUA: No sir.

BETTY: I expect an apology.

JOSHUA: I apologise, madam.

CLIVE: There now. It won't happen again, my dear. I'm very shocked Joshua, very shocked.

[CLIVE *winks at* JOSHUA, *unseen by* BETTY. JOSHUA *goes*.]

CLIVE: I think another drink, and send for the children, and isn't that Harry riding down the hill? Wave, wave. Just in time before dark. Cuts it fine, the blighter. Always a hothead, Harry.

BETTY: Can he see us?

CLIVE: Stand further forward. He'll see your white dress. There, he waved back.

BETTY: Do you think so? I wonder what he saw. Sometimes sunset is so terrifying I can't bear to look.

CLIVE: It makes me proud. Elsewhere in the empire the sun is rising.

BETTY: Harry looks so small on the hillside.

[ELLEN *comes*.]

ELLEN: Shall I bring the children?

BETTY: Shall Ellen bring the children?

CLIVE: Delightful.

BETTY: Yes, Ellen, make sure they're warm. The night air is deceptive. Victoria was looking pale yesterday.

CLIVE: My love.

[MAUD *comes from inside the house*.]

MAUD: Are you warm enough Betty?

BETTY: Perfectly.

MAUD: The night air is deceptive.

BETTY: I'm quite warm. I'm too warm.

MAUD: You're not getting a fever, I hope? She's not strong, you know, Clive. I don't know how long you'll keep her in this climate.

CLIVE: I look after Her Majesty's demains. I think you can trust me to look after my wife.

[ELLEN *comes carrying* VICTORIA, *age 2.* EDWARD, *aged 9, lags behind.*

BETTY: Victoria, my pet, say good evening to papa.

[CLIVE *takes* VICTORIA *on his knee*.]

CLIVE: There's my sweet little Vicky. What have we done today?

BETTY: She wore Ellen's hat.

CLIVE: Did she wear Ellen's big hat like a lady? What a pretty.

BETTY: And Joshua gave her a piggy back. Tell papa. Horsy with Joshy?

ELLEN: She's tired.

CLIVE: Nice Joshy played horsy. What a big strong Joshy. Did you have a gallop? Did you make him stop and go? Not very chatty tonight are we?

BETTY: Edward, say good evening to papa.

CLIVE: Edward my boy. Have you done your lessons well?

EDWARD: Yes papa.

256

CLIVE: Did you go riding?

EDWARD: Yes papa.

CLIVE: What's that you're holding?

BETTY: It's Victoria's doll. What are you doing with it, Edward?

EDWARD: Minding her.

BETTY: Well I should give it to Ellen quickly. You don't want papa to see you with a doll.

CLIVE: No, we had you with Victoria's doll once before, Edward.

ELLEN: He's minding it for Vicky. He's not playing with it.

BETTY: He's not playing with it, Clive. He's minding it for Vicky.

CLIVE: Ellen minds Victoria, let Ellen mind the doll.

ELLEN: Come, give it to me.

[ELLEN *takes the doll.*]

EDWARD: Don't pull her about. Vicky's very fond of her. She likes me to have her.

BETTY: He's a very good brother.

CLIVE: Yes, it's manly of you Edward, to take care of your little sister. We'll say no more about it. Tomorrow I'll take you riding with me and Harry Bagley. Would you like that?

EDWARD: Is he here?

CLIVE: He's just arrived. There Betty, take Victoria now. I must go and welcome Harry.

[CLIVE *tosses* VICTORIA *to* BETTY, *who gives her to* ELLEN.]

EDWARD: Can I come, papa?

BETTY: Is he warm enough?

EDWARD: Am I warm enough?

CLIVE: Never mind the women, Ned. Come and meet Harry.

[*They go. The women are left. There is a silence.*]

MAUD: I daresay Mr Bagley will be out all day and we'll see nothing of him.

BETTY: He plays the piano. Surely he will sometimes stay at home with us.

MAUD: We can't expect it. The men have their duties and we have ours.

BETTY: He won't have seen a piano for a year. He lives a very rough life.

ELLEN: Will it be exciting for you, Betty?

MAUD: Whatever do you mean, Ellen?

ELLEN: We don't have very much society.

BETTY: Clive is my society.

MAUD: It's time Victoria went to bed.

ELLEN: She'd like to stay up and see Mr Bagley.

MAUD: Mr Bagley can see her tomorrow.

[ELLEN *goes.*]

MAUD: You let that girl forget her place, Betty.

BETTY: Mother, she is governess to my son. I know what her place is. I think my friendship does her good. She is not very happy.

MAUD: Young women are never happy.

BETTY: Mother, what a thing to say.

MAUD: Then when they're older they look back and see that comparatively speaking they were ecstatic.

BETTY: I'm perfectly happy.

MAUD: You are looking very pretty tonight. You were such a success as a young girl. You have made a most fortunate marriage. I'm sure you will be an excellent hostess to Mr Bagley.

BETTY: I feel quite nervous at the thought of entertaining.

MAUD: I can always advise you if I'm asked.

BETTY: What a long time they're taking. I always seem to be waiting for the men.

MAUD: Betty you have to learn to be patient. I am patient. My mama was very patient.

[CLIVE *approaches, supporting* CAROLINE SAUNDERS.]

CLIVE: It is a pleasure. It is an honour. It is positively your duty to seek my help. I would be hurt, I would be insulted by any show of independence. Your husband would have been one of my dearest friends if he had lived. Betty, look who has come, Mrs Saunders. She has ridden here all alone, amazing spirit. What will you have? Tea or something stronger? Let her lie down, she is overcome. Betty, you will know what to do.

[MRS SAUNDERS *lies down.*]

MAUD: I knew it. I heard drums. We'll be killed in our beds.

CLIVE: Now, please, calm yourself.

MAUD: I am perfectly calm. I am just outspoken. If it comes to being killed I shall take it as calmly as anyone.

CLIVE: There is no cause for alarm. Mrs Saunders has been alone since her husband died last year, amazing spirit. Not surprisingly, the strain has told. She has come to us as her nearest neighbours.

MAUD: What happened to make her come?

CLIVE: This is not an easy country for a woman.

MAUD: Clive, I heard drums. We are not children.

CLIVE: Of course you heard drums. The tribes are constantly at war, if the term is not too grand to grace their squabbles. Not unnaturally Mrs Saunders would like the company of white women. The piano. Poetry.

BETTY: We are not her nearest neighbours.

CLIVE: We are among her nearest neighbours and I was a dear friend of her late husband. She knows that she will find a welcome here. She will not be disappointed. She will be cared for.

MAUD: Of course we will care for her.

BETTY: Victoria is in bed. I must go and say goodnight. Mother, please, you look after Mrs Saunders.

CLIVE: Harry will be here at once.

[BETTY goes.]

MAUD: How rash to go out after dark without a shawl.

CLIVE: Amazing spirit. Drink this.

MRS SAUNDERS: Where am I?

MAUD: You are quite safe.

MRS SAUNDERS: Clive? Clive? Thank God. This is very kind. How do you do? I am sorry to be a nuisance. Charmed. Have you a gun? I have a gun.

CLIVE: There is no need for guns I hope. We are all friends here.

MRS SAUNDERS: I think I will lie down again.

[HARRY BAGLEY and EDWARD have approached.]

MAUD: Ah, here is Mr Bagley.

EDWARD: I gave his horse some water.

CLIVE: You don't know Mrs Saunders, do you Harry? She has at present collapsed, but she is recovering thanks to the good offices of my wife's mother who I think you've met before. Betty will be along in a minute. Edward will go home to school shortly. He is quite a young man since you saw him.

HARRY: I hardly knew him.

MAUD: What news have you for us, Mr Bagley?

CLIVE: Do you know Mrs Saunders, Harry? Amazing spirit.

EDWARD: Did you hardly know me?

HARRY: Of course I knew you. I mean you have grown.

EDWARD: What do you expect?

HARRY: That's quite right, people don't get smaller.

MAUD: Edward. You should be in bed.

EDWARD: No, I'm not tired, I'm not tired am I Uncle Harry?

HARRY: I don't think he's tired.

CLIVE: He is overtired. It is past his bedtime. Say goodnight.

EDWARD: Goodnight, sir.

CLIVE: And to your grandmother.

EDWARD: Goodnight, grandmother.

[EDWARD goes.]

MAUD: Shall I help Mrs Saunders indoors? I'm afraid she may get a chill.

CLIVE: Shall I give her an arm?

MAUD: How kind of you Clive. I think I am strong enough.

[MAUD helps MRS SAUNDERS into the house.]

CLIVE: Not a word to alarm the women.

HARRY: Absolutely.

CLIVE: I did some good today I think. Kept up some alliances. There's a lot of affection there.

HARRY: They're affectionate people. They can be very cruel of course.

CLIVE: Well they are savages.

HARRY: Very beautiful people many of them.

CLIVE: Joshua! [To HARRY.] I think we should sleep with guns.

HARRY: I haven't slept in a house for six months. It seems extremely safe.

[JOSHUA comes.]

CLIVE: Joshua, you will have gathered there's a spot of bother. Rumours of this and that. You should be armed I think.

JOSHUA: There are many bad men, sir. I pray about it. Jesus will protect us.

CLIVE: He will indeed and I'll also get you a weapon. Betty, come and keep Harry company. Look in the barn, Joshua, every night.

[CLIVE *and* JOSHUA *go.* BETTY *comes.*]

HARRY: I wondered where you were.

BETTY: I was singing lullabies.

HARRY: When I think of you I always think of you with Edward in your lap.

BETTY: Do you think of me sometimes then?

HARRY: You have been thought of where no white woman has ever been thought of before.

BETTY: It's one way of having adventures. I suppose I will never go in person.

HARRY: That's up to you.

BETTY: Of course it's not. I have duties.

HARRY: Are you happy, Betty?

BETTY: Where have you been?

HARRY: Built a raft and went up the river. Stayed with some people. The king is always very good to me. They have a lot of skulls around the place but not white men's I think. I made up a poem one night. If I should die in this forsaken spot, There is a loving heart without a blot, Where I will live – and so on.

BETTY: When I'm near you it's like going out into the jungle. It's like going up the river on a raft. It's like going out in the dark.

HARRY: And you are safety and light and peace and home.

BETTY: But I want to be dangerous.

HARRY: Clive is my friend.

BETTY: I am your friend.

HARRY: I don't like dangerous women.

BETTY: Is Mrs Saunders dangerous?

HARRY: Not to me. She's a bit of an old boot.

[JOSHUA *comes, unobserved.*]

BETTY: Am I dangerous?

HARRY: You are rather.

BETTY: Please like me.

HARRY: I worship you.

BETTY: Please want me.

HARRY: I don't want to want you. Of course I want you.

BETTY: What are we going to do?

HARRY: I should have stayed on the river. The hell with it.

[*He goes to take her in his arms, she runs away into the house.* HARRY *stays where he is. He becomes aware of* JOSHUA.]

HARRY: Who's there?

JOSHUA: Only me sir.

HARRY: Got a gun now have you?

JOSHUA: Yes sir.

HARRY: Where's Clive?

JOSHUA: Going round the boundaries sir.

HARRY: Have you checked there's nobody in the barns?

JOSHUA: Yes sir.

HARRY: Shall we go in a barn and fuck? It's not an order.

JOSHUA: That's all right, yes.

[*They go off.*]

SCENE TWO

An open space some distance from the house. MRS SAUNDERS *alone, breathless. She is carrying a riding crop.* CLIVE *arrives.*

CLIVE: Why? Why?

MRS SAUNDERS: Don't fuss, Clive, it makes you sweat.

CLIVE: Why ride off now? Sweat, you would sweat if you were in love with somebody as disgustingly capricious as you are. You will be shot with poisoned arrows. You will miss the picnic. Somebody will notice I came after you.

MRS SAUNDERS: I didn't want you to come after me. I wanted to be alone.

CLIVE: You will be raped by cannibals.

MRS SAUNDERS: I just wanted to get out of your house.

CLIVE: My God, what women put us through. Cruel, cruel. I think you are the sort of woman who would enjoy whipping somebody. I've never met one before.

MRS SAUNDERS: Can I tell you something, Clive?

CLIVE: Let me tell you something first. Since you came to the house I have had an erection twenty-four hours a day except for ten minutes after the time we had intercourse.

MRS SAUNDERS: I don't think that's physically possible.

CLIVE: You are causing me appalling physical suffering. Is this the way to treat a benefactor?

MRS SAUNDERS: Clive, when I came to your house the other night I came because I was afraid. The cook was going to let his whole tribe in through the window.

CLIVE: I know that, my poor sweet. Amazing –

MRS SAUNDERS: I came to you although you are not my nearest neighbour –

CLIVE: Rather than to the old major of seventy-two.

MRS SAUNDERS: Because the last time he came to visit me I had to defend myself with a shotgun and I thought you would take no for an answer.

CLIVE: But you've already answered yes.

MRS SAUNDERS: I answered yes once. Sometimes I want to say no.

CLIVE: Women, my God. Look the picnic will start, I have to go to the picnic. Please Caroline –

MRS SAUNDERS: I think I will have to go back to my own house.

CLIVE: Caroline, if you were shot with poisoned arrows do you know what I'd do? I'd fuck your dead body and poison myself. Caroline, you smell amazing. You terrify me. You are dark like this continent. Mysterious. Treacherous. When you rode to me through the night. When you fainted in my arms. When I came to you in your bed, when I lifted the mosquito netting, when I said let me in, let me in. Oh don't shut me out, Caroline, let me in.

[*He has been caressing her feet and legs. He disappears completely under her skirt.*]

MRS SAUNDERS: Please stop. I can't concentrate. I want to go home. I wish I didn't enjoy the sensation because I don't like you, Clive. I do like living in your house where there's plenty of guns. But I don't like you at all. But I do like the sensation. Well I'll have it then. I'll have it, I'll have it –

[*Voices are heard singing The First Noël.*]

263

Don't stop. Don't stop.

[CLIVE *comes out from under her skirt.*]

CLIVE: The Christmas picnic. I came.

MRS SAUNDERS: I didn't.

CLIVE: I'm all sticky.

MRS SAUNDERS: What about me? Wait.

CLIVE: All right, are you? Come on. We mustn't be found.

MRS SAUNDERS: Don't go now.

CLIVE: Caroline, you are so voracious. Do let go. Tidy yourself up. There's a hair in my mouth.

[CLIVE *and* MRS SAUNDERS *go off.* BETTY *and* MAUD *come, with* JOSHUA *carrying hamper.*]

MAUD: I never would have thought a guinea fowl could taste so like a turkey.

BETTY: I had to explain to the cook three times.

MAUD: You did very well dear.

[JOSHUA *sits apart with gun.* EDWARD *and* HARRY *with* VICTORIA *on his shoulder, singing The First Noël.* MAUD *and* BETTY *are unpacking the hamper.* CLIVE *arrives separately.*]

MAUD: This tablecloth was one of my mama's.

BETTY: Uncle Harry playing horsy.

EDWARD: Crackers crackers.

BETTY: Not yet, Edward.

CLIVE: And now the moment we have all been waiting for.

[CLIVE *opens champagne. General acclaim.*]

CLIVE: Oh dear, stained my trousers, never mind.

EDWARD: Can I have some?

MAUD: Oh no Edward, not for you.

CLIVE: Give him half a glass.

MAUD: If your father says so.

CLIVE: All rise please. To Her Majesty Queen Victoria, God bless her, and her husband and all her dear children.

ALL: The Queen.

EDWARD: Crackers crackers.

[*General cracker pulling, hats.* CLIVE *and* HARRY *discuss champagne.*]

HARRY: Excellent, Clive, wherever did you get it?

CLIVE: I know a chap in French Equatorial Africa.

EDWARD: I won, I won mama.

[ELLEN *arrives*.]

BETTY: Give a hat to Joshua, he'd like it.

> [EDWARD *takes hat to* JOSHUA. BETTY *takes a ball from the hamper and plays catch with* ELLEN. *Murmurs of surprise and congratulations from the men whenever they catch the ball.*]

EDWARD: Mama, don't play. You know you can't catch a ball.

BETTY: He's perfectly right. I can't throw either.

> [BETTY *sits down.* ELLEN *has the ball.*]

EDWARD: Ellen, don't you play either. You're no good. You spoil it.

> [EDWARD *takes* VICTORIA *from* HARRY *and gives her to* ELLEN. *He takes the ball and throws it to* HARRY. HARRY, CLIVE *and* EDWARD *play ball.*]

BETTY: Ellen come and sit with me. We'll be spectators and clap.

> [EDWARD *misses the ball.*]

CLIVE: Butterfingers.

EDWARD: I'm not.

HARRY: Throw straight now.

EDWARD: I did, I did.

CLIVE: Keep your eye on the ball.

EDWARD: You can't throw.

CLIVE: Don't be a baby.

EDWARD: I'm not, throw a hard one, throw a hard one –

CLIVE: Butterfingers. What will Uncle Harry think of you?

EDWARD: It's your fault. You can't throw. I hate you.

> [*He throws the ball wildly in the direction of* JOSHUA.]

CLIVE: Now you've lost the ball. He's lost the ball.

EDWARD: It's Joshua's fault. Joshua's butterfingers.

CLIVE: I don't think I want to play any more. Joshua, find the ball will you?

EDWARD: Yes, please play. I'll find the ball. Please play.

CLIVE: You're so silly and you can't catch. You'll be no good at cricket.

MAUD: Why don't we play hide and seek?

EDWARD: Because it's a baby game.

BETTY: You've hurt Edward's feelings.

CLIVE: A boy has no business having feelings.

HARRY: Hide and seek. I'll be it. Everybody must hide. This is the base, you have to get home to base.

EDWARD: Hide and seek, hide and seek.

HARRY: Can we persuade the ladies to join us?

MAUD: I'm playing. I love games.

BETTY: I always get found straight away.

ELLEN: Come on, Betty, do. Vicky wants to play.

EDWARD: You won't find me ever.

[*They all go except* CLIVE, HARRY, JOSHUA.]

HARRY: It is safe, I suppose?

CLIVE: They won't go far. This is very much my territory and it's broad daylight. Joshua will keep an open eye.

HARRY: Well I must give them a hundred. You don't know what this means to me, Clive. A chap can only go on so long alone. I can climb mountains and go down rivers, but what's it for? For Christmas and England and games and women singing. This is the empire, Clive. It's not me putting a flag in new lands. It's you. The empire is one big family. I'm one of its black sheep, Clive. And I know you think my life is rather dashing. But I want you to know I admire you. This is the empire, Clive, and I serve it. With all my heart.

CLIVE: I think that's about a hundred.

HARRY: Ready or not, here I come!

[*He goes.*]

CLIVE: Harry Bagley is a fine man, Joshua. You should be proud to know him. He will be in history books.

JOSHUA: Sir, while we are alone.

CLIVE: Joshua of course, what is it? You always have my ear. Any time.

JOSHUA: Sir, I have some information. The stable boys are not to be trusted. They whisper. They go out at night. They visit their people. Their people are not my people. I do not visit my people.

CLIVE: Thank you, Joshua. They certainly look after Beauty. I'll be sorry to have to replace them.

JOSHUA: They carry knives.

CLIVE: Thank you, Joshua.

JOSHUA: And, sir.

CLIVE: I appreciate this, Joshua, very much.

JOSHUA: Your wife.

CLIVE: Ah, yes?

JOSHUA: She also thinks Harry Bagley is a fine man.

CLIVE: Thank you, Joshua.

JOSHUA: Are you going to hide?

CLIVE: Yes, yes I am. Thank you. Keep your eyes open Joshua.

JOSHUA: I do, sir.

[CLIVE *goes.* JOSHUA *goes.* HARRY *and* BETTY *race back to base.*]

BETTY: I can't run, I can't run at all.

HARRY: There, I've caught you.

BETTY: Harry, what are we going to do?

HARRY: It's impossible, Betty.

BETTY: Shall we run away together?

[MAUD *comes.*]

MAUD: I give up. Don't catch me. I have been stung.

HARRY: Nothing serious I hope.

MAUD: I have ointment in my bag. I always carry ointment. I shall just sit down and rest. I am too old for all this fun. Hadn't you better be seeking, Harry?

[HARRY *goes.* MAUD *and* BETTY *are alone for some time. They don't speak.* HARRY *and* EDWARD *race back.*]

EDWARD: I won, I won, you didn't catch me.

HARRY: Yes I did.

EDWARD: Mama, who was first?

BETTY: I wasn't watching. I think it was Harry.

EDWARD: It wasn't Harry. You're no good at judging. I won, didn't I grandma?

MAUD: I expect so, since it's Christmas.

EDWARD: I won, Uncle Harry. I'm better than you.

BETTY: Why don't you help Uncle Harry look for the others?

EDWARD: Shall I?

HARRY: Yes, of course.

BETTY: Run along then. He's just coming.

[EDWARD *goes.*]

Harry, I shall scream.

HARRY: Ready or not, here I come.

[HARRY *runs off*.]

BETTY: Why don't you go back to the house, mother, and rest your insect-bite?

MAUD: Betty, my duty is here. I don't like what I see. Clive wouldn't like it, Betty. I am your mother.

BETTY: Clive gives you a home because you are my mother.

[HARRY *comes back*.]

HARRY: I can't find anyone else. I'm getting quite hot.

BETTY: Sit down a minute.

HARRY: I can't do that. I'm he. How's your sting?

MAUD: It seems to be swelling up.

BETTY: Why don't you go home and rest? Joshua will go with you. Joshua!

HARRY: I could take you back.

MAUD: That would be charming

BETTY: You can't go. You're he.

[JOSHUA *comes*.]

BETTY: Joshua, my mother wants to go back to the house. Will you go with her please.

JOSHUA: Sir told me I have to keep an eye.

BETTY: I am telling you to go back to the house. Then you can come back here and keep an eye.

MAUD: Thank you Betty. I know we have our little differences, but I always want what is best for you.

[JOSHUA *and* MAUD *go*.]

HARRY: Don't give way. Keep calm.

BETTY: I shall kill myself.

HARRY: Betty, you are a star in my sky. Without you I would have no sense of direction. I need you, and I need you where you are, I need you to be Clive's wife. I need to go up rivers and know you are sitting here thinking of me.

BETTY: I want more than that. Is that wicked of me?

HARRY: Not wicked, Betty. Silly.

[EDWARD *calls in the distance*.]

EDWARD: Uncle Harry, where are you?

BETTY: Can't we ever be alone?

HARRY: You are a mother. And a daughter. And a wife.

BETTY: I think I shall go and hide again.

[BETTY *goes*. HARRY *goes*. CLIVE *chases* MRS SAUNDERS *across the stage*. EDWARD *and* HARRY *call in the distance*.]

EDWARD: Uncle Harry!

HARRY: Edward!

[EDWARD *comes*.]

EDWARD: Uncle Harry!

[HARRY *comes*.]

There you are. I haven't found anyone have you?

HARRY: I wonder where they all are.

EDWARD: Perhaps they're lost forever. Perhaps they're dead. There's trouble going on isn't there, and nobody says because of not frightening the women and children.

HARRY: Yes, that's right.

EDWARD: Do you think we'll be killed in our beds?

HARRY: Not very likely.

EDWARD: I can't sleep at night. Can you?

HARRY: I'm not used to sleeping in a house.

EDWARD: If I'm awake at night can I come and see you? I won't wake you up. I'll only come in if you're awake.

HARRY: You should try to sleep.

EDWARD: I don't mind being awake because I make up adventures. Once we were on a raft going down to the rapids. We've lost the paddles because we used them to fight off the crocodiles. A crocodile comes at me and I stab it again and again and the blood is everywhere and it tips up the raft and it has you by the leg and it's biting your leg right off and I take my knife and stab it in the throat and rip open its stomach and it lets go of you but it bites my hand but it's dead. And I drag you onto the river bank and I'm almost fainting with pain and we lie there in each other's arms.

HARRY: Have I lost my leg?

EDWARD: I forgot about the leg by then.

HARRY: Hadn't we better look for the others?

EDWARD: Wait. I've got something for you. It was in mama's box but she never wears it.

[EDWARD *gives* HARRY *a necklace*.]

You don't have to wear it either but you might like it to look at.

HARRY: It's beautiful. But you'll have to put it back.

EDWARD: I wanted to give it to you.

HARRY: You did. It can go back in the box. You still gave it to me. Come on now, we have to find the others.

EDWARD: Harry, I love you.

HARRY: Yes I know. I love you too.

EDWARD: You know what we did when you were here before. I want to do it again. I think about it all the time. I try to do it to myself but it's not as good. Don't you want to any more?

HARRY: I do, but it's a sin and a crime and it's also wrong.

EDWARD: But we'll do it anyway won't we?

HARRY: Yes of course.

EDWARD: I wish the others would all be killed. Take it out now and let me see it.

HARRY: No.

EDWARD: Is it big now?

HARRY: Yes.

EDWARD: Let me touch it.

HARRY: No.

EDWARD: Just hold me.

HARRY: When you can't sleep.

EDWARD: We'd better find the others then. Come on.

HARRY: Ready or not, here we come.

[*They go out with whoops and shouts.* BETTY *and* ELLEN *come.*]

BETTY: Ellen, I don't want to play any more.

ELLEN: Nor do I, Betty.

BETTY: Come and sit here with me. Oh Ellen, what will become of me?

ELLEN: Betty, are you crying? Are you laughing?

BETTY: Tell me what you think of Harry Bagley.

ELLEN: He's a very fine man.

BETTY: No, Ellen, what you really think.

ELLEN: I think you think he's very handsome.

BETTY: And don't you think he is? Oh Ellen, you're so good and I'm so wicked.

ELLEN: I'm not so good as you think.

[EDWARD *comes.*]

EDWARD: I've found you.

ELLEN: We're not hiding Edward.

EDWARD: But I found you.

ELLEN: We're not playing, Edward, now run along.

EDWARD: Come on, Ellen, do play. Come on, mama.

ELLEN: Edward, don't pull your mama like that.

BETTY: Edward, you must do what your governess says. Go and play with Uncle Harry.

EDWARD: Uncle Harry!

[EDWARD *goes.*]

BETTY: Ellen, can you keep a secret?

ELLEN: Oh yes, yes please.

BETTY: I love Harry Bagley. I want to go away with him. There, I've said it, it's true.

ELLEN: How do you know you love him?

BETTY: I kissed him.

ELLEN: Betty.

BETTY: He held my hand like this. Oh I want him to do it again. I want him to stroke my hair.

ELLEN: Your lovely hair. Like this, Betty?

BETTY: I want him to put his arm around my waist.

ELLEN: Like this, Betty?

BETTY: Yes, oh I want him to kiss me again.

ELLEN: Like this Betty?

[ELLEN *kisses* BETTY.]

BETTY: Ellen, whatever are you doing? It's not a joke.

ELLEN: I'm sorry, Betty. You're so pretty. Harry Bagley doesn't deserve you. You wouldn't really go away with him?

BETTY: Oh Ellen, you don't know what I suffer. You don't know what love is. Everyone will hate me, but it's worth it for Harry's love.

ELLEN: I don't hate you, Betty, I love you.

BETTY: Harry says we shouldn't go away. But he says he worships me.

ELLEN: I worship you Betty.

BETTY: Oh Ellen, you are my only friend.

[*They embrace. The others have all gathered together.* MAUD *has rejoined the party, and* JOSHUA.]

271

CLIVE: Come along everyone, you mustn't miss Harry's conjuring trick.

[BETTY *and* ELLEN *go to join the others.*]

MAUD: I didn't want to spoil the fun by not being here.

HARRY: What is it that flies all over the world and is up my sleeve?

[HARRY *produces a union jack from up his sleeve. General acclaim.*]

CLIVE: I think we should have some singing now. Ladies, I rely on you to lead the way.

ELLEN: We have a surprise for you. I have taught Joshua a Christmas carol. He has been singing it at the piano but I'm sure he can sing it unaccompanied, can't you, Joshua?

JOSHUA:

In the deep midwinter
Frosty wind made moan,
Earth stood hard as iron,
Water like a stone.
Snow had fallen snow on snow
Snow on snow,
In the deep midwinter
Long long ago.

What can I give him
Poor as I am?
If I were a shepherd
I would bring a lamb.
If I were a wise man
I would do my part
What I can I give him,
Give my heart.

272

Inside the house. BETTY, MRS SAUNDERS, MAUD *with* VICTORIA. *The blinds are down so the light isn't bright though it is day outside.* CLIVE *looks in.*

CLIVE: Everything all right? Nothing to be frightened of.

[CLIVE *goes. Silence.*]

MAUD: Clap hands, daddy comes, with his pockets full of plums. All for Vicky.

[*Silence.*]

MRS SAUNDERS: Who actually does the flogging?

MAUD: I don't think we want to imagine.

MRS SAUNDERS: I imagine Joshua.

BETTY: Yes I think it would be Joshua. Or would Clive do it himself?

MRS SAUNDERS: Well we can ask them afterwards.

MAUD: I don't like the way you speak of it, Mrs Saunders.

MRS SAUNDERS: How should I speak of it?

MAUD: The men will do it in the proper way, whatever it is. We have our own part to play.

MRS SAUNDERS: Harry Bagley says they should just be sent away. I don't think he likes to see them beaten.

BETTY: Harry is so tender hearted. Perhaps he is right.

MAUD: Harry Bagley is not altogether — He has lived in this country a long time without any responsibilities. It is part of his charm but it hasn't improved his judgment. If the boys were just sent away they would go back to the village and make more trouble.

MRS SAUNDERS: And what will they say about us in the village if they've been flogged?

BETTY: Perhaps Clive should keep them here.

MRS SAUNDERS: That is never wise.

BETTY: Whatever shall we do?

MAUD: I don't think it is up to us to wonder. The men don't tell us what is going on among the tribes, so how can we possibly make a judgment?

MRS SAUNDERS: I know a little of what is going on.

BETTY: Tell me what you know. Clive tells me nothing.

MAUD: You would not want to be told about it, Betty. It is enough for you that Clive knows what is happening. Clive will know what to do. Your father always knew what to do.

BETTY: Are you saying you would do something different, Caroline?

MRS SAUNDERS: I would do what I did at my own home. I left. I can't see any way out except to leave. I will leave here. I will keep leaving everywhere I suppose.

MAUD: Luckily this household has a head. I am squeamish myself. But luckily Clive is not.

BETTY: You are leaving here then, Caroline?

MRS SAUNDERS: Not immediately. I'm sorry.

[Silence.]

MRS SAUNDERS: I wonder if it's over.

[EDWARD comes in.]

BETTY: Shouldn't you be with the men, Edward?

EDWARD: I didn't want to see any more. They got what they deserved. Uncle Harry said I could come in.

MRS SAUNDERS: I never allowed the servants to be beaten in my own house. I'm going to find out what's happening.

[MRS SAUNDERS goes out.]

BETTY: Will she go and look?

MAUD: Let Mrs Saunders be a warning to you, Betty. She is alone in the world. You are not, thank God. Since your father died, I know what it is to be unprotected. Vicky is such a pretty little girl. Clap hands, daddy comes, with his pockets full of plums. All for Vicky.

[EDWARD, meanwhile, has found the doll and is playing clap hands with her.]

BETTY: Edward, what have you got there?

EDWARD: I'm minding her.

BETTY: Edward, I've told you before, dolls are for girls.

MAUD: Where is Ellen? She should be looking after Edward. [She goes to the door.] Ellen! Betty, why do you let that girl mope about in her own room? That's not what she's come to Africa for.

274

BETTY: You must never let the boys at school know you like dolls. Never, never. No one will talk to you, you won't be on the cricket team, you won't grow up to be a man like your papa.

EDWARD: I don't want to be like papa. I hate papa.

MAUD: Edward! Edward!

BETTY: You're a horrid wicked boy and papa will beat you. Of course you don't hate him, you love him. Now give Victoria her doll at once.

EDWARD: She's not Victoria's doll, she's my doll. She doesn't love Victoria and Victoria doesn't love her. Victoria never even plays with her.

MAUD: Victoria will learn to play with her.

EDWARD: She's mine and she loves me and she won't be happy if you take her away, she'll cry, she'll cry, she'll cry.

[BETTY *takes the doll away, slaps him, bursts into tears.* ELLEN *comes in.*]

BETTY: Ellen, look what you've done. Edward's got the doll again. Now, Ellen, will you please do your job.

ELLEN: Edward, you are a wicked boy. I am going to lock you in the nursery until supper time. Now go upstairs this minute.

[*She slaps* EDWARD, *who bursts into tears and goes out.*]
I do try to do what you want. I'm so sorry.

[ELLEN *bursts into tears and goes out.*]

MAUD: There now, Vicky's got her baby back. Where did Vicky's naughty baby go? Shall we smack her? Just a little smack [MAUD *smacks the doll hard.*] There, now she's a good baby. Clap hands, daddy comes, with his pockets full of plums. All for Vicky's baby. When I was a child we honoured our parents. My mama was an angel.

[JOSHUA *comes in. He stands without speaking.*]

BETTY: Joshua?

JOSHUA: Madam?

BETTY: Did you want something?

JOSHUA: Sent to see the ladies are all right, madam.

[MRS SAUNDERS *comes in.*]

MRS SAUNDERS: We're very well thank you, Joshua, and how are you?

JOSHUA: Very well thank you, Mrs Saunders.

MRS SAUNDERS: And the stable boys?

JOSHUA: They have had justice, madam.

MRS SAUNDERS: So I saw. And does your arm ache?

MAUD: This is not a proper conversation, Mrs Saunders.

MRS SAUNDERS: You don't mind beating your own people?

JOSHUA: Not my people, madam.

MRS SAUNDERS: A different tribe?

JOSHUA: Bad people.

[HARRY *and* CLIVE *come in.*]

CLIVE: Well this is all very gloomy and solemn. Can we have the shutters open? The heat of the day has gone, we could have some light, I think. And cool drinks on the verandah, Joshua. Have some lemonade yourself. It is most refreshing.

[*Sunlight floods in as the shutters are opened.* EDWARD *comes.*]

EDWARD: Papa, papa, Ellen tried to lock me in the nursery. Mama is going to tell you of me. I'd rather tell you myself. I was playing with Vicky's doll again and I know it's very bad of me. And I said I didn't want to be like you and I said I hated you. And it's not true and I'm sorry, I'm sorry and please beat me and forgive me.

CLIVE: Well there's a brave boy to own up. You should always respect and love me, Edward, not for myself, I may not deserve it, but as I respected and loved my own father, because he was my father. Through our father we love our Queen and our God, Edward. Do you understand? It is something men understand.

EDWARD: Yes papa.

CLIVE: Then I forgive you and shake you by the hand. You spend too much time with the women. You may spend more time with me and Uncle Harry, little man.

EDWARD: I don't like women. I don't like dolls. I love you, papa, and I love you, Uncle Harry.

CLIVE: There's a fine fellow. Let us go out onto the verandah.

[*They all start to go.* EDWARD *takes* HARRY's *hand and goes with him.* CLIVE *draws* BETTY *back. They embrace.*]

BETTY: Poor Clive.

CLIVE: It was my duty to have them flogged. For you and Edward and Victoria, to keep you safe.

BETTY: It is terrible to feel betrayed.

CLIVE: You can tame a wild animal only so far. They revert to their true nature and savage your hand. Sometimes I feel the natives are the enemy. I know that is wrong. I know I have a responsibility towards them, to care for them and bring them all to be like Joshua. But there is something dangerous. Implacable. This whole continent is my enemy. I am pitching my whole mind and will and reason and spirit against it to tame it, and I sometimes feel it will break over me and swallow me up.

BETTY: Clive, Clive, I am here. I have faith in you.

CLIVE: Yes, I can show you my moments of weakness, Betty, because you are my wife and because I trust you. I trust you, Betty, and it would break my heart if you did not deserve that trust. Harry Bagley is my friend. It would break my heart if he did not deserve my trust.

BETTY: I'm sorry, I'm sorry. Forgive me. It is not Harry's fault, it is all mine. Harry is noble. He has rejected me. It is my wickedness, I get bored, I get restless, I imagine things. There is something so wicked in me, Clive.

CLIVE: I have never thought of you having the weakness of your sex, only the good qualities.

BETTY: I am bad, bad, bad—

CLIVE: You are thoughtless, Betty, that's all. Women can be treacherous and evil. They are darker and more dangerous than men. The family protects us from that, you protect me from that. You are not that sort of woman. You are not unfaithful to me, Betty. I can't believe you are. It would hurt me so much to cast you off. That would be my duty.

BETTY: No, no, no.

CLIVE: Joshua has seen you kissing.

BETTY: Forgive me.

CLIVE: But I don't want to know about it. I don't want to know I wonder of course, I wonder constantly. If Harry Bagley was not my friend I would shoot him. If I shot you every British man and woman would applaud me. But no. It was a moment of passion such as women are too weak to resist. But you must resist it, Betty, or it will destroy us. We must fight against it. We must resist this dark female lust, Betty, or it will swallow us up.

BETTY: I do, I do resist. Help me. Forgive me.

CLIVE: Yes I do forgive you. But I can't feel the same about you as I did. You are still my wife and we still have duties to the household.

[*They go out arm in arm. As soon as they have gone* EDWARD *sneaks back to get the doll, which has been dropped on the floor. He picks it up and comforts it.* JOSHUA *comes through with a tray of drinks.*]

JOSHUA: Baby. Sissy. Girly.

[JOSHUA *goes.* BETTY *calls from off.*]

BETTY: Edward?

[BETTY *comes in.*]

BETTY: There you are, my darling. Come, papa wants us all to be together. Uncle Harry is going to tell how he caught a crocodile. Mama's sorry she smacked you.

[*They embrace.* JOSHUA *comes in again, passing through.*]

BETTY: Joshua, fetch me some blue thread from my sewing box. It is on the piano.

JOSHUA: You've got legs under that skirt.

BETTY: Joshua.

JOSHUA: And more than legs.

BETTY: Edward, are you going to stand there and let a servant insult your mother?

EDWARD: Joshua, get my mother's thread.

JOSHUA: Oh little Eddy, playing at master. It's only a joke.

EDWARD: Don't speak to my mother like that again.

JOSHUA: Ladies have no sense of humour. You like a joke with Joshua.

EDWARD: You fetch her sewing at once, do you hear me? You move when I speak to you, boy.

JOSHUA: Yes sir, master Edward sir.

[JOSHUA *goes.*]

BETTY: Edward, you were wonderful.

[*She goes to embrace him but he moves away.*]

EDWARD: Don't touch me.

SONG – A Boy's Best Friend – ALL.

While plodding on our way, the toilsome road of life,
How few the friends that daily there we meet.

278

Not many will stand in trouble and in strife,
With counsel and affection ever sweet.
But there is one whose smile will ever on us beam,
Whose love is dearer far than any other;
And wherever we may turn
This lesson we will learn
A boy's best friend is his mother.

Then cherish her with care
And smooth her silv'ry hair,
When gone you will never get another.
And wherever we may turn
This lesson we shall learn,
A boy's best friend is his mother.

SCENE FOUR

The verandah as in Scene One. Early morning. Nobody there.
JOSHUA *comes out of the house slowly and stands for some time doing nothing.* EDWARD *comes out.*

EDWARD: Tell me another bad story, Joshua. Nobody else is even awake yet.

JOSHUA: First there was nothing and then there was the great goddess. She was very large and she had golden eyes and she made the stars and the sun and the earth. But soon she was miserable and lonely and she cried like a great waterfall and her tears made all the rivers in the world. So the great spirit sent a terrible monster, a tree with hundreds of eyes and a long green tongue, and it came chasing after her and she jumped into a lake and the tree jumped in after her, and she jumped right up into the sky. And the tree couldn't follow, he was stuck in the mud. So he picked up a big handful of mud and he threw it at her, up among the stars, and it hit her on the head. And she fell down onto the earth into his arms and the ball of mud is the moon in the sky. And then they had children which is all of us.

EDWARD: It's not true, though.

JOSHUA: Of course it's not true. It's a bad story. Adam and Eve is true. God made man white like him and gave him the bad woman who liked the snake and gave us all this trouble.

[CLIVE *and* HARRY *come out.*]

CLIVE: Run along now, Edward. No, you may stay. You mustn't repeat anything you hear to your mother or your grandmother or Ellen.

EDWARD: Or Mrs Saunders?

CLIVE: Mrs Saunders is an unusual woman and does not require protection in the same way. Harry, there was trouble last night where we expected it. But it's all over now. Everything is under control but nobody should leave the house today I think.

HARRY: Casualties?

CLIVE: No, none of the soldiers hurt thank God. We did a certain amount of damage, set a village on fire and so forth.

HARRY: Was that necessary?

CLIVE: Obviously, it was necessary, Harry, or it wouldn't have happened. The army will come and visit, no doubt. You'll like that, eh, Joshua, to see the British army? And a treat for you, Edward, to see the soldiers. Would you like to be a soldier?

EDWARD: I'd rather be an explorer.

CLIVE: Ah, Harry, like you, you see. I didn't know an explorer at his age. Breakfast, I think, Joshua.

[CLIVE *and* JOSHUA *go in.* HARRY *is following.*]

EDWARD: Uncle.

[HARRY *stops.*]

EDWARD: Harry, why won't you talk to me?

HARRY: Of course I'll talk to you.

EDWARD: If you won't be nice to me I'll tell father.

HARRY: Edward, no, not a word, never, not to your mother, nobody, please. Edward, do you understand? Please.

EDWARD: I won't tell. I promise I'll never tell. I've cut my finger and sworn.

HARRY: There's no need to get so excited Edward. We can't be together all the time. I will have to leave soon anyway, and go back to the river.

EDWARD: You can't, you can't go. Take me with you.

ELLEN: Edward!

HARRY: I have my duty to the Empire.

[HARRY *goes in.* ELLEN *comes out.*]

ELLEN: Edward, breakfast time. Edward.

EDWARD: I'm not hungry.

ELLEN: Betty, please come and speak to Edward.

[BETTY *comes.*]

BETTY: Why what's the matter?

ELLEN: He won't come in for breakfast.

BETTY: Edward, I shall call your father.

EDWARD: You can't make me eat.

[*He goes in.* BETTY *is about to follow.*]

ELLEN: Betty.

[BETTY *stops.*]

ELLEN: Betty, when Edward goes to school will I have to leave?

BETTY: Never mind, Ellen dear, you'll get another place. I'll give you an excellent reference.

ELLEN: I don't want another place, Betty. I want to stay with you forever.

BETTY: If you go back to England you might get married, Ellen. You're quite pretty, you shouldn't despair of getting a husband.

ELLEN: I don't want a husband. I want you.

BETTY: Children of your own, Ellen, think.

ELLEN: I don't want children, I don't like children. I just want to be alone with you, Betty, and sing for you and kiss you because I love you, Betty.

BETTY: I love you too, Ellen. But women have their duty as soldiers have. You must be a mother if you can.

ELLEN: Betty, Betty, I love you so much. I want to stay with you forever, my love for you is eternal, stronger than death. I'd rather die than leave you, Betty.

BETTY: No you wouldn't, Ellen, don't be silly. Come, don't cry. You don't feel what you think you do. It's the loneliness here and the climate is very confusing. Come and have breakfast, Ellen dear, and I'll forget all about it.

[ELLEN *goes,* CLIVE *comes.*]

BETTY: Clive, please forgive me.

CLIVE: Will you leave me alone?

281

[BETTY *goes back into the house.* HARRY *comes.*]

CLIVE: Women, Harry. I envy you going into the jungle, a man's life.

HARRY: I envy you.

CLIVE: Harry, I know you do. I have spoken to Betty.

HARRY: I assure you, Clive –

CLIVE: Please say nothing about it.

HARRY: My friendship for you –

CLIVE: Absolutely. I know the friendship between us, Harry, is not something that could be spoiled by the weaker sex. Friendship between men is a fine thing. It is the noblest form of relationship.

HARRY: I agree with you.

CLIVE: There is the necessity of reproduction. The family is all important. And there is the pleasure. But what we put ourselves through to get that pleasure, Harry. When I heard about our fine fellows last night fighting those savages to protect us I thought yes, that is what I aspire to. I tell you Harry, in confidence, I suddenly got out of Mrs Saunders' bed and came out here on the verandah and looked at the stars.

HARRY: I couldn't sleep last night either.

CLIVE: There is something dark about women, that threatens what is best in us. Between men that light burns brightly.

HARRY: I didn't know you felt like that.

CLIVE: Women are irrational, demanding, inconsistent, treacherous, lustful, and they smell different from us.

HARRY: Clive –

CLIVE: Think of the comradeship of men, Harry, sharing adventures, sharing danger, risking their lives together.

[HARRY *takes hold of* CLIVE.]

CLIVE: What are you doing?

HARRY: Well, you said –

CLIVE: I said what?

HARRY: Between men.

[CLIVE *is speechless.*]

I'm sorry, I misunderstood, I would never have dreamt, I thought –

CLIVE: My God, Harry, how disgusting.

HARRY: You will not betray my confidence.

CLIVE: I feel contaminated.

HARRY: I struggle against it. You cannot imagine the shame. I have tried everything to save myself.

CLIVE: The most revolting perversion. Rome fell, Harry, and this sin can destroy an empire.

HARRY: It is not a sin, it is a disease.

CLIVE: A disease more dangerous than diphtheria. Effeminacy is contagious. How I have been deceived. Your face does not look degenerate. Oh Harry, how did you sink to this?

HARRY: Clive, help me, what am I to do?

CLIVE: You have been away from England too long.

HARRY: Where can I go except into the jungle to hide?

CLIVE: You don't do it with the natives, Harry? My God, what a betrayal of the Queen.

HARRY: Clive, I am like a man born crippled. Please help me.

CLIVE: You must repent.

HARRY: I have thought of killing myself.

CLIVE: That is a sin too.

HARRY: There is no way out. Clive, I beg of you, do not betray my confidence.

CLIVE: I cannot keep a secret like this. Rivers will be named after you, it's unthinkable. You must save yourself from depravity. You must get married. You are not unattractive to women. What a relief that you and Betty were not after all – good God, how disgusting. Now Mrs Saunders. She's a woman of spirit, she could go with you on your expeditions.

HARRY: I suppose getting married wouldn't be any worse than killing myself.

CLIVE: Mrs Saunders! Mrs Saunders! Ask her now, Harry. Think of England.

[MRS SAUNDERS *comes.* CLIVE *withdraws.* HARRY *goes up to* MRS SAUNDERS.]

HARRY: Mrs Saunders, will you marry me?

MRS SAUNDERS: Why?

HARRY: We are both alone.

MRS SAUNDERS: I choose to be alone, Mr Bagley. If I can look after myself, I'm sure you can. Clive, I have something important to tell you. I've just found Joshua putting earth on his head. He tells me his parents were killed last night by the British soldiers. I think you owe him an apology on behalf of the Queen.

CLIVE: Joshua! Joshua!

MRS SAUNDERS: Mr Bagley, I could never be a wife again. There is only one thing about marriage that I like.

[CLIVE comes.]

CLIVE: Joshua, I am horrified to hear what has happened. Good God!

MRS SAUNDERS: His father was shot. His mother died in the blaze.

[MRS SAUNDERS goes.]

CLIVE: Joshua, do you want a day off? Do you want to go to your people?

JOSHUA: Not my people, sir.

CLIVE: But you want to go to your parents' funeral?

JOSHUA: No sir.

CLIVE: Yes, Joshua, yes, your father and mother. I'm sure they were loyal to the crown. I'm sure it was all a terrible mistake.

JOSHUA: My mother and father were bad people.

CLIVE: Joshua, no.

JOSHUA: You are my father and mother.

CLIVE: Well really. I don't know what to say. That's very decent of you. Are you sure there's nothing I can do? You can have the day off you know.

[BETTY comes out followed by EDWARD.]

BETTY: What's the matter? What's happening?

CLIVE: Something terrible has happened. No, I mean some relatives of Joshua's met with an accident.

JOSHUA: May I go sir?

CLIVE: Yes, yes of course. Good God, what a terrible thing. Bring us a drink will you Joshua?

[JOSHUA goes.]

EDWARD: What? What?

BETTY: Edward, go and do your lessons.

EDWARD: What is it, Uncle Harry?

HARRY: Go and do your lessons.

ELLEN: Edward, come in here at once.

EDWARD: What's happened, Uncle Harry?

[HARRY *has moved aside*, EDWARD *follows him*. ELLEN *comes out.*]

HARRY: Go away. Go inside. Ellen!

ELLEN: Go inside, Edward. I shall tell your mother.

BETTY: Go inside, Edward at once. I shall tell your father.

CLIVE: Go inside, Edward. And Betty you go inside too.

[BETTY, EDWARD *and* ELLEN *go*. MAUD *comes out.*]

CLIVE: Go inside. And Ellen, you come outside.

[ELLEN *comes out.*]

Mr Bagley has something to say to you.

HARRY: Ellen. I don't suppose you would marry me?

ELLEN: What if I said yes?

CLIVE: Run along now, you two want to be alone.

[HARRY *and* ELLEN *go out*. JOSHUA *brings* CLIVE *a drink.*]

JOSHUA: The governess and your wife, sir.

CLIVE: What's that, Joshua?

JOSHUA: She talks of love to your wife, sir. I have seen them. Bad women.

CLIVE: Joshua, you go too far. Get out of my sight.

SCENE FIVE

The verandah. A table with a white cloth. A wedding cake and a large knife. Bottles and glasses. JOSHUA *is putting things on the table.* EDWARD *has the doll.* JOSHUA *sees him with it. He holds out his hand.* EDWARD *gives him the doll.* JOSHUA *takes the knife and cuts the doll open and shakes the sawdust out of it.* JOSHUA *throws the doll under the table.*

MAUD: Come along Edward, this is such fun.

[*Everyone enters, triumphal arch for* HARRY *and* ELLEN.]

MAUD: Your mama's wedding was a splendid occasion, Edward. I cried and cried.

[ELLEN *and* BETTY *go aside.*]

ELLEN: Betty, what happens with a man? I don't know what to do.

BETTY: You just keep still.

ELLEN: And what does he do?

BETTY: Harry will know what to do.

ELLEN: And is it enjoyable?

BETTY: Ellen, you're not getting married to enjoy yourself.

ELLEN: Don't forget me, Betty.

[ELLEN goes.]

BETTY: I think my necklace has been stolen Clive. I did so want to wear it at the wedding.

EDWARD: It was Joshua. Joshua took it.

CLIVE: Joshua?

EDWARD: He did, he did, I saw him with it.

HARRY: Edward, that's not true.

EDWARD: It is, it is.

HARRY: Edward, I'm afraid you took it yourself.

EDWARD: I did not.

HARRY: I have seen him with it.

CLIVE: Edward, is that true? Where is it? Did you take your mother's necklace? And to try and blame Joshua, good God.

[EDWARD runs off.]

BETTY: Edward, come back. Have you got my necklace?

HARRY: I should leave him alone. He'll bring it back.

BETTY: I wanted to wear it. I wanted to look my best at your wedding.

HARRY: You always look your best to me.

BETTY: I shall get drunk.

[MRS SAUNDERS comes.]

MRS SAUNDERS: The sale of my property is completed. I shall leave tomorrow.

CLIVE: That's just as well. Whose protection will you seek this time?

MRS SAUNDERS: I shall go to England and buy a farm there. I shall introduce threshing machines.

CLIVE: Amazing spirit.

[He kisses her. BETTY launches herself on MRS SAUNDERS. They fall to the ground.]

286

CLIVE: Betty – Caroline – I don't deserve this – Harry, Harry.

    [HARRY *and* CLIVE *separate them.* HARRY *holding* MRS SAUNDERS, CLIVE BETTY.]

CLIVE: Mrs Saunders, how can you abuse my hospitality? How dare you touch my wife? You must leave here at once.

BETTY: Go away, go away. You are a wicked woman.

MAUD: Mrs Saunders, I am shocked. This is your hostess.

CLIVE: Pack your bags and leave the house this instant.

MRS SAUNDERS: I was leaving anyway. There's no place for me here. I have made arrangements to leave tomorrow, and tomorrow is when I will leave. I wish you joy, Mr Bagley.

    [MRS SAUNDERS *goes.*]

CLIVE: No place for her anywhere I should think. Shocking behaviour.

BETTY: Oh Clive, forgive me, and love me like you used to.

CLIVE: Were you jealous my dove? My own dear wife!

MAUD: Ah, Mr Bagley, one flesh, you see.

    [EDWARD *comes back with the necklace.*]

CLIVE: Good God, Edward, it's true.

EDWARD: I was minding it for mama because of the troubles.

CLIVE: Well done, Edward, that was very manly of you. See Betty? Edward was protecting his mama's jewels from the rebels. What a hysterical fuss over nothing. Well done, little man. It is quite safe now. The bad men are dead. Edward, you may do up the necklace for mama.

    [EDWARD *does up* BETTY*'s necklace, supervised by* CLIVE, JOSHUA *is drinking steadily.* ELLEN *comes back.*]

MAUD: Ah, here's the bride. Come along, Ellen, you don't cry at your own wedding, only at other people's.

CLIVE: Now, speeches, speeches. Who is going to make a speech? Harry, make a speech.

HARRY: I'm no speaker. You're the one for that.

ALL: Speech, speech.

HARRY: My dear friends – what can I say – the empire – the family – the married state to which I have always aspired – your shining example of domestic bliss – my great good fortune in winning Ellen's love – happiest day of my life.

    [*Applause.*]

CLIVE: Cut the cake, cut the cake.

    [HARRY *and* ELLEN *take the knife to cut the cake.* HARRY *steps on the doll under the table.*]

HARRY: What's this?

ELLEN: Oh look.

BETTY: Edward.

EDWARD: It was Joshua. It was Joshua. I saw him.

CLIVE: Don't tell lies again.

    [*He hits* EDWARD *across the side of the head.*]

Unaccustomed as I am to public speaking –

    [*Cheers.*]

  Harry, my friend. So brave and strong and supple.

  Ellen, from neath her veil so shyly peeking.

  I wish you joy. A toast – the happy couple.

  Dangers are past. Our enemies are killed.

  – Put your arm round her, Harry, have a kiss –

  All murmuring of discontent is stilled.

  Long may you live in peace and joy and bliss.

    [*While he is speaking* JOSHUA *raises his gun to shoot* CLIVE. *Only* EDWARD *sees. He does nothing to warn the others. He put his hands over his ears.*]

    BLACK.

ACT TWO

SCENE ONE

Winter afternoon. Inside the hut of a one o'clock club, a children's playcentre in a park, VICTORIA *and* LIN, *mothers.* CATHY, LIN's *daughter, age 4, played by a man, clinging to* LIN. VICTORIA *reading a book.*

CATHY Yum yum bubblegum.
  Stick it up your mother's bum.
  When it's brown
  Pull it down
  Yum yum bubblegum.
LIN: Like your shoes, Victoria.
CATHY Jack be nimble, Jack be quick,
  Jack jump over the candlestick.
  Silly Jack, he should jump higher,
  Goodness gracious, great balls of fire.
LIN: Cathy, do stop. Do a painting.
CATHY: You do a painting.
LIN: You do a painting.
CATHY: What shall I paint?
LIN: Paint a house.
CATHY: No.
LIN: Princess.
CATHY: No.
LIN: Pirates.
CATHY: Already done that.
LIN: Spacemen.
CATHY: I never paint spacemen. You know I never.
LIN: Paint a car crash and blood everywhere.
CATHY: No, don't tell me. I know what to paint.
LIN: Go on then. You need an apron, where's an apron. Here.
CATHY: Don't want an apron.
LIN: Lift up your arms. There's a good girl.
CATHY: I don't want to paint.

289

LIN: Don't paint. Don't paint.

CATHY: What shall I do? You paint. What shall I do mum?

VICTORIA: There's nobody on the big bike, Cathy, quick.

[CATHY *goes out.* VICTORIA *is watching the children playing outside.*]

VICTORIA: Tommy, it's Jimmy's gun. Let him have it. What the hell.

[*She goes on reading. She reads while she talks.*]

LIN: I don't know how you can concentrate.

VICTORIA: You have to or you never do anything.

LIN: Yeh, well. It's really warm in here, that's one thing. It's better than standing out there. I got chilblains last winter.

VICTORIA: It is warm.

LIN: I suppose Tommy doesn't let you read much. I expect he talks to you while you're reading.

VICTORIA: Yes, he does.

LIN: I didn't get very far with that book you lent me.

VICTORIA: That's all right.

LIN: I was glad to have it, though. I sit with it on my lap while I'm watching telly. Well, Cathy's off. She's frightened I'm going to leave her. It's the babyminder didn't work out when she was two, she still remembers. You can't get them used to other people if you're by yourself. It's no good blaming me. She clings round my knees every morning up the nursery and they don't say anything but they make you feel you're making her do it. But I'm desperate for her to go to school. I did cry when I left her the first day. You wouldn't, you're too fucking sensible. You'll call the teacher by her first name. I really fancy you.

VICTORIA: What?

LIN: Put your book down will you for five minutes. You didn't hear a word I said.

VICTORIA: I don't get much time to myself.

LIN: Do you ever go to the movies?

VICTORIA: Tommy's very funny who he's left with. My mother babysits sometimes.

LIN: Your husband could babysit.

VICTORIA: But then we couldn't go to the movies.

LIN: You could go to the movies with me.

VICTORIA: Oh I see.

LIN: Couldn't you?

VICTORIA: Well yes, I could.

LIN: Friday night?

VICTORIA: What film are we talking about?

LIN: Does it matter what film?

VICTORIA: Of course it does.

LIN: You choose then. Friday night.

[CATHY *comes in with gun, shoots them saying Kiou kiou kiou, and runs off again.*]

Not in a foreign language, ok. You don't go in the movies to read.

[LIN *watches the children playing outside.*]

Don't hit him, Cathy, kill him. Point the gun, kiou, kiou, kiou. That's the way.

VICTORIA: They've just banned war toys in Sweden.

LIN: The kids'll just hit each other more.

VICTORIA: Well, psychologists do differ in their opinions as to whether or not aggression is innate.

LIN: Yeh?

VICTORIA: I'm afraid I do let Tommy play with guns and just hope he'll get it out of his system and not end up in the army.

LIN: I've got a brother in the army.

VICTORIA: Oh I'm sorry. Whereabouts is he stationed?

LIN: Belfast.

VICTORIA: Oh dear.

LIN: I've got a friend who's Irish and we went on a Troops Out march. Now my dad won't speak to me.

VICTORIA: I don't get on too well with my father either.

LIN: And your husband? How do you get on with him?

VICTORIA: Oh, fine. Up and down. You know. Very well. He helps with the washing up and everything.

LIN: I left mine two years ago. He let me keep Cathy and I'm grateful for that.

VICTORIA: You shouldn't be grateful.

LIN: I'm a lesbian.

VICTORIA: You still shouldn't be grateful.

LIN: I'm grateful he didn't hit me harder than he did.

VICTORIA: I suppose I'm very lucky with Martin.

LIN: Don't get at me about how I bring up Cathy, ok?

VICTORIA: I didn't.

LIN: Yes you did. War toys. I'll give her a rifle for Christmas and blast Tommy's pretty head off for a start.

[VICTORIA *goes back to her book.*]

LIN: I hate men.

VICTORIA: You have to look at it in a historical perspective in terms of learnt behaviour since the industrial revolution.

LIN: I just hate the bastards.

VICTORIA: Well it's a point of view.

[*By now* CATHY *has come back in and started painting in many colours, without an apron.* EDWARD *comes in.*]

EDWARD: Victoria, mother's in the park. She's walking round all the paths very fast.

VICTORIA: By herself?

EDWARD: I told her you were here.

VICTORIA: Thanks.

EDWARD: Come on.

VICTORIA: Ten minutes talking to my mother and I have to spend two hours in a hot bath.

[VICTORIA *goes out.*]

LIN: Shit, Cathy, what about an apron. I don't mind you having paint on your frock but if it doesn't wash off just don't tell me you can't wear your frock with paint on, ok?

CATHY: Ok.

LIN: You're gay, aren't you?

EDWARD: I beg your pardon?

LIN: I really fancy your sister. I thought you'd understand. You do but you can go on pretending you don't, I don't mind. That's lovely Cathy, I like the green bit.

EDWARD: Don't go around saying that. I might lose my job.

LIN: The last gardener was ever so straight. He used to flash at all the little girls.

EDWARD: I wish you hadn't said that about me. It's not true.

LIN: It's not true and I never said it and I never thought it and I never will think it again.

EDWARD: Someone might have heard you.

LIN: Shut up about it then.

[BETTY *and* VICTORIA *come up.*]

BETTY: It's quite a nasty bump.

VICTORIA: He's not even crying.

BETTY: I think that's very worrying. You and Edward always cried. Perhaps he's got concussion.

VICTORIA: Of course he hasn't mummy.

BETTY: That other little boy was very rough. Should you speak to somebody about him?

VICTORIA: Tommy was hitting him with a spade.

BETTY: Well he's a real little boy. And so brave not to cry. You must watch him for sighs of drowsiness. And nausea. If he's sick in the night, phone an ambulance. Well, you're looking very well darling, a bit tired, a bit peaky. I think the fresh air agrees with Edward. He likes the open air life because of growing up in Africa. He misses the sunshine, don't you, darling? We'll soon have Edward back on his feet. What fun it is here.

VICTORIA: This is Lin. And Cathy.

BETTY: Oh Cathy what a lovely painting. What is it? Well I think it's a house on fire. I think all that red is a fire. Is that right? Or do I see legs, is it a horse? Can I have the lovely painting or is it for mummy? Children have such imagination, it makes them so exhausting. [*To* LIN.] I'm sure you're wonderful, just like Victoria. I had help with my children. One does need help. That was in Africa of course so there wasn't the servant problem. This is my son Edward. This is —

EDWARD: Lin.

BETTY: Lin, this is Lin. Edward is doing something such fun, he's working in the park as a gardener. He does look exactly like a gardener.

EDWARD: I am a gardener.

BETTY: He's certainly making a stab at it. Well it will be a story to tell. I expect he will write a novel about it, or perhaps a television series. Well what a pretty child Cathy is. Victoria was a pretty child just like a little doll — you can't be certain how they'll grow up. I think Victoria's very pretty but she doesn't make the most of herself, do you darling, it's not the fashion I'm told but there are still women who dress out of *Vogue*, well we hope that's not what Martin looks for, though in many ways I wish it was, I don't know what it is Martin looks for and nor does he I'm afraid poor Martin. Well I am rattling on. I like your skirt dear but your shoes won't do at all. Well do they have lady gardeners, Edward, because I'm going to leave your father and I think I might need to get a job, not a gardener really of course. I haven't got green fingers I'm afraid, everything I touch shrivels straight up. Vicky gave me a poinsettia last Christmas and the leaves all fell off on Boxing Day. Well good heavens, look what's happened to that lovely painting.

[CATHY *has slowly and carefully been going over the whole sheet with black paint. She has almost finished.*]

LIN: What you do that for silly? It was nice.

CATHY: I like your earrings.

VICTORIA: Did you say you're leaving Daddy?

BETTY: Do you darling? Shall I put them on you? My ears aren't pierced, I never wanted that, they just clip on the lobe.

LIN: She'll get paint on you, mind.

BETTY: There's a pretty girl. It doesn't hurt does it? Well you'll grow up to know you have to suffer a little bit for beauty.

CATHY: Look mum I'm pretty, I'm pretty, I'm pretty.

LIN: Stop showing off Cathy.

VICTORIA: It's time we went home. Tommy, time to go home. Last go then, all right.

EDWARD: Mum did I hear you right just now?

CATHY: I want my ears pierced.

BETTY: Ooh, not till you're big.

CATHY: I know a girl got her ears pierced and she's three. She's got real gold.

BETTY: I don't expect she's English, darling. Can I give her a sweety? I know they're not very good for the teeth, Vicky gets terribly cross with me. What does mummy say?

LIN: Just one, thank you very much.

CATHY: I like your beads.

BETTY: Yes they are pretty. Here you are.

[*It is the necklace from ACT ONE.*]

CATHY: Look at me, look at me. Vicky, Vicky, Vicky look at me.

LIN: You look lovely, come on now.

CATHY: And your hat, and your hat.

LIN: No, that's enough.

BETTY: Of course she can have my hat.

CATHY: Yes, yes, hat, hat. Look look look.

LIN: That's enough, please, stop it now. Hat off, bye bye hat.

CATHY: Give me my hat.

LIN: Bye bye beads.

BETTY: It's just fun.

LIN: It's very nice of you.

CATHY: I want my beads.

LIN: Where's the other earring?

CATHY: I want my beads.

> [CATHY *has the other earring in her hand. Meanwhile* VICTORIA *and* EDWARD *look for it.*]

EDWARD: Is it on the floor?

VICTORIA: Don't step on it.

EDWARD: Where?

CATHY: I want my beads. I want my beads.

LIN: You'll have a smack.

> [LIN *gets the earring from* CATHY.]

CATHY: I want my beads.

BETTY: Oh dear oh dear. Have you got the earring? Thank you darling.

CATHY: I want my beads, you're horrid, I hate you, mum, you smell.

BETTY: This is the point you see where one had help. Well it's been lovely seeing you dears and I'll be off again on my little walk.

VICTORIA: You're leaving him? Really?

BETTY: Yes you hear aright, Vicky, yes. I'm finding a little flat, that will be fun.

> [BETTY *goes.*]

Bye bye Tommy, granny's going now. Tommy don't hit that little girl, say goodbye to granny.

VICTORIA: Fucking hell.

EDWARD: Puking Jesus.

LIN: That was news was it, leaving your father?

EDWARD: They're going to want so much attention.

VICTORIA: Does everybody hate their mothers?

EDWARD: Mind you, I wouldn't live with him.

LIN: Stop snivelling, pigface. Where's your coat? Be quiet now and we'll have doughnuts for tea and if you keep on we'll have dogshit on toast.

[CATHY *laughs so much she lies on the floor.*]

VICTORIA: Tommy, you've had two last goes. Last last last last go.

LIN: Not that funny, come on, coat on.

EDWARD: Can I have your painting?

CATHY: What for?

EDWARD: For a friend of mine.

CATHY: What's his name?

EDWARD: Gerry.

CATHY: How old is he?

EDWARD: Thirty-two.

CATHY: You can if you like. I don't care. Kiou kiou kiou kiou.

[CATHY *goes out. Edward takes the painting and goes out.*]

LIN: Will you have sex with me?

VICTORIA: I don't know what Martin would say. Does it count as adultery with a woman?

LIN: You'd enjoy it.

SCENE TWO

Spring. Swing, bench, pond nearby. EDWARD *is gardening.* GERRY *sitting on a bench.*

EDWARD: I sometimes pretend we don't know each other. And you've come to the park to eat your sandwiches and look at me.

GERRY: That would be more interesting, yes. Come and sit down.

EDWARD: If the superintendent comes I'll be in trouble. It's not my dinner time yet. Where were you last night? I think you owe me an explanation. We always do tell each other everything.

GERRY: Is that a rule?

EDWARD: It's what we agreed.

GERRY: It's a habit we've got into. Look, I was drunk. I woke up at 4 o'clock on somebody's floor. I was sick. I hadn't any money for a cab. I went back to sleep.

EDWARD: You could have phoned.

GERRY: There wasn't a phone.

EDWARD: Sorry.

GERRY: There was a phone and I didn't phone you. Leave it alone, Eddy, I'm warning you.

EDWARD: What are you going to do to me, then?

GERRY: I'm going to the pub.

EDWARD: I'll join you in ten minutes.

GERRY: I didn't ask you to come. [EDWARD *goes*.] Two years I've been with Edward. You have to get away sometimes or you lose sight of yourself. The train from Victoria to Clapham still has those compartments without a corridor. As soon as I got on the platform I saw who I wanted. Slim hips, tense shoulders, trying not to look at anyone. I put my hand on my packet just long enough so that he couldn't miss it. The train came in. You don't want to get in too fast or some straight dumbo might get in with you. I sat by the window. I couldn't see where the fuck he'd got to. Then just as the whistle went he got in. Great. It's a six-minute journey so you can't start anything you can't finish. I stared at him and he unzipped his flies. then he stopped. So I stood up and took my cock out. He took me in his mouth and shut his eyes tight. He was sort of mumbling it about as if he wasn't sure what to do, so I said, 'A bit tighter son' and he said 'Sorry' and then got on with it. He was jerking off with his left hand, and I could see he'd got a fairsized one. I wished he'd keep still so I could see his watch. I was getting really turned on. What if we pulled into Clapham Junction now. Of course by the time we sat down again the train was just slowing up. I felt wonderful. Then he started talking. It's better if nothing is said. Once you find he's a librarian in Walthamstow with a special interest in science fiction and lives with his aunt, then forget it. He said I hope you don't think I do this all the time. I said I hope you will from now on. He said he would if I was on the train, but why don't we go out for a meal? I opened the door before the train stopped. I told him I live with somebody, I don't want to know. He was jogging sideways to keep up. He said

'What's your phone number, you're my ideal physical type, what sign of the zodiac are you? Where do you live? Where are you going now? It's not fair, I saw him at Victoria a couple of months later and I went straight down to the end of the platform and I picked up somebody really great who never said a word, just smiled.

[CATHY *is on the swing.*]

CATHY: Batman and Robin
Had a batmobile.
Robin done a fart
And paralysed the wheel.
The wheel couldn't take it,
The engine fell apart,
All because of Robin
And his supersonic fart.

[CATHY *goes.* MARTIN, VICTORIA *and* BETTY *walking slowly.*]

MARTIN: Tom!

BETTY: He'll fall in.

VICTORIA: No he won't.

MARTIN: Don't go too near the edge Tom. Throw the bread from there. The ducks can get it.

BETTY: I'll never be able to manage. If I can't even walk down the street by myself. Everything looks so fierce.

VICTORIA: Just watch Tommy feeding the ducks.

BETTY: He's going to fall in. Make Martin make him move back.

VICTORIA: He's not going to fall in.

BETTY: It's since I left your father.

VICTORIA: Mummy, it really was the right decision.

BETTY: Everything comes at me from all directions. Martin despises me.

VICTORIA: Of course he doesn't, mummy.

BETTY: Of course he does.

MARTIN: Throw the bread. That's the way. The duck can get it. Quack quack quack quack quack.

BETTY: I don't want to take pills. Lin says you can't trust doctors.

VICTORIA: You're not taking pills. You're doing very well.

BETTY: But I'm so frightened.

298

VICTORIA: What are you frightened of?

BETTY: Victoria, you always ask that as if there was suddenly going to be an answer.

VICTORIA: Are you all right sitting there?

BETTY: Yes, yes. Go and be with Martin.

[VICTORIA *joins* MARTIN, BETTY *stays sitting on the bench.*

MARTIN: You take the job, you go to Manchester. You turn it down, you stay in London. People are making decisions like this every day of the week. It needn't be for more than a year. You get long vacations. Our relationship might well stand the strain of that, and if it doesn't we're better out of it. I don't want to put any pressure on you. I'd just like to know so we can sell the house. I think we're moving into an entirely different way of life if you go to Manchester because it won't end there. We could keep the house as security for Tommy but he might as well get used to the fact that life nowadays is insecure. You should ask your mother what she thinks and then do the opposite. I could just take that room in Barbara's house, and then we could babysit for each other. You think that means I want to fuck Barbara. I don't. Well, I do, but I won't. And even if I did, what's a fuck between friends? What are we meant to do it with; strangers? Whatever you want to do, I'll be delighted. If you could just let me know what it is I'm to be delighted about. Don't cry again, Vicky, I'm not the sort of man who makes women cry.

[LIN *has come in and sat down with* BETTY, CATHY *joins them. She is wearing a pink dress and carrying a rifle.*]

LIN: I've bought her three new frocks. She won't wear jeans to school any more because Tracy and Mandy called her a boy.

CATHY: Tracy's got a perm.

LIN: You should have shot them.

CATHY: They're coming to tea and we've got to have trifle. Not trifle you make, trifle out of a packet. And you've got to wear a skirt. And tights.

LIN: Tracy's mum wears jeans.

CATHY: She does not. She wears velvet.

299

BETTY: Well I think you look very pretty. And if that gun has caps in it please take it a long way away.

CATHY: It's got red caps. They're louder.

MARTIN: Do you think you're well enough to do this job? You don't have to do it. No one's going to think any the less of you if you stay here with me. There's no point being so liberated you make yourself cry all the time. You stay and we'll get everything sorted out. What it is about sex, when we talk while it's happening I get to feel it's like a driving lesson. Left, right, a little faster, carry on, slow down –

[CATHY *shoots* VICTORIA.]

CATHY: You're dead Vicky.

VICTORIA: Aaaargh.

CATHY: Fall over.

VICTORIA: I'm not falling over, the ground's wet.

CATHY: You're dead.

VICTORIA: Yes, I'm dead.

CATHY: The Dead Hand Gang fall over. They said I had to fall over in the mud or I can't play. That duck's a mandarin.

MARTIN: Which one? Look, Tommy.

CATHY: That's a diver. It's got a yellow eye and it dives. That's a goose. Tommy doesn't know it's a goose, he thinks it's a duck. The babies get eaten by weasels. Kiou kiou.

[CATHY *goes.*]

MARTIN: So I lost my erection last night not because I'm not prepared to talk, it's just that taking in technical information is a different part of the brain and also I don't like to feel that you do it better to yourself. I have read the Hite report. I do know that women have to learn to get their pleasure despite our clumsy attempts at expressing undying devotion and ecstasy, and that what we spent our adolescence thinking was an animal urge we had to suppress is in fact a fine art we have to acquire. I'm not like whatever percentage of American men have become impotent as a direct result of women's liberation, which I am totally in favour of, more I sometimes think than you are yourself. Nor am I one of your villains who sticks it in, bangs away, and falls asleep. My one aim is to give you pleasure. My one aim is to give you rolling orgasms like I do other women. So why the hell don't you have them? My analysis for what it's worth is that despite all my efforts you still feel dominated by me. I in fact think it's very sad that you don't feel able to take that job. It makes me feel very guilty. I don't want you to do it just because I encourage you to do it. But don't you think you'd feel better if you did take the job? You're the one who's talked about freedom. You're the one who's experimenting with bi-sexuality, and I don't stop you, I think women have something to give each other. You seem to need the mutual support. You find me too overwhelming. So follow it through, go away, leave me and Tommy alone for a bit, we can manage perfectly well without you. I'm not putting any pressure on you but I don't think you're being a whole person. God knows I do everything I can to make you stand on your own two feet. Just be yourself. You don't seem to realise how insulting it is to me that you can't get yourself together.

[MARTIN *and* VICTORIA *go.*]

BETTY: You must be very lonely yourself with no husband. You don't miss him?

LIN: Not really, no.

BETTY: Maybe you like being on your own.

LIN: I'm seeing quite a lot of Vicky. I don't live alone. I live with Cathy.

BETTY: I would have been frightened when I was your age. I thought, the poor children, their mother all alone.

LIN: I've a lot of friends.

BETTY: I find when I'm making tea I put out two cups. It's strange not having a man in the house. You don't know who to do things for.

LIN: Yourself.

BETTY: Oh, that's very selfish.

LIN: Have you any women friends?

BETTY: I've never been so short of men's company that I've had to bother with women.

LIN: Don't you like women?

BETTY: They don't have such interesting conversations as men. There has never been a woman composer of genius. They don't have a sense of humour. They spoil things for themselves with their emotions. I can't say I do like women very much, no.

LIN: But you're a woman.

BETTY: There's nothing says you have to like yourself.

LIN: Do you like me?

BETTY: There's no need to take it personally, Lin.

[MARTIN and VICTORIA come back.]

MARTIN: Did you know if you put cocaine on your prick you can keep it up all night? The only thing is of course it goes numb so you don't feel anything. But you would, that's the main thing. I just want to make you happy.

BETTY: Vicky, I'd like to go home.

VICTORIA: Yes, mummy, of course.

BETTY: I'm sorry, dear.

VICTORIA: I think Tommy would like to stay out a bit longer.

LIN: Hello, Martin. We do keep out of each other's way.

MARTIN: I think that's the best thing to do.

BETTY: Perhaps you'd walk home with me, Martin. I do feel safer with a man. The park is so large the grass seems to tilt.

MARTIN: Yes, I'd like to go home and do some work. I'm writing a novel about women from the women's point of view.

[MARTIN and BETTY go. LIN and VICTORIA are alone. They embrace.]

VICTORIA: Why the hell can't he just be a wife and come with me? Why does Martin make me tie myself in knots? No wonder we can't just have a simple fuck. No, not Martin, why do I make myself tie myself in knots. It's got to stop, Lin. I'm not like that with you. Would you love me if I went to Manchester?

LIN: Yes.

VICTORIA: Would you love me if I went on a climbing expedition in the Andes mountains?

LIN: Yes.

VICTORIA: Would you love me if my teeth fell out?

LIN: Yes.

VICTORIA: Would you love me if I loved ten other people?

LIN: And me?

VICTORIA: Yes.

LIN: Yes.

VICTORIA: And I feel apologetic for not being quite so subordinate as I was. I am more intelligent than him. I am brilliant.

LIN: Leave him Vic. Come and live with me.

VICTORIA: Don't be silly.

LIN: Silly, Christ, don't then. I'm not asking because I need to live with someone. I'd enjoy it, that's all, we'd both enjoy it. Fuck you. Cathy, for fuck's sake stop throwing stones at the ducks. The man's going to get you.

VICTORIA: What man? Do you need a man to frighten your child with?

LIN: My mother said it.

VICTORIA: You're so inconsistent, Lin.

LIN: I've changed who I sleep with, I can't change everything.

VICTORIA: Like when I had to stop you getting a job in a boutique and collaborating with sexist consumerism.

LIN: I should have got that job, Cathy would have liked it. Why shouldn't I have some decent clothes? I'm sick of dressing like a boy, why can't I look sexy, wouldn't you love me?

VICTORIA: Lin, you've no analysis.

LIN: No but I'm good at kissing aren't I? I give Cathy guns, my mum didn't give me guns. I dress her in jeans, she wants to wear dresses. I don't know. I can't work it out, I don't want to. You read too many books, you get at me all the time, you're worse to me than Martin is to you, you piss me off, my brother's been killed. I'm sorry to win the argument that way but there it is.

VICTORIA: What do you mean win the argument?

LIN: I mean be nice to me.

VICTORIA: In Belfast?

LIN: I heard this morning. Don't don't start. I've hardly seem him for two years. I rung my father. You'd think I'd shot himself. He doesn't want me to go the funeral.

[CATHY approaches.]

VICTORIA: What will you do?

LIN: Go of course.

CATHY: What is it? Who's killed? What?

LIN: It's Bill. Your uncle. In the army. Bill that gave you the blue teddy.

CATHY: Can I have his gun?

LIN: It's time we went home. Time you went to bed.

CATHY: No it's not.

LIN: We go home and you have tea and you have a bath and you go to bed.

CATHY: Fuck off.

LIN: Cathy, shut up.

VICTORIA: It's only half past five, why don't we —

LIN: I'll tell you why she has to go to bed —

VICTORIA: She can come home with me.

LIN: Because I want her out the fucking way.

VICTORIA: She can come home with me.

CATHY: I'm not going to bed.

LIN: I want her home with me not home with you, I want her in bed, I want today over.

CATHY: I'm not going to bed.

[LIN *hits* CATHY, CATHY *cries*.]

LIN: And shut up or I'll give you something to cry for.

CATHY: I'm not going to bed.

VICTORIA: Cathy —

LIN: You keep out of it.

VICTORIA: Lin for God's sake.

[*They are all shouting.* CATHY *runs off.* LIN *and* VICTORIA *are silent. Then they laugh and embrace.*]

LIN: Where's Tommy?

VICTORIA: What? Didn't he go with Martin?

LIN: Did he?

VICTORIA: God oh God.

LIN: Cathy! Cathy!

VICTORIA: I haven't thought about him. How could I not think about him? Tommy!

LIN: Cathy! Come on, quick, I want some help.

VICTORIA: Tommy! Tommy!

[CATHY *comes back*.]

LIN: Where's Tommy? Have you seen him? Did he go with Martin? Do you know where he is?

CATHY: I showed him the goose. We went in the bushes.

LIN: Then what?

CATHY: I came back on the swing.

VICTORIA: And Tommy? Where was Tommy?

CATHY: He fed the ducks.

LIN: No that was before.

CATHY: He did a pee in the bushes. I helped him with his trousers.

VICTORIA: And after that?

CATHY: He fed the ducks.

VICTORIA: No no.

CATHY: He liked the ducks. I expect he fell in.

LIN: Did you see him fall in?

VICTORIA: Tommy! Tommy!

LIN: What's the last time you saw him?

CATHY: He did a pee.

VICTORIA: Mummy said he would fall in. Oh God, Tommy!

LIN: We'll go round the pond. We'll go opposite ways round the pond.

ALL [Shout]: Tommy!

> [VICTORIA and LIN go off opposite sides. CATHY climbs the bench.

CATHY: Georgie Best, superstar
Walks like a woman and wears a bra.

There he is! I see him! Mum! Vicky! There he is! He's in the bushes.

> [LIN comes back.]

LIN: Come on Cathy love, let's go home.

CATHY: Vicky's got him.

LIN: Come on.

CATHY: Is she cross?

LIN: No. Come on.

CATHY: I found him.

LIN: Yes. Come on.

> [CATHY gets off the bench. CATHY and LIN hug.]

CATHY: I'm watching telly.

LIN: Ok.

CATHY: After the news.

LIN: Ok.

CATHY: I'm not going to bed.

LIN: Yes you are.

CATHY: I'm not going to bed now.

LIN: Not now but early.

CATHY: How early?

LIN: Not late.

CATHY: How not late?

LIN: Early.

CATHY: How early?

LIN: Not late.

[*They go off together.* GERRY *comes on. He waits.* EDWARD *comes.*]

EDWARD: I've got some fish for dinner. I thought I'd make a cheese sauce.

GERRY: I won't be in.

EDWARD: Where are you going?

GERRY: For a start I'm going to a sauna. Then I'll see.

EDWARD: All right. What time will you be back? We'll eat then.

GERRY: You're getting like a wife.

EDWARD: I don't mind that.

GERRY: Why don't I do the cooking sometime?

EDWARD: You can if you like. You're just not so good at it that's all. Do it tonight.

GERRY: I won't be in tonight.

EDWARD: Do it tomorrow. If we can't eat it we can always go to a restaurant.

GERRY: Stop it.

EDWARD: Stop what?

GERRY: Just be yourself.

EDWARD: I don't know what you mean. Everyone's always tried to stop me being feminine and now you are too.

GERRY: You're putting it on.

EDWARD: I like doing the cooking. I like being fucked. You do like me like this really.

GERRY: I'm bored, Eddy.

EDWARD: Go to the sauna.

GERRY: And you'll stay home and wait up for me.

EDWARD: No, I'll go to bed and read a book.

GERRY: Or knit. You could knit me a pair of socks.

EDWARD: I might knit. I like knitting.

GERRY: I don't mind if you knit. I don't want to be married.

EDWARD: I do.

GERRY: Well I'm divorcing you.

EDWARD: I wouldn't want to keep a man who wants his freedom.

GERRY: Eddy, do stop playing the injured wife, it's not funny.

EDWARD: I'm not playing. It's true.

GERRY: I'm not the husband so you can't be the wife.

EDWARD: I'll always be here, Gerry, if you want to come back. I know you men like to go off by yourselves. I don't think I could love deeply more than once. But I don't think I can face life on my own so don't leave it too long or it may be too late.

GERRY: What are you trying to turn me into?

EDWARD: A monster, darling, which is what you are.

GERRY: I'll collect my stuff from the flat in the morning.

[GERRY *goes.* EDWARD *sits on the bench. It gets darker.* VICTORIA *comes.*]

VICTORIA: Tommy dropped a toy car somewhere, you haven't seen it? It's red. He says it's his best one. Oh the hell with it. Martin's reading him a story. There, isn't it quiet?

[*They sit on the bench, holding hands.*]

EDWARD: I like women.

VICTORIA: That should please mother.

EDWARD: No listen Vicky. I'd rather be a woman. I wish I had breasts like that, I think they're beautiful. Can I touch them?

VICTORIA: What, pretending they're yours?

EDWARD: No, I know it's you.

VICTORIA: I think I should warn you I'm enjoying this.

EDWARD: I'm sick of men.

VICTORIA: I'm sick of men.

EDWARD: I think I'm a lesbian.

SCENE THREE

The park. Summer night. VICTORIA, LIN *and* EDWARD *drunk.*

LIN: Where are you?

VICTORIA: Come on.

EDWARD: Do we sit in a circle?

VICTORIA: Sit in a triangle.

EDWARD: You're good at mathematics. She's good at mathematics.

VICTORIA: Give me your hand. We all hold hands.

EDWARD: Do you know what to do?

LIN: She's making it up.

VICTORIA: We start off by being quiet.

EDWARD: What?

LIN: Hush.

EDWARD: Will something appear?

VICTORIA: It was your idea.

EDWARD: It wasn't my idea. It was your book.

LIN: You said call up the goddess.

EDWARD: I don't remember saying that.

LIN: We could have called her on the telephone.

EDWARD: Don't be so silly, this is meant to be frightening.

LIN: Kiss me.

VICTORIA: Are we going to do it?

LIN: We're doing it.

VICTORIA: A ceremony.

LIN: It's very sexy, you said it is. You said the women were priests in the temples and fucked all the time. I'm just helping.

VICTORIA: As long as it's sacred.

LIN: It's very sacred.

VICTORIA: Innin, Innana, Nana, Nut, Anat, Anahita, Istar, Isis.

LIN: I can't remember all that.

VICTORIA: Lin! Innin, Innana, Nana, Nut, Anat, Anahita, Istar, Isis.

[LIN *and* EDWARD *join in and continue the chant under* VICTORIA's *speech.*]

Goddess of many names, oldest of the old, who walked in chaos and created life, hear us calling you back through time, before Jehovah, before Christ, before men drove you out and burnt your temples, hear us, Lady, give us back what we were, give us the history we haven't had, make us the women we can't be.

ALL: Innin, Innana, Nana, Nut, Anat, Anahita, Istar, Isis.

[*Chant continues under other speeches.*]

LIN: Come back, goddess.

VICTORIA: Goddess of the sun and the moon her brother, little goddess of Crete with snakes in your hands.

LIN: Goddess of breasts.

VICTORIA: Goddess of cunts.

LIN: Goddess of fat bellies and babies. And blood blood blood.

[*Chant continues.*]

I see her.

EDWARD: What?

[*They stop chanting.*]

LIN: I see her. Very tall. Snakes in her hands. Light light light – look out! Did I give you a fright?

EDWARD: I was terrified.

VICTORIA: Don't spoil it Lin.

LIN: It's all out of a book.

VICTORIA: Innin Innana – I can't do it now. I was really enjoying myself.

LIN: She won't appear with a man here.

VICTORIA: They had men, they had sons and lovers.

EDWARD: They had eunuchs.

LIN: Don't give us ideas.

VICTORIA: There's Attis and Tammuz, they're torn to pieces.

EDWARD: Tear me to pieces, Lin.

VICTORIA: The priestess chose a lover for a year and he was king because she chose him and then he was killed at the end of the year.

EDWARD: Hurray.

VICTORIA: And the women had the children and nobody knew it was done by fucking so they didn't know about fathers and nobody cared who the father was and the property was passed down through the maternal line –

LIN: Don't turn it into a lecture, Vicky, it's meant to be an orgy.

VICTORIA: It never hurts to understand the theoretical background. You can't separate fucking and economics.

LIN: Give us a kiss.

EDWARD: Shut up, listen.

LIN: What?

EDWARD: There's somebody there.

LIN: Where?

EDWARD: There.

VICTORIA: The priestesses used to make love to total strangers.

LIN: Go on then, I dare you.

EDWARD: Go on, Vicky.

VICTORIA: He won't know it's a sacred rite in honour of the goddess.

EDWARD: We'll know.

LIN: We can tell him.

EDWARD: It's not what he thinks, it's what we think.

LIN: Don't tell him till after, he'll run a mile.

VICTORIA: Hello. We're having an orgy. Do you want me to suck your cock?

[*The stranger approaches. It is* MARTIN.]

MARTIN: There you are. I've been looking everywhere. What the hell are you doing? Do you know what the time is? You're all pissed out of your minds.

[*They leap on* MARTIN, *pull him down and start to make love to him.*]

MARTIN: Well that's all right. If all we're talking about is having a lot of sex there's no problem. I was all for the sixties when liberation just meant fucking.

[*Another stranger approaches.*]

LIN: Hey you, come here. Come and have sex with us.

VICTORIA: Who is it?

[*The stranger is a soldier.*]

LIN: It's my brother.

EDWARD: Lin, don't.

LIN: It's my brother.

VICTORIA: It's her sense of humour, you get used to it.

LIN: Shut up Vicky, it's my brother. Isn't it? Bill?

SOLDIER: Yes it's me.

LIN: And you are dead.

SOLDIER: Fucking dead all right yeh.

LIN: Have you come back to tell us something?

SOLDIER: No I've come for a fuck. That was the worst thing in the fucking army. Never fucking let out. Can't fucking talk to Irish girls. Fucking bored out of my fucking head. That or shit scared. For five minutes I'd be glad I wasn't bored, then I was fucking scared. Then we'd come in and I'd be glad I wasn't scared and then I was fucking bored. Spent the day reading fucking porn and the fucking night wanking. Man's fucking life in the fucking army? No fun when the fucking kids hate you. I got so I fucking wanted to kill someone and I got fucking killed myself and I want a fuck.

LIN: I miss you. Bill. Bill.

[LIN *collapses.* SOLDIER *goes.* VICTORIA *comforts* LIN.]

EDWARD: Let's go home.

LIN: Victoria, come home with us. Victoria's coming to live with me and Edward.

MARTIN: Tell me about it in the morning.

LIN: It's true.

VICTORIA: It is true.

MARTIN: Tell me when you're sober.

[EDWARD, LIN, VICTORIA *go off together.* MARTIN *goes off alone.* GERRY *comes on.*]

GERRY: I come here sometimes at night and pick somebody up. Sometimes I come here at night and don't pick anybody up. I do also enjoy walking about at night. There's never any trouble finding someone. I can have sex any time. You might not find the type you most fancy every day of the week, but there's plenty of people about who just enjoy having a good time. I quite like living alone. If I live with someone I get annoyed with them. Edward always put on Capital radio when he got up. The silence gets wasted. I wake up at four o'clock sometimes. Birds. Silence. If I bring somebody home I never let them stay the night. Edward! Edward!

[EDWARD *from Act One comes on.*]

EDWARD: Gerry I love you.

GERRY: Yes, I know. I love you, too.

EDWARD: You know what we did? I want to do it again. I think about it all the time. Don't you want to any more?

GERRY: Yes, of course.

CLOUD NINE

SONG Cloud Nine [ALL.]
It'll be fine when you reach Cloud Nine.

Mist was rising and the night was dark.
Me and my baby took a walk in the park.
He said Be mine and you're on Cloud Nine.

Better watch out when you're on Cloud Nine.

Smoked some dope on the playground swings
Higher and higher on true love's wings
He said Be mine and you're on Cloud Nine.

Twenty-five years on the same Cloud Nine.

Who did she meet on her first blind date?
The guys were no surprise but the lady was great
They were women in love, they were on Cloud Nine.

Two the same, they were on Cloud Nine.

The bride was sixty-five, the groom was seventeen,
They fucked in the back of the black limousine.
It was divine in their silver Cloud Nine.

Simply divine in their silver Cloud Nine.

The wife's lover's children and my lover's wife,
Cooking in my kitchen, confusing my life.
And it's upside down when you reach Cloud Nine.

Upside down when you reach Cloud Nine.

The park. Afternoon in late summer. MARTIN, CATHY, EDWARD.

CATHY: Under the bramble bushes,
 Under the sea boom boom boom,
 True love for you my darling,
 True love for me my darling,
 When we are married,
 We'll raise a family.
 Boy for you, girl for me,
 Boom tiddley oom boom
 SEXY.

EDWARD: You'll have Tommy and Cathy tonight then ok? Tommy's still on antibiotics, do make him finish the bottle, he takes it in Ribena. It's no good in orange, he spits it out. Remind me to give you Cathy's swimming things.

CATHY: I did six strokes, didn't I Martin? Did I do a width? How many strokes is a length? How many miles is a swimming pool? I'm going to take my bronze and silver and gold and diamond.

MARTIN: Is Tommy still wetting the bed?

EDWARD: Don't get angry with him about it.

MARTIN: I just need to go to the launderette so I've got a spare sheet. Of course I don't get fucking angry, Eddy, for God's sake. I don't like to say he is my son but he is my son. I'm surprised I'm not wetting the bed myself.

CATHY: I don't wet the bed ever. Do you wet the bed Martin?

MARTIN: No.

CATHY: You said you did.

 [BETTY *comes.*]

BETTY: I do miss the sun living in England but today couldn't be more beautiful. You appreciate the weekend when you're working. Betty's been at work this week, Cathy. It's terrible tiring, Martin, I don't know how you've done it all these years. And the money, I feel like a child with the money, Clive always paid everything but I do understand it perfectly well. Look Cathy let me show you my money.

CATHY: I'll count it. Let me count it. What's that?

313

BETTY: Five pounds, Five and five is —?

CATHY: One two three —

BETTY: Five and five is ten, and five —

CATHY: If I get it right can I have one?

EDWARD: No you can't.

[CATHY *goes on counting the money.*]

BETTY: I never like to say anything, Martin, or you'll think I'm being a mother-in-law.

EDWARD: Which you are.

BETTY: Thank you, Edward, I'm not talking to you. Martin, I think you're being wonderful. Vicky will come back. Just let her stay with Lin till she sorts herself out. It's very nice for a girl to have a friend; I had friends at school, that was very nice. But I'm sure Lin and Edward don't want her with them all the time. I'm not at all shocked that Lin and Edward aren't married and she already has a child, we all know first marriages don't always work out. But really Vicky must be in the way. And poor little Tommy. I hear he doesn't sleep properly and he's had a cough.

MARTIN: No, he's fine, Betty, thank you.

CATHY: My bed's horrible. I want to sleep in the big bed with Lin and Vicky and Eddy and I do get in if I've got a bad dream, and my bed's got a bump right in my back. I want to sleep in a tent.

BETTY: Well Tommy has got a nasty cough, Martin, whatever you say.

EDWARD: He's over that. He's got some medicine.

MARTIN: He takes it in Ribena.

BETTY: Well I'm glad to hear it. Look what a lot of money, Cathy, and I sit behind a desk of my own and I answer the telephone and keep the doctor's appointment book and it really is great fun.

CATHY: Can we go camping, Martin, in a tent? We could take the Dead Hand Gang.

BETTY: Not those big boys, Cathy? They're far too big and rough for you. They climb back into the park after dark. I'm sure mummy doesn't let you play with them, does she Edward? Well I don't know.

[*Ice cream bells.*]

CATHY: Ice cream. Martin you promised. I'll have a double ninety-

314

nine. No I'll have a shandy lolly. Betty, you have a shandy lolly and I'll have a lick. No, you have a double ninety-nine and I'll have the chocolate.

[MARTIN, CATHY *and* BETTY *go, leaving* EDWARD. GERRY *comes.*]

GERRY: Hello, Eddy. Thought I might find you here.

EDWARD: Gerry.

GERRY: Not working today then?

EDWARD: I don't work here any more.

GERRY: Your mum got you into a dark suit?

EDWARD: No of course not. I'm on the dole. I am working, though, I do housework.

GERRY: Whose wife are you now then?

EDWARD: Nobody's. I don't think like that any more. I'm living with some women.

GERRY: What women?

EDWARD: It's my sister, Vic, and her lover. They go out to work and I look after the kids.

GERRY: I thought for a moment you said you were living with women.

EDWARD: We do sleep together, yes.

GERRY: I was passing the park anyway so I thought I'd look in. I was in the sauna the other night and I saw someone who looked like you but it wasn't. I had sex with him anyway.

EDWARD: I do go to the sauna sometimes.

[CATHY *comes, gives* EDWARD *an ice cream, goes.*]

GERRY: I don't think I'd like living with children. They make a lot of noise don't they?

EDWARD: I tell them to shut up and they shut up. I wouldn't want to leave them at the moment.

GERRY: Look why don't we go for a meal sometime?

EDWARD: Yes I'd like that. Where are you living now?

GERRY: Same place.

EDWARD: I'll come round for you tomorrow night about 7.30.

GERRY: Great.

[EDWARD *goes.* HARRY *comes.* HARRY *and* GERRY *pick each other up. They go off.* BETTY *comes back.*]

BETTY: No, the ice cream was my treat, Martin. Off you go. I'm going to have a quiet sit in the sun.

[MAUD *comes.*]

MAUD: Let Mrs Saunders be a warning to you, Betty. I know what it is to be unprotected.

BETTY: But mother, I have a job. I earn money.

MAUD: I know we have our little differences but I always want what is best for you.

[ELLEN *comes.*]

ELLEN: Betty, what happens with a man?

BETTY: You just keep still.

ELLEN: And is it enjoyable? Don't forget me, Betty.

[MAUD *and* ELLEN *go.*]

BETTY: I used to think Clive was the one who liked sex. But then I found I missed it. I used to touch myself when I was very little, I thought I'd invented something wonderful. I used to do it to go to sleep with or to cheer myself up, and one day it was raining and I was under the kitchen table, and my mother saw me with my hand under my dress rubbing away, and she dragged me out so quickly I hit my head and it bled and I was sick, and nothing was said, and I never did it again till this year. I thought if Clive wasn't looking at me there wasn't a person there. And one night in bed in my flat I was so frightened I started touching myself. I thought my hand might go through space. I touched my face, it was there, my arm, my breast, and my hand went down where I thought it shouldn't, and I thought well there is somebody there. It felt very sweet, it was a feeling from very long ago, it was very soft, just barely touching, and I felt myself gathering together more and more and I felt angry with Clive and angry with my mother and I went on and on defying them, and there was this vast feeling growing in me and all round me and they couldn't stop me and no one could stop me and I was there and coming and coming. Afterwards I thought I'd betrayed Clive. My mother would kill me. But I felt triumphant because I was a separate person from them. And I cried because I didn't want to be. But I don't cry about it any more. Sometimes I do it three times in one night and it really is great fun.

[VICTORIA *and* LIN *come in.*]

VICTORIA: So I said to the professor, I don't think this is an occasion for invoking the concept of structural causality — oh hello mummy.

BETTY: I'm going to ask you a question, both of you. I have a little money from your grandmother. And the three of you are living in that tiny flat with two children. I wonder if we could get a house and all live in it together? It would give you more room.

VICTORIA: But I'm going to Manchester anyway.

LIN: We'd have a garden, Vicky.

BETTY: You do seem to have such fun all of you.

VICTORIA: I don't want to.

BETTY: I didn't think you would.

LIN: Come on, Vicky, she knows we sleep together, and Eddy.

BETTY: I think I've known for quite a while but I'm not sure. I don't usually think about it, so I don't know if I know about it or not.

VICTORIA: I don't want to live with my mother.

LIN: Don't think of her as your mother, think of her as Betty.

VICTORIA: But she thinks of herself as my mother.

BETTY: I am your mother.

VICTORIA: But mummy we don't even like each other.

BETTY: We might begin to.

    [CATHY *comes on howling with a nosebleed.*]

LIN: Oh Cathy what happened?

BETTY: She's been assaulted.

VICTORIA: It's a nosebleed.

CATHY: Took my ice cream.

LIN: Who did?

CATHY: Took my money.

    [MARTIN *comes.*]

MARTIN: Is everything all right?

LIN: I thought you were looking after her.

CATHY: They hit me. I can't play. They said I'm a girl.

BETTY: Those dreadful boys, the gang, the Dead Hand.

MARTIN: What do you mean you thought I was looking after her?

LIN: Last I saw her she was with you getting an ice cream. It's your afternoon.

MARTIN: Then she went off to play. She goes off to play. You don't keep an eye on her every minute.

LIN: She doesn't get beaten up when I'm looking after her.

CATHY: Took my money.

MARTIN: Why the hell should I look after your child anyway? I just want Tommy. Why should he live with you and Vicky all week?

LIN: I don't mind if you don't want to look after her but don't say you will and then this happens.

VICTORIA: When I get to Manchester everything's going to be different anyway, Lin's staying here, and you're staying here, we're all going to have to sit down and talk it through.

MARTIN: I'd really enjoy that.

CATHY: Hit me on the face.

LIN: You were the one looking after her and look at her now, that's all.

MARTIN: I've had enough of you telling me.

LIN: Yes you know it all.

MARTIN: Now stop it. I work very hard at not being like this, I could do with some credit.

LIN: Ok you're quite nice, try and enjoy it. Don't make me sorry for you, Martin, it's hard for me too. We've better things to do than quarrel. I've got to go and sort those little bastards out for a start. Where are they, Cathy?

CATHY: Don't kill them, mum, hit them. Give them a nosebleed, mum.

[LIN goes.]

VICTORIA: Tommy's asleep in the pushchair. We'd better wake him up or he won't sleep tonight.

MARTIN: Sometimes I keep him up watching television till he falls asleep on the sofa so I can hold him. Come on, Cathy, we'll get another ice cream.

CATHY: Chocolate sauce and nuts.

VICTORIA: Betty, would you like an ice cream?

BETTY: No thank you, the cold hurts my teeth, but what a nice thought, Vicky, thank you.

[VICTORIA goes. BETTY alone. GERRY comes.]

BETTY: I think you used to be Edward's flatmate.

GERRY: You're his mother. He's talked about you.

BETTY: Well never mind. Children are always wrong about their parents. It's great problem knowing where to live and who to share with. I live by myself just now.

GERRY: Good, So do I. You can do what you like.

BETTY: I don't really know what I like.

GERRY: You'll soon find out.

BETTY: What do you like?

GERRY: Waking up at four in the morning.

BETTY: I like listening to music in bed and sometimes for supper I just have a big piece of bread and dip it in very hot lime pickle. So you don't get lonely by yourself? Perhaps you have a lot of visitors. I've been thinking I should have some visitors, I could give a little dinner party. Would you come? There wouldn't just be bread and lime pickle.

GERRY: Thank you very much.

BETTY: Or don't wait to be asked to dinner. Just drop in informally. I'll give you the address shall I? I don't usually give strange men my address but then you're not a strange man, you're a friend of Edward's. I suppose I seem a different generation to you but you are older than Edward. I was married for so many years it's quite hard to know how to get acquainted. But if there isn't a right way to do things you have to invent one. I always thought my mother was far too old to be attractive but when you get to an age yourself it feels quite different.

GERRY: I think you could be quite attractive.

BETTY: If what?

GERRY: If you stop worrying.

BETTY: I think when I do more about things I worry about them less. So perhaps you could help me do more.

GERRY: I might be going to live with Edward again.

BETTY: That's nice, but I'm rather surprised if he wants to share a flat. He's rather involved with a young woman he lives with, or two young women, I don't understand Edward but never mind.

GERRY: I'm very involved with him.

BETTY: I think Edward did try to tell me once but I didn't listen. So what I'm being told now is that Edward is 'gay' is that right?

And you are too. And I've being making rather a fool of myself. But Edward does also sleep with women.

GERRY: He does, yes, I don't.

BETTY: Well people always say it's the mother's fault but I don't intend to start blaming myself. He seems perfectly happy.

GERRY: I could still come and see you.

BETTY: So you could, yes. I'd like that. I've never tried to pick up a man before.

GERRY: Not everyone's gay.

BETTY: No, that's lucky isn't it.

[GERRY goes. CLIVE comes.]

CLIVE: You are not that sort of woman, Betty. I can't believe you are. I can't feel the same about you as I did. And Africa is to be communist I suppose. I used to be proud to be British. There was a high ideal. I came out onto the verandah and looked at the stars.

[CLIVE goes. BETTY from Act One comes. BETTY and BETTY embrace.]

Bloomsbury Methuen Drama World Classics

include

Jean Anouilh (two volumes)
Brendan Behan
Aphra Behn
Bertolt Brecht (eight volumes)
Büchner
Bulgakov
Calderón
Čapek
Anton Chekhov
Noël Coward (eight volumes)
Feydeau
Eduardo De Filippo
Max Frisch
John Galsworthy
Gogol
Gorky (two volumes)
Harley Granville Barker
  (two volumes)
Victor Hugo
Henrik Ibsen (six volumes)
Jarry

Lorca (three volumes)
Marivaux
Mustapha Matura
David Mercer (two volumes)
Arthur Miller (five volumes)
Molière
Musset
Peter Nichols (two volumes)
Joe Orton
A. W. Pinero
Luigi Pirandello
Terence Rattigan
  (two volumes)
W. Somerset Maugham
  (two volumes)
August Strindberg
  (three volumes)
J. M. Synge
Ramón del Valle-Inclán
Frank Wedekind
Oscar Wilde

Bloomsbury Methuen Drama Modern Plays

include work by

Edward Albee
Jean Anouilh
John Arden
Margaretta D'Arcy
Peter Barnes
Sebastian Barry
Brendan Behan
Dermot Bolger
Edward Bond
Bertolt Brecht
Howard Brenton
Anthony Burgess
Simon Burke
Jim Cartwright
Caryl Churchill
Noël Coward
Lucinda Coxon
Sarah Daniels
Nick Darke
Nick Dear
Shelagh Delaney
David Edgar
David Eldridge
Dario Fo
Michael Frayn
John Godber
Paul Godfrey
David Greig
John Guare
Peter Handke
David Harrower
Jonathan Harvey
Iain Heggie
Declan Hughes
Terry Johnson
Sarah Kane
Charlotte Keatley
Barrie Keeffe
Howard Korder

Robert Lepage
Doug Lucie
Martin McDonagh
John McGrath
Terrence McNally
David Mamet
Patrick Marber
Arthur Miller
Mtwa, Ngema & Simon
Tom Murphy
Phyllis Nagy
Peter Nichols
Sean O'Brien
Joseph O'Connor
Joe Orton
Louise Page
Joe Penhall
Luigi Pirandello
Stephen Poliakoff
Franca Rame
Mark Ravenhill
Philip Ridley
Reginald Rose
Willy Russell
Jean-Paul Sartre
Sam Shepard
Wole Soyinka
Shelagh Stephenson
Peter Straughan
C. P. Taylor
Theatre de Complicite
Theatre Workshop
Sue Townsend
Judy Upton
Timberlake Wertenbaker
Roy Williams
Snoo Wilson
Victoria Wood